# Financial Statements for
# Public Companies

# Financial Statements for Public Companies

Hazel Powling

Ken Rigelsford

Isobel Sharp

*Arthur Andersen*

Accountancy Books
40 Bernard Street
London WC1N 1LD
Tel: +44 (0) 171 920 8991
Fax: +44 (0) 171 920 8992
E-mail: abgbooks@icaew.co.uk
Website: www.icaew.co.uk/books.htm

© 1999 Arthur Andersen

ISBN 1 85355 830 3

This book is based on legislation and regulation extant at 1 January 1999.

**British Library Cataloguing-in-Publication Data**

A catalogue record for this book is available from the British Library.

Typeset by York House Typographic Ltd, London
Printed in Great Britain by Bemrose Security Printing, Derby

# Contents

# Contents

## Chapter 6: Directors' transactions, emoluments and interests 37

## Chapter 7: Approval and publication of accounts 49

Contents

# Preface

The 1998/99 reporting season promises to be a bumper time for changes in company accounts. The introduction of six new and one revised Financial Reporting Standards, four new UITF Abstracts, new Listing Rules on corporate governance matters and a non-mandatory statement on preliminary announcements must be digested, discussed and determined. The output from this process is a company's annual report and accounts revised as necessary for the new rules. The purpose of this book is to provide guidance on what must be presented.

While this is the first edition of *Financial Statements for Public Companies*, the book's format has been around for some 15 years in the form of our firm's 'Accounting and reporting requirements' to which many have contributed over the years and for which we are grateful. Unlike its predecessors, however, its focus is now solely on public company reporting, with private companies' rules being considered briefly, principally to illustrate the different regimes.

The book is organised into two parts, of which Part II will probably be the more popular. It contains model accounts, accompanied by a detailed commentary, to illustrate the principal statutory, professional and Stock Exchange requirements for public listed company accounts extant at 1 January 1999 and assuming all have been implemented. The report pages are a staggering 80 pages and yet only a proportion of the rules have been illustrated, albeit it is hoped a very high proportion. The aim is to present the most common disclosure requirements and then via the commentary pages opposite to cover the requirements which are driving those disclosures. Reference should be made to the relevant source material for the full text.

The purpose of Part I is to set the scene. The chapters therein cover the framework within which public companies report.

In preparing this book, we are grateful to our colleagues at Arthur Andersen for their help and in particular for the assistance of our secretary, Vanessa Reid, who handled calmly and competently the endless changes required to the accounts pages.

*Hazel Powling*
*Ken Rigelsford*
*Isobel Sharp*
*January 1999*

# Part I – Discussion of regulatory framework

# Chapter 1 Regulatory framework for company accounts

## 1.1 Introduction

The statutory framework for company accounts is established by Part VII of the Companies Act 1985 ('the 1985 Act'). This is supported by a wider regulatory framework encompassing the accounting and disclosure requirements set out in Financial Reporting Standards (FRSs), Statements of Standard Accounting Practice (SSAPs) and Urgent Issues Task Force (UITF) Abstracts. Listed companies are subject to additional disclosure requirements imposed by the London Stock Exchange (see Chapter 8).

The regulatory framework for company accounts reflects UK practice which has developed over many years, but it has also been heavily influenced by European Directives. In particular, the 1985 Act incorporates the provisions of the Fourth Directive on single company accounts, first enacted in the UK by the Companies Act 1981 (subsequently consolidated into the 1985 Act), and the Seventh Directive on group accounts, implemented by the Companies Act 1989 ('the 1989 Act') which amended the 1985 Act.

The chapters in this Part discuss the accounting and reporting requirements for companies. Part II contains a set of model accounts, together with a detailed commentary. These illustrate many of the statutory and other disclosure requirements applicable to a listed group, as well as the form and content of auditors' reports.

## 1.2 Statutory requirements

*85 s226*
*85 s227*

The directors of every company in Great Britain must prepare accounts for each financial year. These accounts must include a balance sheet, a profit and loss account and additional information in accompanying notes to the accounts. If, at its year end, the company has subsidiary undertakings then it is also required to prepare group accounts, unless it can take advantage of certain exemptions (see Chapter 5).

The form and content of individual company accounts are governed by Schedule 4 to the 1985 Act. Schedule 4A imposes additional requirements for group accounts. Schedules 5 and 6 set out disclosure requirements relating to investments and directors' emoluments and transactions respectively. Many of these disclosure requirements are illustrated in the model accounts in Part II.

There are separate disclosure requirements for banks and insurance companies which are discussed in Chapter 9, which deals with special categories of companies. There are also separate disclosure requirements for small companies which are not dealt with in this book but are discussed in another publication *Financial Statements for Smaller Companies*, the second edition of which was published in 1998 by Accountancy Books.

# 1.3 True and fair view

The accounts of both an individual company and a group are required to give a true and fair view of the profit or loss for the financial year and the state of affairs at the end of it. This paramount principle underpins all the accounting requirements of the 1985 Act and accounting standards. If accounts drawn up in compliance with the 1985 Act do not provide sufficient information to give a true and fair view, then the necessary additional information must be given.

*85 s226(2), s227(3)*

*85 s226(4), s227(5)*

## 1.3.1 Use of true and fair override

In special circumstances, it is possible that compliance with one or more of the requirements of the 1985 Act, even when supplemented by additional information, is inconsistent with the requirement for the accounts to show a true and fair view. In these cases the directors must depart from the specific requirements to the extent necessary to show a true and fair view and must disclose in a note the particulars of the departure, the reasons for it and its effect. These statutory disclosure requirements have been further clarified by the UITF.

*85 s226(5), s227(6)*

*UITF 7*

## 1.3.2 Interpretation of 'special circumstances'

There is no statutory definition of the 'special circumstances' in which such a departure may be acceptable. It is generally accepted that the requirement to show a true and fair view does not authorise blanket departures from other statutory requirements for all companies. It has been used, as in SSAP 19 *Accounting for Investment Properties*, to authorise such a departure for companies with a particular type of asset. In contrast, FRS 2 *Accounting for Subsidiary Undertakings* recognises, in the context of the calculation of goodwill when an associated undertaking becomes a subsidiary undertaking, that a company should only use the true and fair override where the statutory calculation of goodwill would be misleading.

*SSAP 19(17)*

*FRS 2(89)*

# 1.4 Authority of accounting standards

The 1985 Act sets out the framework for accounts, including the formats for the balance sheet and profit and loss account and the basic disclosure requirements for the notes. Detailed rules for accounting, presentation and disclosure are laid down in accounting standards. These take three forms: SSAPs, issued by the Accounting Standards Committee (ASC), the former standard-setting body, and subsequently adopted by its successor body, the Accounting Standards Board (ASB); FRSs, issued by the ASB itself; and UITF Abstracts developed by the UITF and issued by the ASB.

The authority of accounting standards is set out in the Foreword to Accounting Standards. This states:

> *'Accounting standards are authoritative statements of how particular types of transaction and other events should be reflected in financial statements and accordingly compliance with accounting standards will normally be necessary for financial statements to give a true and fair view.'*

*Foreword to Accounting Standards 16*

## 1.4.1 Legal status

The 1985 Act recognises the existence of accounting standards by authorising government funding of bodies concerned with their issue. This status is currently granted to the ASB. The 1985 Act also requires all large companies to disclose whether their accounts have been prepared in accordance with applicable accounting standards and to give particulars of, and the reasons for, any material departure from those standards. In addition, the 1985 Act recognises the Financial Reporting Review Panel ('the Review Panel') as a body which may apply to the courts for a

*85 s256*

*SI 1990 No. 1667*

*85 4 Sch 36A*

determination of whether a particular set of accounts shows a true and fair view. Both the ASB and the Review Panel are accountable to their parent body, the Financial Reporting Council.

*85 s245B, SI 1991 No. 13*

### 1.4.2 Counsel's Opinion on accounting standards

The ASB sought legal opinion from Miss Mary Arden QC (now the Honourable Mrs Justice Arden DBE) on the status of accounting standards in the context of the requirement for accounts to show a true and fair view. Her Opinion, 'The true and fair requirement', is attached to the Foreword to Accounting Standards. The Opinion recognises that the immediate effect of the issue of an accounting standard is to make it likely that the courts will deem compliance with this standard necessary to show a true and fair view. It also acknowledges that the statutory recognition of both accounting standards and the ASB as a standard-setting body has reinforced the status of accounting standards. This effectively makes compliance with accounting standards mandatory, other than in the exceptional circumstances of an individual company where a departure is necessary for a true and fair view.

*Counsel's Opinion 10*

*Foreword to Accounting Standards 19*

### 1.4.3 Authority of UITF Abstracts

The authority of UITF Abstracts is comparable with that of accounting standards. Consequently, they are regarded as part of the body of accounting practices which are relevant in determining whether a set of accounts shows a true and fair view. Departures from the requirements of a UITF Abstract are envisaged only in the exceptional circumstances where this is necessary for a true and fair view.

### 1.4.4 Enforcement of accounting standards

Both the Review Panel and the Department of Trade and Industry (DTI) have procedures for reviewing and investigating departures from the accounting requirements of the 1985 Act, including any departure from the requirement to show a true and fair view. The two bodies are therefore able to investigate departures from accounting standards. These investigatory powers are backed by statutory powers to apply to the court for an order requiring the directors to reissue their accounts if they do not comply with the 1985 Act. This provides a mechanism for the enforcement of both the statutory accounting requirements and the requirements of accounting standards.

*85 s245B*

# 1.5 The accountancy profession

The Consultative Committee of Accountancy Bodies (CCAB) consists of the six main professional accounting bodies in the UK and the Republic of Ireland:

- the Institute of Chartered Accountants in England and Wales (ICAEW);
- the Institute of Chartered Accountants of Scotland (ICAS);
- the Institute of Chartered Accountants in Ireland (ICAI);
- the Association of Chartered Certified Accountants (ACC');
- the Chartered Institute of Management Accountants (CIMA); and
- the Chartered Institute of Public Finance and Accountancy (CIPFA).

As the accountancy profession's umbrella body, the CCAB is committed to promoting and supporting compliance with accounting standards by its member bodies and their members, whether they are acting as auditors or preparers of accounts. Members of CCAB bodies may therefore be investigated by the appropriate disciplinary committees if they fail to observe accounting standards or to ensure adequate disclosure of significant departures.

*Foreword to Accounting Standards 9–11*

### 1.5.1 The standard-setting process

The standard-setting process is the responsibility of the ASB, which consists of a Chairman and Technical Director, both of whom are full-time, together with up to eight part-time board members drawn from public practice, industry, academia and user groups.

The following process of research and consultation is followed before an accounting standard is issued on a particular topic:

(a) an individual topic is identified either from the ASB's own research or from external sources, including submissions from interested parties and the work programmes of other standard-setters such as the International Accounting Standards Committee;

(b) the topic is researched by the ASB's staff, who carry out informal consultations with interested parties and present issues to the board for detailed debate;

(c) a discussion paper is issued for comment, identifying, where possible, the preliminary views of the ASB on the preferred treatments;

(d) a Financial Reporting Exposure Draft (FRED) is issued for comment to allow an opportunity for all interested parties to comment on the proposals and for the ASB to gauge the appropriateness and level of acceptance of those proposals; and

*Foreward to Accounting Standards 23–26* (e) the FRED is refined in the light of these comments and may be subject to further consultation prior to the issue of an FRS.

The consultative process may be extended for particular topics by the publication of additional discussion papers or exposure drafts to present alternative proposals and by holding public hearings to permit more open debate of complex or controversial issues.

### 1.5.2 Reviews of accounting standards

*Foreward to Accounting Standards 33* The ASB recognises that accounting standards need to evolve with the business environment in which they are set. Consequently, it accepts the need to review the effectiveness of individual accounting standards once they have been in place for a reasonable period.

### 1.5.3 Relationship with international accounting standards

*Foreward to Accounting Standards 36* The ASB, in common with its predecessor body the ASC, supports the International Accounting Standards Committee in its aim to harmonise international financial reporting. Consequently, each FRS and most SSAPs contain a section which explains how they relate to the international accounting standard (IAS) dealing with the same topic and identifies areas of difference. In most cases compliance with an FRS or SSAP ensures compliance with the relevant IAS, although there are significant notable exceptions. In recent years co-operation among standard-setters has increased and UK FRSs are now often directly linked with international equivalents. Examples of these are FRS 12 on provisions and FRS 14 on earnings per share.

### 1.5.4 Urgent issues

The standard-setting process is inevitably a lengthy one to allow for adequate consultation. The ASB has therefore established a sub-committee, the UITF, which has responsibility for reviewing important or significant accounting issues where unsatisfactory or inconsistent interpretations of existing accounting standards or provisions of companies' legislation have arisen in practice. The UITF operates by seeking a consensus as to the accounting treatment which should be adopted, and issues Abstracts (following a brief period of public consultation) setting out this consensus.

# Chapter 2  Keeping accounting records

## 2.1  Introduction

Proper accounting records are essential to enable companies to produce accounts that show a true and fair view. This chapter summarises the legal requirements concerning the maintenance and retention of accounting records.

## 2.2  Statutory requirements

*85 s221*
Every company must keep accounting records that are adequate to show and explain the company's transactions and to enable the directors to ensure that the annual audited accounts give a true and fair view of the company's state of affairs and profit or loss for the financial year. Proper accounting records must enable the company's financial position to be disclosed, with reasonable accuracy, at any time and, in particular, must contain the following information:

(a) day-to-day entries of sums received and paid and the matters in respect of which the income is earned or the expenditure is incurred;
(b) a record of the company's assets and liabilities;
(c) a statement of stock held at the financial year end (if the company's business involves dealing in goods);
(d) all underlying stocktaking records from which the above was, or will be, prepared; and
(e) statements capable of identifying all goods sold (and the buyers) and purchased (and the sellers) if the company's business involves dealing in goods, other than by way of ordinary retail trade.

The 1985 Act imposes penalties on directors who fail to comply with these requirements unless they can show that they acted honestly and that, in the circumstances in which the company's business was carried on, the default was excusable.

### 2.2.1  Parent companies

*85 s221(4)*
A parent company with a subsidiary undertaking that is not subject to the above requirements (e.g., a partnership or a body incorporated overseas) must take reasonable steps to ensure that the subsidiary undertaking keeps accounting records that will enable the directors of the parent to prepare accounts complying with the 1985 Act.

## 2.3  Form and content

*85 s723*
Accounting records may be maintained in any form. This includes the use of computers, provided that the underlying records can be reproduced in a legible format. If accounting records are not kept in bound book form, the 1985 Act requires

*85 s722*    adequate precautions to be taken for guarding against falsification and facilitating discovery. Failure to take such precautions may result in penalties.

*85 s237*    The auditors are required to make a specific reference in their report if, in their opinion, proper accounting records have not been kept. The 1985 Act does not specifically define what is meant by the term 'proper accounting records' which will generally depend on the size, nature and complexity of the business concerned. Guidance on the interpretation of the statutory accounting records requirements can be found in a Technical Release, FRAG 5/92, issued by the ICAEW.

### 2.3.1 Relationship with statutory accounts requirements

*85 4 Sch 1*

*85 4 Sch 55, 56, 33(3)*

The form and content of accounting records is driven by the choice of accounts formats under Schedule 4 of the 1985 Act and the mandatory disclosure requirements. This includes, for example, the analysis of turnover and profit by activity or geographical segment, the breakdown of staff costs or the historical cost equivalent of revalued fixed assets. Any requirements to make specific information available to regulatory and fiscal authorities, overseas parents, banks and other external bodies will also influence the format of the accounting records.

*85 4 Sch 2*

Voluntary choices relating to the form and extent of disclosure may also require the format of the accounting records to be adapted to provide the necessary information. For example, they may have to provide more detail than would otherwise be the case if the balance sheet caption 'accruals and deferred income' is included in creditors rather than shown as a separate sub-total. If the former disclosure is adopted, any accruals and deferred income must be split between amounts due within one year and those due after more than one year. If they are shown separately, no such analysis is required. The 1985 Act also permits a change in the format of accounts in certain circumstances and this could require changes in the underlying accounting records. Moreover, if any item in the accounts is to be shown in more detail than required by the statutory format, the underlying records have to be capable of producing the necessary information.

*85 s330–347, 6 Sch*
*Part II, FRS 8*

Another area which may influence the form of accounting records concerns directors' loans and other transactions with directors, where the 1985 Act provides limits and reliefs for different purposes and different types of transaction and where FRS 8 *Related Party Disclosures* requires, principally, disclosure of transactions and balances with related parties. Adequate underlying records will again be helpful in avoiding unintended breaches of the requirements.

## 2.4 Access to accounting records

*85 s222*

*85 s744*

*85 s389A*

Accounting records must be kept either at the company's registered office or wherever else the directors consider appropriate. They must in any event be open to inspection by the company's officers (defined as including its directors, secretary and managers) at all times. The auditors also have a right of access at all times to the company's accounting records, but not directly to the accounting records of any subsidiary undertakings, unless they are also the auditors of those subsidiaries. They, however, have rights to obtain information regarding subsidiary undertakings, either from the subsidiary directly, if it is incorporated in the UK, or via the parent company if the subsidiary is unincorporated or incorporated elsewhere.

### 2.4.1 Accounting records kept overseas

If a company's accounting records are kept outside Great Britain (e.g., in the case of a UK subsidiary managed abroad), accounts and returns concerning the business

*85 s222(2)*

*85 s222(3)*

dealt with in the relevant records must be sent to, and retained in, Great Britain, where they must be open to inspection by the company's officers and auditors at all times. These accounts and returns must at least be adequate to disclose with reasonable accuracy, at six-monthly intervals, the financial position of the relevant business. They must also allow the directors to prepare true and fair annual accounts. There is no requirement to maintain them in the English language or to denominate them in sterling.

# 2.5 Retention of accounting records

*85 s222(5)*

A public company must retain its accounting records for at least six years, and private companies for at least three years, from the date on which they are made. These retention periods are subject to any directions which may be made under the winding-up rules and may be overridden by other statutory regulations, such as those referred to below.

## 2.5.1 Regulatory requirements

It is usually helpful to discuss policy on the retention of records (especially microfilming or optical scanning) with the auditors before originals are destroyed. It may also be necessary to discuss such policy with Customs & Excise where VAT matters are concerned. The more common regulations which may need to be considered in establishing company policy on retained records are summarised below.

*VAT Act 1994 11 Sch 6(3)*

**VAT**: Organisations registered for VAT must keep their records and other documentation for six years following the period to which they relate.

*The Income Tax (Employments) Regulations 1993*

**PAYE**: To avoid disputes later, employers must keep payroll records for at least three years after the income tax year to which they relate.

*Taxes Management Act 1970*

**Corporation tax**: The Inland Revenue may require production of records relevant to tax liability. An assessment may normally be raised at any time up to six years after the end of the chargeable period to which the assessment relates. In cases of wilful default or fraud, there is no time limit.

*Finance Act 1998 18 Sch 21*

Under the new corporation tax self-assessment rules which apply to accounting periods ending on or after 1 July 1999 a company must keep such records as are required to enable it to deliver a correct and complete return for the period concerned. These records must be preserved for six years after the end of the period concerned or until any outstanding enquiry into the period is completed. Supporting documents must also be preserved.

*Limitation Act 1980*

**Contracts**: An action under a sealed contract may be brought within 12 years of the event which gives rise to the action. A judgment debt is barred after 12 years. An action under a simple contract may be brought within six years. Interest on a judgment debt cannot be recovered more than six years after it accrues. Certain records may need to be kept with these time limits in mind.

*Data Protection Act 1984*

**Data protection**: Personal data held in computerised form for any purpose must not be kept longer than necessary for that purpose. Appropriate security measures must be taken to prevent unauthorised access to, or alteration, disclosure, destruction or accidental loss of, personal data.

**New Stock Exchange listings**: A company seeking a listing will normally have to produce accounting information for the preceding three years (i.e., records will

*SE 3.3*   have to be kept for four years).

*Charities Act 1993 s41(3)*   **Charities:** The trustees of an incorporated charity are subject to the provisions of both the 1985 Act and the Charities Act 1993. The latter requires trustees to preserve records for at least six years.

## 2.5.2 Company policy on retention of records

Records should generally be retained only as long as they are really needed for commercial or legal purposes. Company policy on this matter may be dictated by economic considerations (e.g., the cost of staff, equipment, space and supplies), legal and related requirements (e.g., specific retention periods required by law, audit considerations and enforceability of contracts), actual or potential demand for copies and historical value (e.g., policy decisions, precedents and technical or scientific archives). Important documents may need to be kept indefinitely or for long periods, possibly in their original form, whereas it may be possible to dispose of others as soon as permitted by the law.

*AD 352*   Further guidance on this subject is given in an *Accountants' Digest* on the management and retention of business documents, published by Accountancy Books. This discusses the different types of records which companies may have and the legal and other regulatory requirements which influence retention periods. The Digest provides detailed guidelines on determining when a document is likely to cease to have value and includes an Appendix suggesting retention periods for specific types of document.

# Chapter 3 The financial year

## 3.1 Introduction

*85 s223*

*85 s223(2)*

A financial year is the period in respect of which the profit and loss account is made up. Normally, it will be a period of 12 months beginning the day after the date to which the last accounts were prepared and ending on the accounting reference date (ARD) registered with the Registrar of Companies. As discussed below, however, it may be longer or shorter than 12 months in certain circumstances. In any year, a company may opt to make up its accounts to a date not more than seven days either side of the ARD. This effectively allows companies to prepare accounts using a 52- or 53-week period, even though their accounting reference period (the period between ARDs) is a full year.

*85 s224(4)*
*85 s225(6)*

*85 s223(5)*

*85 5 Sch 4*

There is no stated minimum period for a financial year other than for the initial period (see below). However, it may not generally in any case exceed 18 months (the maximum length of the accounting reference period) by more than seven days. Directors of a parent company must ensure that the financial years of the parent and its subsidiary undertakings coincide unless there are good reasons to the contrary. In such cases, the parent, if it is not required to prepare group accounts, must disclose in its accounts the details of the subsidiary's last financial year ending prior to the parent's year end.

## 3.2 Initial accounting reference date

*85 s224(3A)*

For a company incorporated on or after 1 April 1996, its first ARD falls on the last day of the month in which the anniversary of incorporation falls.

*85 s224(4)*

*85 s224(6)*

The first accounting reference period of a company may not normally be less than six months and cannot be more than 18 months (calculated from the date of incorporation). It is, however, possible to choose to have a first period of less than six months by changing the 'allocated' ARD. This can be done by serving notice of a change in ARD in accordance with section 225 so that the first accounting reference period comes to an end less than six months after the date of incorporation. This is because section 224(6) provides that section 224 is subject to the provisions of section 225 relating to the change of accounting reference date; section 225 allows any accounting reference period to be shortened without restriction. It is worth remembering that where a first accounting reference period is longer than 12 months, the normal time for filing accounts may be reduced.

## 3.3 Change of accounting reference date

A company may change its accounting reference date either during the financial year (in respect of current and future years) or after the year end (in respect of the financial year just ended). The rules are summarised below.

### 3.3.1 Change of accounting reference date during year

*85 s225(1)*

A company may change the ARD of its current and future financial years at any time during the current financial year by applying to the Registrar of Companies. The company must state whether its financial year is to be shortened or extended. No minimum length for the new accounting reference period is specified, but the notice will not be valid if the new accounting reference period would exceed 18 months. Notice to extend a financial year will also be invalid where a previous application to extend an accounting reference period has been granted, unless the period was last extended more than five years before, or it is being changed to coincide with the ARD of another European Economic Area company which is either its parent or subsidiary undertaking. Extensions are also permitted where an administration order is in force under Part II of the Insolvency Act 1986 or the Secretary of State so directs.

### 3.3.2 Change of accounting reference date after year end

Until 1 April 1996 it was only possible after the end of an accounting reference period for a company to give notice changing the ARD which had already passed where the company was a parent or subsidiary undertaking of another company and the new ARD coincided with that of the other company. However, since 1 April 1996 the rules for changes to a previous accounting period are the same as those for a current accounting reference period (see above) subject to the additional rule that the period for laying and delivering accounts in respect of the old accounting refer-

*85 s225(5)* ence period has not expired.

# Chapter 4  Form and content of accounts

## 4.1  Introduction

*85 s226*

The directors of each company are required to prepare accounts annually which include a balance sheet, profit and loss account and additional information in accompanying notes. These accounts must comply with the requirements of the 1985 Act as to their form and content.

*85 s227*

If at the year end the company has subsidiary undertakings, then it is also required, subject to certain exceptions, to prepare group accounts. Group accounts are considered further in Chapter 5.

The accounts of both an individual company and a group are required to give a true and fair view. As explained in Chapter 1 this effectively imposes a requirement to comply with accounting standards except in very rare and exceptional circumstances.

Accounting standards impose a requirement for two additional non-statutory primary statements: the cash flow statement and the statement of total recognised gains and losses. Where these are presented, they must be given equal prominence with the balance sheet and profit and loss account. Additional disclosure requirements which influence the content of the primary statements can be found in other accounting standards.

If the company is listed on the London Stock Exchange it must also give the information specified in Chapter 12 of the Listing Rules (Yellow Book). These requirements are considered in Chapter 8.

This chapter summarises the requirements of the 1985 Act and some of the more significant accounting standards relating to the form and content of company accounts.

## 4.2  Statutory formats

*85 4 Sch 1, 8*

The 1985 Act requires all companies to adopt specified formats for their balance sheet and profit and loss account and to adopt the terminology and order of presentation prescribed in Schedule 4 to the 1985 Act. This Schedule is not totally prescriptive since it provides a choice of two balance sheet formats (horizontal and vertical) and four profit and loss account formats. The contents of the two balance sheet formats are virtually the same, but the presentation of the information differs. In contrast, the four profit and loss account formats provide two sets of different information, analysing costs either according to type of expenditure (e.g., raw materials or wages and salaries) or by function (e.g., cost of sales or distribution costs). The commonly used statutory formats are set out in Appendix 1.

### 4.2.1 Numbers and letters

Each item in the statutory formats is preceded by letters, Roman numerals or Arabic numerals, which are not intended to be reproduced in the published accounts. They are used in the statutory formats for the following reasons:

*85 4 Sch 3*

(a) letters and Roman numerals indicate items which must always be shown on the face of the balance sheet and profit and loss account;

(b) Arabic numerals indicate items which may be amalgamated and analysed in notes to the accounts;

(c) Arabic numerals also indicate where headings must be adapted or rearranged to suit the special nature of the company's business;

(d) letters are used to identify those items which should be aggregated to determine the 'balance sheet total' in order to establish whether a company meets the small or medium-sized company criteria (see Chapter 7); and

*85 s247*

(e) Arabic numerals identify those items which need not be disclosed in the abbreviated accounts filed by small companies (see Chapter 7).

### 4.2.2 Presentation of balance sheet

The vertical balance sheet format (Format 1) is the most common format used in Great Britain. The 1985 Act does not specify a balance sheet total in this format, but it is common practice to break at Item J (i.e., total assets less total liabilities), with Item K 'capital and reserves' as the balancing section. Alternatively, a break can be made at Item G 'total assets less current liabilities', a mandatory caption, thus allowing long-term creditors and loan capital to be included in the financing section of the balance sheet.

### 4.2.3 Analysis of creditors

Format 1 requires long- and short-term creditors to be presented as separate captions, allowing the disclosure of net current assets (or liabilities) and total assets less current liabilities. Format 2, on the other hand, which analyses the balance sheet horizontally between total assets on one side and total liabilities, capital and reserves on the other, groups all creditors together. A separate analysis between creditors due within and after one year is nevertheless required to be given either on the face of the balance sheet or in the notes.

*Statutory format note 13*

### 4.2.4 Analysis of assets

The 1985 Act requires all assets to be analysed between fixed assets, defined as 'assets which are intended for use on a continuing basis in the company's activities' and all other assets, described as current assets. Consequently, debtors' balances which fall due after more than one year are included within current assets. In most cases it is sufficient to disclose the amount due after more than one year in the notes to the accounts. There will be instances, however, where the amount of debtors falling due after more than one year is so material in the context of the total net current assets that they will need to be disclosed separately on the face of the balance sheet so as to reduce the possibility that the accounts will be misinterpreted.

*85 s262*
*Statutory format note 5*

*UITF 4(3)*

### 4.2.5 Profit and loss account

Profit or loss on ordinary activities before taxation, dividends paid or proposed, and actual or proposed transfers to or from reserves must always be disclosed separately on the face of the profit and loss account. They are not included in the statutory profit and loss account formats since all items in the latter are preceded by Arabic numerals and can therefore be amalgamated and relegated to the notes. These mandatory captions provide vital information which must therefore be disclosed on the face of the profit and loss account.

*85 4 Sch 3*

# 4.3 Departure from statutory formats

Despite the 1985 Act's prescriptive approach to the layout of accounts there is still flexibility in certain areas.

(a) Departure from the statutory formats is required where compliance conflicts with giving a true and fair view.

*85 s226, s227, UITF 7*

(b) Any item preceded by an Arabic numeral may be given in the notes rather than on the face of the accounts, and certain headings may be amalgamated, if this is more convenient in assessing the company's state of affairs or financial results. Where the individual items concerned are material they must be disclosed in the notes to the accounts. Clarity, significance, relevance and the need for a true and fair presentation will determine the appropriate treatment in individual cases.

*85 4 Sch 3(4)*

(c) Amounts which are not material in the context of a particular provision of Schedule 4 may be disregarded. The ASB considers information to be material if it could influence users' decisions taken on the basis of financial statements. If that information is misstated or if certain information is omitted, the materiality of the misstatement or omission depends on the size and nature of the item in question judged in the particular circumstances of the case. The ICAEW has issued guidance on the interpretation of materiality in financial reporting. The guidance stresses that materiality is a matter of judgement and depends on the item's size, nature and circumstances. Because the nature and circumstances of an item are qualitative matters, materiality is not capable of general mathematical definition. Accounting standards need not be applied to immaterial items.

*85 4 Sch 86*

*Draft SOP 2.7*

*ICAEW Handbook 2.401*
*Foreword to Accounting*
*Standards 13*

(d) In special cases (which are not defined), certain rules may be ignored (e.g., the basic prohibition on recognising development costs as a fixed asset) and the company's normal format may be changed.

*85 4 Sch 20*
*85 4 Sch 2*

(e) The directors may provide summarised information about certain items, such as indebtedness and investments, where they are of the opinion that full disclosure would result in a statement of excessive length.

*85 s231, 4 Sch 48*

(f) The segmental analysis of turnover and profit may be omitted if, in the opinion of the directors, it would be 'seriously prejudicial to the interests of the company' and provided the omission is noted. The reasons for omitting the information do not have to be disclosed.

*85 4 Sch 55*

(g) More detail concerning statutory items may be given if the directors so wish, and information not covered by the formats may also be provided.

*85 4 Sch 3*

## 4.3.1 Terminology

As explained above, items preceded by Arabic numerals (i.e., all items in the statutory profit and loss account formats and certain items in the balance sheet formats) are required to be adapted both as to order and description wherever the special nature of the business requires it. The inference is that the captions may not be adapted (e.g., by using different terminology) in any other case although it is not unknown for companies to do so. Captions may be combined to produce new subtotals not envisaged by the statutory formats, which gives additional flexibility.

# 4.4 Comparatives

Comparative amounts (adjusted for consistency if necessary) are required for all items in the balance sheet and profit and loss account, even where there is a nil balance in the current year. However, no caption is required where there is a nil entry for both the current year and prior year. Where non-statutory information is voluntarily given on the face of the balance sheet or profit and loss account,

*85 4 Sch 4*

comparatives also have to be shown. Accounting standards impose similar requirements for comparatives in respect of the additional non-statutory primary statements discussed above.

*FRS 1(48), FRS 3(30)*

In addition, comparatives usually have to be given for any information disclosed in the notes to the accounts for the current year, even if disclosure is voluntary. There are specific exemptions from this rule for certain details regarding acquisitions, investments, transactions with directors or non-director officers, and movements on fixed assets and on provisions and reserves. Comparative information is not specifically required in the directors' report other than for directors' interests.

*85 4 Sch 58*

# 4.5 Profit and loss account presentation

The statutory formats for the profit and loss account are enhanced by the additional presentation requirements of FRS 3 *Reporting Financial Performance*. This highlights a number of important components of financial performance that need separate disclosure on the face of the profit and loss account. These include:

(a) the results of continuing operations (including the results of acquisitions);
(b) the results of discontinued operations; and
(c) non-operating exceptional items (i.e., profits or losses on the sale or termination of an operation, costs of a fundamental reorganisation or restructuring, profits or losses on the disposal of fixed assets and provisions in respect of any of these items).

These items are illustrated in the model accounts in Part II.

# 4.6 Cash flow statement

There is no statutory requirement for a cash flow statement but FRS 1, which was revised in 1996, requires one to be included in all financial statements intended to show a true and fair view, subject to the following exemptions:

*FRS 1(5)*

(a) those entities (including entities which would be so entitled were they companies incorporated under the 1985 Act) which would be entitled to the exemptions in section 246 available to small companies for filing abbreviated accounts with the Registrar;
(b) subsidiary undertakings 90 per cent of whose voting rights are controlled within the group, provided that consolidated financial statements in which the subsidiary undertakings are included are publicly available;
(c) building societies with accounting periods ending before 23 March 1999;
(d) mutual life assurance companies;
(e) pension funds; and
(f) open-ended investment companies that meet certain specified conditions.

## 4.6.1 Format of cash flow statement

The cash flow statement should show the inflows and outflows of cash for the period classified under the following standard headings:

*FRS 1(7)*

(a) operating activities;
(b) dividends from joint ventures and associates;
(c) returns on investments and servicing of finance;
(d) taxation;
(e) capital expenditure and financial investment;

(f) acquisitions and disposals;
(g) equity dividends paid;
(h) management of liquid resources; and
(i) financing.

*FRS 1(8)*

The statement must show a total for each standard heading although cash flows relating to the management of liquid resources and financing can be combined under a single heading provided that the cash flows relating to each are shown separately and separate subtotals are given. Except for cash flows from operating activities, and certain cash flows which are permitted by the standard to be shown net, the individual categories of inflows and outflows under the standard headings must be shown either on the face of the statement or in a note.

*FRS 1(7)*

*FRS 1(12)*

There are two methods of deriving cash flows from operations: the indirect method, which arrives at operating cash flows from operating profit by adding back non-cash items and adjusting for movements in working capital, and the direct method, which builds up from actual receipts from customers and payments to suppliers. The mandatory inclusion of a reconciliation between operating profit and operating cash flows effectively means that the accounts must give the information required by the indirect method. In practice, almost all companies use the indirect method.

*FRS 1(33)*

In addition to the reconciliation of operating profit to operating cash flows mentioned above, the standard requires a reconciliation between the movement in cash in the period and the movement in net debt. The movement in net debt should identify certain prescribed items and reconcile to the opening and closing balance sheet amounts.

# 4.7 Total recognised gains and losses

*FRS 3(27)*

The statement of total recognised gains and losses is another non-statutory primary statement required by accounting standards. This should be presented with the same prominence as the other primary statements wherever there are gains and losses in the year which are not recognised in the profit and loss account.

*FRS 3(56)*

The requirement to present this statement recognises that the profit and loss account is often an incomplete picture of performance since certain gains and losses are specifically permitted or are required to be taken directly to reserves. The most common examples are unrealised gains and losses resulting from the revaluation of fixed assets and foreign currency translation differences arising from the retranslation of net investments in foreign subsidiary undertakings.

# 4.8 Other statements

Both the 1985 Act and accounting standards require additional information to be disclosed in notes to the accounts. These are illustrated, where appropriate, in the model accounts in Part II. The following two statements are sometimes presented adjacent to the primary statements.

## 4.8.1 Reconciliation of movements in shareholders' funds

A reconciliation of the opening and closing totals of shareholders' funds for the period must be given in the accounts. The purpose of this reconciliation is to highlight any changes in the financial position of the company other than those disclosed by the profit and loss account and statement of total recognised gains and

*FRS 3(28,59)* losses. Examples of such changes include the issue of shares and redemption or repurchase of shares. This note is usually included as one of the notes to the accounts, although some companies have chosen to give it equal prominence with the statement of total recognised gains and losses and the note of historical cost *FRS 3(59)* profits or losses, as permitted by FRS 3.

### 4.8.2  Historical cost profits or losses

Where there is a material difference between the results as disclosed in the profit and loss account and the results on an unmodified historical cost basis, a note of the historical cost profit or loss for the period should be presented immediately following the profit and loss account or the statement of total recognised gains and *FRS 3(26)* losses. The purpose of the note is to eliminate the effects of any revaluation of assets and to show the results on a pure historical cost basis, thus facilitating a comparison of reported profits of different companies.

The note should incorporate:

(a)  a reconciliation of the reported profit on ordinary activities before taxation to the historical cost equivalent; and

(b)  the retained profit for the year on the historical cost basis.

Such notes are comparatively rare because the extra depreciation resulting from revaluations of assets is often immaterial to the reported results.  However, the difference can become much more material when revalued assets are sold.

## 4.9  Fundamental accounting principles

*85 4 Sch 9–14,*  Any amounts to be included in respect of items shown in a company's accounts
*SSAP 2(14)*  should be determined in accordance with the following five fundamental accounting principles:

- consistency;
- prudence;
- accruals;
- going concern; and
- separate determination.

### 4.9.1  Consistency

*85 4 Sch 11,*  The consistency principle requires like items to be treated consistently both within
*SSAP 2(14)(c)*  the same set of accounts and from one financial year to the next. This effectively prohibits selective application of accounting policies for similar items or between financial years.

### 4.9.2  Prudence

The prudence concept prohibits the recognition of unrealised profits in the profit and loss account and requires the recognition of all foreseeable losses, including *85 4 Sch 12,* those adjusting post balance sheet events which provide additional evidence of con-
*SSAP 2(14)(d)* ditions existing at the balance sheet date. The prudence concept has particular rel-
*SSAP 17(19,22)* evance in the determination of realised and distributable profits as discussed in Chapter 10.

### 4.9.3  Accruals

The accruals or matching principle requires all income and expenditure to be recog-

*85 4 Sch 13,*
*SSAP 2(14)(b)*

nised in the financial year to which it relates, irrespective of the date of receipt or payment. The application of this is subject to the overriding principle of prudence. The application of the accruals principle may result in the accelerated recognition of provisions for future expenditure where a loss is foreseeable, or the deferral of income recognition where it does not yet meet the test for a realised profit. However, with effect for financial statements ending on or after 23 March 1999, FRS 12 *Provisions, Contingent Liabilities and Contingent Assets* provides further rules in this area.

### 4.9.4  Going concern

*85 4 Sch 10,*
*SSAP 2(14)(a)*
*SAS 130*

The going concern principle recognises the presumption that the company for which the accounts have been prepared is expected to continue in operational existence for the foreseeable future without any intention or necessity to liquidate or curtail significantly the scale of operations. Where this presumption is inappropriate, it should be clearly stated and necessary adjustments made. The Auditing Practices Board (APB) has issued guidance on the interpretation of 'the foreseeable future' for this purpose and on the disclosures which might be expected to give a true and fair view when there is concern about the application of the going concern basis.

### 4.9.5  Separate determination

*85 4 Sch 14*

In determining the aggregate amount of any balance sheet item, the amount of each individual asset and liability must be determined separately. This rule is generally regarded as prohibiting the pooling of stocks or current investments for the purposes of determining whether they need to be written down to net realisable value where this is lower than cost.

### 4.9.6  Departure from statutory principles

*85 4 Sch 15, SSAP 2(17)*

*UITF 7*

*SSAP 20(65)*

Departures are permitted from these statutory principles where there are special reasons for doing so, but they must be disclosed, explained and quantified. 'Special reasons' are not defined but would probably include compliance with a relevant accounting standard or with the particular circumstances of the company (possibly reflecting industry practice). Such departures should generally be rare, although SSAP 20 *Foreign Currency Translation* specifically recognises that a departure from the principle of prudence may be necessary where unrealised foreign exchange gains on unsettled long-term monetary items are taken to the profit and loss account in accordance with that standard.

### 4.9.7  Disclosure of accounting policies

*85 4 Sch 36, SSAP 2(18)*

*85 4 Sch 36A*

There is a general requirement to disclose the particular accounting policies adopted by the company in arriving at balance sheet items and those which are material in determining the profit or loss for the year. All companies other than those defined as small or medium-sized (see Chapter 7) are required to state in their accounts whether they comply with all applicable accounting standards and to disclose any material departures from them.

In 1992 some companies proposed to state in their accounts that their accounting policies were in accord with accounting standards without further elaboration. This was considered by the Financial Reporting Review Panel. The Panel took legal advice about the effect of paragraph 36A of Schedule 4 to the 1985 Act on the accounting policy disclosure requirements of paragraph 36 of that Schedule. The advice confirmed that the requirements of the two paragraphs were separate and distinct. Thus, the inclusion in the notes to the accounts of a statement that the accounts had been prepared in accordance with applicable accounting standards did not satisfy the requirement to state the accounting policies of the company.

# 4.10  Substance over form

*FRS 5(14)*

*FRS 5(2)*

In addition to the five statutory accounting principles discussed above, a company's accounts should also reflect the substance of the transactions into which it has entered where this differs from the legal form. It is recognised that the legal form of complex transactions may not adequately express their true substance. Where this is the case, companies are required to determine the extent to which assets and liabilities have been acquired or disposed of as a result of transactions and to account for them accordingly.

# 4.11  Offsetting

*85 4 Sch 5, FRS 5(29)*

The 1985 Act prohibits setting off assets or income against liabilities or expenditure, and vice versa. FRS 5 recognises this statutory prohibition but permits debit and credit balances to be offset where the following conditions apply:

(a)  the reporting entity and the other party owe each other determinable monetary amounts in freely convertible currencies;

(b)  the reporting entity has the ability to insist on net settlement – a contingent right to net settlement will suffice provided the entity can insist on this in all circumstances of default and the right would survive the insolvency of the other party; and

(c)  the reporting entity's ability to insist on a net settlement is assured beyond doubt.

# 4.12  Statutory valuation methods

*85 4 Sch 16–34*

Most accounts are prepared in accordance with historical cost principles which require fixed assets to be shown at cost less provisions for impairment and current assets at the lower of cost and net realisable value. It is common, however, for companies to adopt the alternative accounting rules to a limited extent to permit the revaluation of certain assets, particularly property.

## 4.12.1  Historical cost rules

*85 4 Sch 17*

*85 4 Sch 18*

Fixed assets are included at their purchase price or production cost, less any provision for depreciation or diminution in value. The purchase price or production cost less any residual value of all fixed assets which have limited useful lives must be written off systematically over those lives.

Under both the historical cost and alternative accounting rules, the 1985 Act requires provision to be made for diminution in value of a fixed asset if the reduction in its value is expected to be permanent. FRS 11 *Impairment of Fixed Assets and Goodwill* was issued by the ASB in 1998 to provide more consistency concerning when such provisions are required and how they should be calculated. FRS 11 uses the term 'impairment' in place of the more traditional 'permanent diminution in value', but they mean the same thing for most practical purposes.

Current assets are included at the lower of purchase price or production cost (as appropriate) and net realisable value. Where any provision that has been made to write a current asset down to its net realisable value is no longer required, it must be written back to the extent that it is no longer necessary.

The purchase price or production cost of stocks, and of any 'fungible' assets, may be determined by application of the FIFO (first in, first out), weighted average price, or any other similar method (instead of strict calculation of the actual cost of each individual asset), provided that the asset chosen is one which appears to the directors to be appropriate in the circumstances of the company. Fungible assets are those which are substantially indistinguishable one from another – for example, wooden pallets or nuts and bolts. Investments are specifically included in this category. Where one of these methods is used and the balance sheet amount of stocks or fungible assets differs materially from their replacement cost at the balance sheet *85 4 Sch 27* date, the amount of that difference must be disclosed in a note to the accounts.

Raw materials and consumables may be included at a fixed quantity and value (e.g., the base stock method) in circumstances where they are constantly being replaced, their overall value is not material in assessing the company's state of affairs and *85 4 Sch 25* their quantity, value and composition are not subject to material variation.

## 4.12.2  Alternative accounting rules

The alternative accounting rules can be applied to some, or all, assets provided that:

*85 4 Sch 33(2)* (a)  the items affected and the basis of valuation are disclosed; and
(b)  the historical cost, or the difference between historical cost and the value at which the asset is stated, in both the current and preceding year is shown separately in the accounts or notes, with similar disclosure applying to deprecia-
*85 4 Sch 32* tion calculations.

## 4.12.3  Valuation methods

The alternative accounting rules may be summarised as follows.

(a)  Intangible assets, other than goodwill, may be included at their current cost. However, this freedom is constrained by FRS 10 *Goodwill and Intangible Assets* which severely restricts the circumstances in which intangible assets may be revalued.
(b)  Tangible fixed assets may be included either at their market value as at the date of their last valuation or at their current cost. FRS 15 *Measurement of Tangible Fixed Assets* will require such valuations to be conducted on a consistent basis and kept up to date.
(c)  Investments shown under fixed assets may be included either at their market value as at the date of their last valuation or at a value determined on any basis which the directors consider to be appropriate in the circumstances. In the latter case, particulars of the method of valuation adopted and of the reason for adopting it must be disclosed in a note to the accounts.
(d)  Investments shown under current assets may be included at their current cost.
(e)  Stocks may be included at their current cost.

The term 'current cost' is not defined in the 1985 Act but is generally taken to mean the lower of net current replacement cost and recoverable amount, where recoverable amount is the higher of net realisable value and value in use. This basis implies that the valuation must be current at each balance sheet date and may be contrasted with 'market value at the date of their last valuation' which need not be kept up to date. In practice, the use of current cost valuations has been rare although the basis has been used to value intangible assets such as brands prior to the implementation of FRS 10.

Where the value of any asset is determined on the basis of one of the alternative rules above, that value is the starting point for determining the amount of deprecia-
*85 4 Sch 32* tion to be included in respect of that asset.

### 4.12.4 Revaluation reserve

*85 4 Sch 34*

Revaluation surpluses and deficits must be taken to a revaluation reserve which appears as a separate heading in the balance sheet. The calculation of the surplus or deficit should be based on the written-down value of the asset prior to revaluation. The rules apply to assets revalued from time to time (e.g., property) and those which are revalued annually (e.g., investment properties dealt with in accordance with SSAP 19).

*85 4 Sch 34(3B)*

Amounts may not be transferred from the revaluation reserve other than in the following circumstances:

*85 4 Sch 34(3)*

(a)  where the amount was previously charged to the profit and loss account (e.g., additional depreciation charged following an upward revaluation surplus); or

*85 4 Sch 34(3,3A)*

(b)  on capitalisation (where it is used to issue fully or partly paid shares to the members of the company).

The revaluation reserve must be reduced to the extent that amounts transferred to it are no longer necessary for the purposes of the valuation method used. This would apply where a revalued asset is disposed of and the revaluation surplus relating to that asset is realised.

# Chapter 5  Groups and group accounts

## 5.1  Introduction

Where companies operate in groups rather than individually, single entity accounts for each member of the group are not normally sufficient on their own to provide financial information about their economic activities. Group accounts therefore need to be presented as well. This chapter sets out the main requirements concerning the preparation, presentation and publication of group accounts.

## 5.2  Regulatory framework

The statutory framework for groups and group accounts is established by the 1985 Act, which covers the following key areas:

(a)  the fundamental requirement to prepare group accounts and the exemptions from that requirement;
(b)  the form of group accounts;
(c)  the definitions of parent and subsidiary undertakings;
(d)  the exemption of subsidiaries from consolidation;
(e)  business combinations; and
(f)  the treatment of associates and joint ventures.

The legislation is supported, extended and interpreted by the following accounting standards:

- FRS 2     *Accounting for Subsidiary Undertakings*;
- FRS 5     *Reporting the Substance of Transactions*;
- FRS 6     *Acquisitions and Mergers*;
- FRS 7     *Fair Values in Acquisition Accounting*;
- FRS 9     *Associates and Joint Ventures*; and
- FRS 10    *Goodwill and Intangible Assets*.

These two regulatory sources (the 1985 Act and accounting standards) together establish current UK accounting practice for groups.

## 5.3  Definition of a group

*85 s258, s259*  There are essentially two different definitions of a group. For accounting purposes there is a wider definition incorporating a parent and its subsidiary undertakings. A subsidiary undertaking may be a body corporate, a partnership, or an unincorporated association carrying on a trade or business with or without a view to profit. For other statutory purposes there is a narrower definition of a holding company *85 s736*  and its subsidiary companies.

## 5.3.1 Parent and subsidiary undertakings

*85 s258, FRS 2(14)*

An entity will be a parent undertaking (P) in relation to another subsidiary undertaking (S) in any of the following circumstances:

*85 s258(2)(a), 10A Sch 2*

**Direct control of voting rights:** P holds a majority of the voting rights in S. These voting rights should be exercisable in relation to all, or substantially all, matters.

*85 s258(2)(d)*

**Control of voting rights by shareholders' agreement:** P is a member of S and controls a majority of the voting rights in S as a result of an agreement with the other members of S.

*85 s258(2)(b), 10A Sch 3*

**Control of board:** P is a member of S and has the right to appoint or remove a majority of its board of directors. This relates to directors who have a majority of the voting rights at board meetings on all, or substantially all, matters. If a director can be appointed only with the consent of another party, that appointment should not be taken into account.

*85 s258(2)(c), 10A Sch 4*

**Constitutional control of policy:** P need not be a member of S but has the right to exercise dominant influence over S by virtue of provisions in S's Memorandum or Articles. In this context, dominant influence refers to the ability to give directions with respect to the financial and operating policies of S which the directors of S are obliged to comply with, whether or not they are for the benefit of S.

*85 s258(2)(c), 10A Sch 4(2)*

**Contractual control of policy:** As above, but P's right to exercise dominant influence over S is by virtue of a control contract of a kind which S is authorised to enter into under its Memorandum and Articles and which is permitted under the domestic law under which S is incorporated. This is unlikely to be applicable to a subsidiary undertaking incorporated under UK law, since its directors would be obliged to act in the best interests of the company, but such an arrangement is permitted, for example, under German law.

*85 s258(4)(a), s260*

**Control through exercise of dominant influence:** P has a participating interest in S and actually exercises dominant influence over S. A participating interest is defined as an interest (including options) in the shares of another undertaking held for the long term for the purpose of securing a contribution to its activities by the exercise of control or influence. A holding of 20 per cent or more of the shares is presumed to be a participating interest unless the contrary is shown. Actual exercise of dominant influence is defined as 'the exercise of an influence that achieves the result that the operating and financial policies of the undertaking influenced are set in accordance with the wishes of the holder of the influence and for the holder's benefit whether or not those wishes are explicit'. It is identified by its effect in practice rather than the means by which it is exercised, which can be either interventionist or non-interventionist.

*FRS 2(7)(b)*
*FRS 2(71–73)*

**Control through unified management:** P has a participating interest in S and both P and S are managed on a unified basis. For this to apply, the whole of the operations of P and S must be integrated and managed as a single unit. It is not sufficient for them to have the same management team.

*85 s258(4)(b), FRS 2(12)*

**Sub-subsidiaries:** P is a parent of S if S is itself a subsidiary undertaking of another subsidiary undertaking of P.

*85 s258(5)*

Where any of the rights discussed above are only exercisable in certain circumstances, they should only be taken into account when those circumstances have actually arisen and still apply, or where they are within the control of the person having the rights.

*85 10A Sch 5*

### 5.3.2  Comparison of 'subsidiary undertaking' and 'subsidiary'

The 1985 Act distinguishes subsidiary undertakings (for accounts purposes) from subsidiaries (for other statutory purposes). Whereas the definition of a group for accounts purposes is essentially based on the ability to exercise control, the definition for other purposes is more restricted and does not include:

*85 s736*

(a)  entities other than bodies corporate (i.e., partnerships and unincorporated associations carrying on a trade or business with or without a view to profit);
(b)  entities controlled constitutionally or contractually;
(c)  entities controlled through the exercise of dominant influence; and
(d)  entities controlled through unified management.

# 5.4  Obligation to prepare group accounts

*85 s227*

If at the end of its financial year a company is a parent company, it must produce group accounts showing a true and fair view of the state of affairs and profit or loss of the parent company and its subsidiary undertakings, unless it is exempt. It also has to produce its own individual accounts, including a profit and loss account, for the board to approve, although the profit and loss account may be omitted in the accounts that are laid before the members and delivered to the Registrar of Companies, provided the accounts disclose the company's profit or loss for the

*85 s230*

financial year. The specific exemptions from the obligation to prepare group accounts are discussed below.

The requirement to produce group accounts only applies if a company is a parent company at the end of its financial year. Thus, if a company disposes of all its subsidiary undertakings during the year, it need not prepare group accounts in respect of that year, even though it was a parent company for part of the year. On the other hand, a company that acquires subsidiary undertakings, even on the last day of its financial year, must produce group accounts for the year, unless it is entitled to any of the exemptions.

# 5.5  Exemptions from consolidation

There are three circumstances in which the 1985 Act exempts a parent company from preparing group accounts. These are discussed in more detail below.

### 5.5.1  EEA parent

*85 s228*

A parent company is exempt from the requirement to prepare group accounts if its immediate parent is established under the law of a European Economic Area (EEA) Member State and either it is a wholly owned subsidiary undertaking or more than 50 per cent of its shares are held by its immediate parent. In the latter case, the exemption is subject to the additional condition that a significant minority of its other shareholders have not requested group accounts to be prepared by serving notice on the company to that effect. A significant minority is defined as shareholders holding:

(a)  more than half the remaining shares in the company; or
(b)  5 per cent of the total shares in the company.

This notice must be served no later than six months after the end of the financial year before that to which it relates: e.g., in relation to both a financial year covering the 18 months ending 30 June 1999 and a financial year covering the 12 months ending 31 December 1998, the minority must serve any notice requiring the preparation of group accounts by 30 June 1998. In both cases, the previous financial year would have ended on 31 December 1997.

The EEA comprises the European Union countries together with Norway, Iceland and Liechtenstein.

*85 s228(2)* This exemption is available only if the following additional conditions are met:

(a) the company must be included in the consolidated accounts of a parent undertaking established under the law of an EEA Member State (not necessarily the immediate parent);
(b) those consolidated accounts must be drawn up and audited, and the accompanying directors' report prepared, in accordance with the EEA Seventh Directive;
(c) the company must disclose in its own accounts that it is taking advantage of the relief and provide details of the identity and location of the EEA parent preparing the consolidated accounts; and
(d) the company must file the consolidated accounts of its parent at Companies House within the filing period applicable to it, together with a certified translation into English if they are not prepared in that language.

*85 s228(3)* The company is not entitled to take advantage of this exemption if any of its securities (e.g., equity shares, preference shares, debentures or loan stock) are listed on any stock exchange within the EEA.

## 5.5.2 Small and medium-sized groups

*85 s248* A parent company need not prepare group accounts if the group headed by that company qualifies as a small or medium-sized group. To be entitled to this exemption, the group must not only meet specified size criteria (discussed below) but must also not be ineligible because of the status of any of its members. This rules out a parent company of a group which includes any of the following:

(a) a public limited company or a body corporate which has the power under its constitution to offer its shares or debentures to the public;
(b) an authorised institution under the Banking Act 1987;
(c) an insurance company to which Part II of the Insurance Companies Act 1982 applies; or
(d) a person authorised under the Financial Services Act 1986.

A group is not regarded as ineligible simply because the parent company of the group seeking the exemption is an intermediate parent and its own parent or a fellow subsidiary falls into one of the categories above.

*85 s249* A newly formed group is treated as small or medium-sized if it satisfies the relevant criteria in respect of its first financial year. There are three situations in which an existing group is treated as small or medium-sized:

(a) it satisfies the relevant criteria for both the previous and the current year;
(b) it qualified in the immediately preceding year (either as a newly incorporated company which met the size criteria or under (a) or (c)) but does not qualify in the current year; or
(c) it meets the relevant size criteria in the current year and also was treated as qualifying the previous year under (b), even though it did not meet the criteria in that year.

*85 s249(4)*  The size criteria may be calculated on either a gross or a net basis. The former requires a simple aggregation of the figures for the group while the latter permits adjustments to be made for intra-group transactions and different accounting policies, as required for the preparation of consolidated accounts in Schedule 4A to the 1985 Act. The small and medium-sized group limits are as follows:

|  | *Net basis* | *Gross basis* |
|---|---|---|
| **Small group** | | |
| Aggregate turnover | £2.8 million | £3.36 million |
| Aggregate balance sheet total | £1.4 million | £1.68 million |
| Aggregate number of employees | 50 | 50 |
| | | |
| **Medium-sized group** | | |
| Aggregate turnover | £11.2 million | £13.44 million |
| Aggregate balance sheet total | £5.6 million | £6.72 million |
| Aggregate number of employees | 250 | 250 |

The monetary amounts of these criteria are subject to regular review by the European Commission and may therefore increase to reflect both inflation and a policy of deregulation for smaller companies. The upper limits are set at the EU level in ECUs and the UK has historically opted to set its own limits at the highest level permitted, although it has not yet taken advantage of the most recent increase.

### 5.5.3 Statutory exemptions for individual subsidiaries

*85 s229*  The third exemption from the requirement to prepare group accounts applies to a parent company, all of whose subsidiary undertakings are subject to individual exemptions from consolidation. Although the 1985 Act requires consolidated accounts to deal with all subsidiary undertakings, it identifies the following five situations where a subsidiary undertaking need not be consolidated. The applicability of these exemptions is clarified further by FRS 2.

*85 s229(2)*  **The inclusion of a subsidiary undertaking is not material for the purpose of giving a true and fair view**: Two or more undertakings may be excluded only if they are not material in aggregate. This possible exclusion therefore needs to be applied on a cumulative basis – a parent company cannot exclude all or most of its subsidiary undertakings from consolidation on the basis that each, individually, is immaterial in group terms, unless they are also immaterial in aggregate.

*85 s229(3)(b)*  **The information necessary for the preparation of group accounts cannot be obtained without disproportionate expense or undue delay**: The 1985 Act does not define the yardstick against which 'disproportionate' should be measured. FRS 2 prohibits the use of this exemption unless the excluded subsidiaries are immaterial in aggregate, on the grounds that this is the only circumstance in which the expense of preparing consolidated accounts can be disproportionate or the delay involved *FRS 2(24)*  can be excessive.

*85 s229(3)(a),*  **Severe long-term restrictions substantially hinder the exercise of the rights of the** *FRS 2(25)(a)*  **parent company over the assets or management of the undertaking**: Whilst the 1985 Act permits the subsidiary undertaking to be excluded in these circumstances, FRS 2 makes exclusion mandatory on the grounds that it is inappropriate to consolidate where there is no control. It is important to note that the restrictions must be over the rights by virtue of which the parent company is deemed to have a subsidiary undertaking (e.g., over the voting rights attached to the shares, the right to appoint or remove the board of directors or the right to exercise dominant influence), not over the underlying assets of the subsidiary. The restrictions must actually be in place and continuing rather than merely threatened because another party has the

*FRS 2(78)(c)*   power to impose such restrictions.

**The interest of the parent company is held exclusively with a view to subsequent resale and the undertaking has not previously been included in group accounts prepared by the parent company:** This applies only where control was intended to be temporary from the date of the acquisition. FRS 2 requires that one of the following conditions must be met:

*85 s229(3)(c), FRS 2(11)*

(a) either a purchaser must have been identified or the search for one must be underway and there must be a reasonable expectation of disposing of the interest within approximately one year of the date of acquisition; or
(b) the interest was acquired as a result of the enforcement of a security (which would most commonly be the case where the interest was now held by a lending institution), unless the interest has become part of the continuing activities of the group or the holder acts as if it intended the interest to become so.

If, for example, a company with a subsidiary undertaking that was acquired some time previously decides to dispose of that subsidiary, it would not be possible to exclude the subsidiary from consolidation on this ground. Conversely, where a company acquires a group of companies with the intention of disposing of some of the subsidiaries acquired, those subsidiaries need not be consolidated, provided the disposals are likely to take place within a year.

**The activities of one or more subsidiary undertakings are so different from those of other undertakings to be included in the consolidation that their inclusion would be incompatible with the obligation to give a true and fair view:** The 1985 Act states specifically that this exemption, which is mandatory if the circumstances arise, does not apply merely because some of the undertakings are industrial and some commercial, or because businesses provide different products and services. FRS 2 recognises that it will be exceptional for such circumstances to arise. No examples are therefore provided of any particular contrast of activities where the necessary incompatibility is likely to arise. In contrast, FRS 2 specifically excludes the following situations from the scope of this exemption:

*85 s229(4), FRS 2(25)(c)*

*FRS 2(78)(e)*

(a) where a subsidiary undertaking is a banking or insurance company and its parent undertaking is not, or vice versa; and
(b) if a subsidiary undertaking is a profit-oriented organisation and its parent undertaking does not trade for profit, or vice versa.

# 5.6 Form and content of group accounts

The 1985 Act requires group accounts to consist of a consolidated balance sheet and a consolidated profit and loss account which together give a true and fair view of the state of affairs and profit or loss of the parent company and its subsidiary undertakings, insofar as the members of the parent company are concerned. In addition, accounting standards require the presentation of a consolidated cash flow statement dealing with the consolidated cash flows of the group and a consolidated statement of total recognised gains and losses. Group accounts in a form other than consolidated accounts would not comply with the 1985 Act or with accounting standards.

*85 s227(2,3)*

*FRS 1(6)*
*FRS 3(27)*

The consolidated balance sheet and profit and loss account must comply with the provisions of Schedule 4A to the 1985 Act, which requires them to be prepared by combining the information contained in the separate balance sheets and profit and loss accounts of the undertaking included in the consolidation and by making such adjustments as may be appropriate in accordance with generally accepted accounting principles or practice. They should comply as far as practicable with the provi-

*85 s227(4), 4A Sch 2*

*85 s227(5)* sions of Schedule 4 as if the group were a single undertaking. However, if compliance with Schedule 4A is not sufficient to present a true and fair view, additional information should be provided.

### 5.6.1 Uniform accounting policies

*85 4A Sch 3(1), FRS 2(40)*

*85 4A Sch 3(2), FRS 2(41)*

*85 4A Sch 4*

The carrying values of a subsidiary undertaking's assets and liabilities should be adjusted for inclusion in the consolidated accounts if accounting policies different from those used in the group accounts have been followed when preparing the accounts of the underlying subsidiaries. Departure from this principle is permitted in special cases provided full disclosure is made of the different policies used, together with an indication of the amounts of assets and liabilities affected, and the reasons. Adjustments that are not material to a true and fair view need not be made. Differences in accounting policies between the parent's own accounts for a financial year and its group accounts should be disclosed and explained in the group accounts.

### 5.6.2 Coterminous years

*85 s223(5), 4A Sch 2*

Directors of parent undertakings must ensure that the financial years of both the parent and each subsidiary undertaking coincide, unless in their opinion there are good reasons not to do so. Where the financial year of a subsidiary undertaking differs from that of the parent, the 1985 Act permits the group accounts to be based on the accounts of:

(a) the most recent financial year of the subsidiary ending before that of the parent (provided it ended no more than three months prior to that of the parent); or
(b) 'interim' accounts made up by the subsidiary as at the parent's year end.

*FRS 2(42)* Wherever practicable, however, FRS 2 requires the accounts of all companies in the group to be made up to the same date and for identical accounting periods.

### 5.6.3 Minority interests

*85 4A Sch 17*

All the assets and liabilities of subsidiaries, including those of subsidiaries which are not wholly owned, should be consolidated. The minority interest in the capital and reserves of the subsidiary undertaking and in its profit or loss for the year must be shown separately in both the balance sheet and profit and loss account. The statutory formats are amended by Schedule 4A to include the relevant captions (see Appendix 1).

### 5.6.4 Intra-group transactions

*FRS 2(39), 85 4A Sch 6*

The 1985 Act requires intra-group transactions to be eliminated unless the impact is immaterial. Where intra-group profits or losses are included in the carrying amount of assets, FRS 2 requires them to be eliminated in full, although the 1985 Act permits partial elimination in proportion to the group's interest in the subsidiary.

### 5.6.5 Treatment of excluded subsidiary undertakings

FRS 2 sets out the appropriate treatment for subsidiaries excluded from consolidation for the reasons set out above.

*FRS 2(27–28)* **Severe long-term restrictions:** The group's investment should be carried as a fixed asset investment and stated at the amount at which it would have been included under the equity method at the date the restrictions came into force. The parent company should not continue to recognise the subsidiary's profits or losses unless it retains a significant influence. If this is the case, the parent should continue to account for the undertaking under the equity method.

*FRS 2(29)* **Held for resale:** The group's investment in the subsidiary should be stated as a current asset at the lower of cost and net realisable value.

*85 4A Sch 18, s243,* **Different activities:** The investment in the subsidiary should be accounted for using
*FRS 2(30)* the equity method. In addition, the 1985 Act requires that the accounts of a subsidiary undertaking excluded from consolidation on grounds of different activities should be attached to the consolidated accounts. This requirement applies, however, only to subsidiary undertakings which are:

(a) incorporated overseas and without an established place of business in Great Britain; or
(b) unincorporated entities.

These entities would not normally have to file accounts at Companies House and the treatment is therefore designed to ensure that information regarding them is available. If the subsidiary's accounts are required by its own domestic law to be audited, a copy of the relevant auditors' report must also be attached.

# 5.7  Business combinations

Business combinations are governed by both the 1985 Act and accounting standards. There are two methods of accounting for a business combination in group accounts: the acquisition method, which is the most common, and the merger method which is required only in limited circumstances.

## 5.7.1  Selection of method

A combination must be accounted for using merger accounting if it meets certain specified criteria (discussed below). Acquisition accounting must be used for all other combinations except group reconstructions. These may be accounted for as mergers if the statutory conditions for applying merger accounting are met, the relative rights of the ultimate shareholders are not changed and no minority interest
*FRS 6(13)* in the net assets of the group is altered by the transfer. A group reconstruction does not, however, have to meet the strict conditions for identifying a merger set out in FRS 6. A group reconstruction is defined in FRS 6 as any of the following arrange-
*FRS 6(2)* ments:

'(a)  *the transfer of a shareholding in a subsidiary undertaking from one group company to another;*
(b)  *the addition of a new parent company to a group;*
(c)  *the transfer of shares in one or more subsidiary undertakings of a group to a new company that is not a group company but whose shareholders are the same as those of the group's parent; or*
(d)  *the combination into a group of two or more companies that before the combination had the same shareholders.'*

The statutory conditions which must be met for merger accounting to be permitted
*85 4A Sch 10* are as follows:

(a) at least 90 per cent of the nominal value of the relevant shares in the undertaking acquired is held by or on behalf of the parent company and its subsidiary undertakings;

(b) the 90 per cent holding was attained by means of an arrangement providing for the issue of equity shares by the parent company or one or more of its subsidiary undertakings;

(c) the fair value of any consideration other than the issue of equity shares given pursuant to the arrangement did not exceed 10 per cent of the nominal value of the equity shares issued; and

(d) the adoption of the merger method of accounting accords with generally accepted accounting principles or practice.

*FRS 6(6–12)*

FRS 6 severely limits the circumstances where merger accounting is permitted other than in the case of group reconstructions. The following strict criteria must all be met for a merger to be recognised and accounted for as such:

(a) no party to the combination is portrayed as either acquirer or acquiree, either by its own board or management or by that of any other party to the combination;

(b) all parties, through their boards or appointees, participate in establishing the management structure of the combined entity (including the selection of management personnel) on the basis of consensus between the parties to the combination rather than through the exercise of voting rights alone;

*FRS 2(68)*

(c) the relative sizes of the combining entities are not so disparate that one party dominates the combined entity by virtue of its relative size. This means effectively that the relative sizes are to be within a 60/40 banding;

(d) no more than an immaterial proportion of the fair value of the consideration received by an equity shareholder is represented by non-equity consideration; and

(e) no equity shareholders retain an interest in the performance of only part of the business.

Where a business combination meets all of the above criteria, including the 1985 Act requirements, merger accounting is mandatory. All other business combinations, other than group reconstructions, are acquisitions.

## 5.7.2 Effective date of acquisition or disposal

*FRS 2(45)*

The effective date for recognising the acquisition and disposal of a subsidiary undertaking is the date on which control of that undertaking passes to its new parent undertaking. This applies even if the acquiring company has the right under the agreement to share in the profits of the acquired business from an earlier date.

## 5.7.3 Acquisition method

Under the acquisition method of accounting in group accounts:

(a) the identifiable assets and liabilities of the undertaking acquired (i.e., those assets and liabilities which are capable of being disposed of or discharged separately, without disposing of the business of the undertaking) are included in

*85 4A Sch 9, FRS 6(20)*

the consolidated balance sheet at their fair values as at the date of acquisition;

(b) the income and expenditure of the undertaking acquired is brought into the group accounts only from the date of acquisition; and

(c) the interest of the parent company and its subsidiary undertakings in the adjusted capital and reserves of the undertaking acquired is set off against the acquisition cost of that interest, with the balancing number being positive or negative goodwill.

The adjusted capital and reserves of the undertaking acquired refers to its capital and reserves at the date of acquisition after adjusting the identifiable assets and liabilities (see (a) above) of the undertaking to reflect their fair values as at that date. The acquisition cost refers to the amount of cash consideration and the fair value of any other consideration, together with any amounts paid in respect of fees and other expenses of acquisition. FRS 7 sets out requirements for establishing the fair values of the assets, liabilities and non-cash consideration in relation to an acquisition. FRS 10 deals with the accounting treatment of the resultant goodwill.

The acquisition method should also be used in the individual accounts of a company which has acquired the trade and assets of another entity.

### 5.7.4 Merger method

*85 4A Sch 11, FRS 6(16)*

Under merger accounting the carrying values of the assets and liabilities of the parties to the combination are not adjusted to reflect fair values on consolidation, although appropriate adjustments should be made to achieve uniformity of accounting policies in the combining entities.

*FRS 6(17)*

The results and cash flows of all the combining entities should be brought into the financial statements of the combined entity from the beginning of the financial year in which the combination occurred. The corresponding figures should be restated by including the results for all the combining entities for the previous period and their balance sheets for the previous balance sheet date. In both cases, adjustments should be made as necessary to achieve uniformity of accounting policies.

*FRS 6(18)*

The difference, if any, between the nominal value of the shares issued plus the fair value of any other consideration given and the nominal value of the shares received in exchange should be shown as a movement on other reserves in the consolidated financial statements. Any existing balance on the share premium account or capital redemption reserve of the new subsidiary undertaking should be brought in by being shown as a movement on other reserves. These movements should be shown in the reconciliation of movements in shareholders' funds. Merger expenses are not included as part of this adjustment but should be charged to the profit and loss account of the combined entity at the effective date of the merger.

*FRS 6(19)*

# 5.8 Business combinations in parent company accounts

Where a parent company has acquired an interest in the shares of a subsidiary undertaking, the normal method of accounting for the acquisition in the parent company's individual accounts is to record the investment at the fair value of the consideration given. If all or part of the consideration given for the acquisition is shares, then the difference between their fair value and nominal value is normally credited to a share premium account.

*FRS 4 App 1(3)*

There are, however, two different types of relief applicable to certain business combinations which reduce or eliminate the need for share premium to be recognised and which may also result in a carrying value for the investment below the fair value. These are merger relief and group reconstruction relief respectively. The application of these reliefs may appear to be in conflict with the requirements in FRS 4 for shares to be stated at the fair value of the net proceeds received. However, the FRS states explicitly that nothing in it affects the availability of statutory merger relief. Moreover, FRS 6 specifically excludes from its scope the form of accounting to be used in the parent company's accounts and states in particular that it does not restrict the availability of merger relief and group reconstruction relief.

### 5.8.1  Merger relief

*85 s130, s131*

Under the merger relief provisions, where the issuing company (i.e., the acquirer) has, by an arrangement which includes the exchange of shares, acquired at least a 90 per cent equity holding in another company, then the requirement to establish a share premium account in respect of those shares does not apply.

*85 s133*

Where merger relief applies, the issuing company can opt to carry the investment in its new subsidiary at the nominal value of the shares it has issued rather than at fair value. If it chooses to carry its investment at fair value, however, any premium which is accounted for should not be credited to the share premium account, since merger relief is mandatory, but taken to some other suitably described reserve (e.g., a 'merger reserve').

Merger relief is not applicable only to transactions that are accounted for on consolidation using merger accounting. It was originally introduced to remove one of the barriers to merger accounting (the requirement to establish a share premium account) and it is essential if merger accounting is to be adopted. Nevertheless, it is common for merger relief to be applicable in business combinations where merger accounting would not be permitted. The combination of merger relief and acquisition accounting gives rise to a merger reserve either in the parent company's own accounts (if the investment is carried at fair value) or on consolidation.

### 5.8.2  Group reconstruction relief

*85 s132*

If a business combination falls within the statutory definition of a group reconstruction, the statutory share premium relief is more restrictive than that allowed by the merger relief provisions. A transaction is considered a group reconstruction for this purpose if:

(a)  the issuing company is a wholly owned subsidiary of its holding company;
(b)  it allots its shares to its holding company or to a fellow wholly owned subsidiary; and
(c)  it must receive in exchange shares in, or other non-cash assets of, another member of the group.

*85 s132(3,5)*

Where group reconstruction relief applies, share premium can be limited to the minimum premium value. This is defined as 'the amount (if any) by which the base value of the consideration for the shares allotted exceeds the aggregate nominal value of those shares'. The base value of the consideration is the lower of the book value or the original cost to the transferor of the net assets transferred. Thus, if the nominal value of the shares issued is greater than or equal to the base value of the net assets acquired, no share premium need be recognised. On the other hand, if the nominal value of the shares is less than the base value of the net assets acquired, the minimum premium value that must be recognised is the difference between the two. This has the effect of at least maintaining the base value of the net assets transferred in the books of the new holding company.

*85 s131(1)*

If a business combination falls within the definition of a group reconstruction then merger relief cannot be used. Moreover, group reconstruction relief does not appear to be mandatory and a company can establish a full share premium account if it wishes to do so.

*85 s133*

Where a company takes advantage of group reconstruction relief, it may also carry the investment at an amount equal to the nominal value of the shares issued plus the minimum premium value recognised.

### 5.8.3 Advantages of merger and group reconstruction relief

The two main advantages of merger relief and group reconstruction relief are as follows:

(a) there is no share premium account (or at least it may be established at a lower level than would otherwise be required), thus enabling the establishment of a non-statutory reserve on consolidation; and

(b) the new subsidiary may be recorded, in the parent's accounts, at a value below its fair value, thus reducing the need to consider making an immediate provision for a diminution in value if pre-acquisition dividends are distributed to the new parent.

*FRS 6 App 1(16)*

# 5.9 Quasi-subsidiaries

The definition of a subsidiary undertaking, which is essentially based on a concept of control, catches many entities which would not fall within the narrower definition of a subsidiary company in the 1985 Act. Nevertheless, controlled entities are sometimes used to house assets and liabilities in a financing arrangement which is structured so that the vehicle does not meet the legal definition of a subsidiary undertaking. The commercial effect of these transactions is no different from that which would result if the vehicle were a subsidiary, since the reporting entity stands to benefit from the overall performance of the vehicle and essentially controls it.

Such vehicles are amongst those that may fall within the following definition of 'quasi-subsidiaries' in FRS 5:

*FRS 5(7)*

> 'A company, trust, partnership or other vehicle that, though not fulfilling the definition of a subsidiary, is directly or indirectly controlled by the reporting entity and gives rise to benefits for that entity that are in substance no different from those that would arise were the vehicle a subsidiary.'

*FRS 5(35,36)*

A company which has quasi-subsidiaries must include the assets, liabilities, profits, losses and cash flows of these quasi-subsidiaries in its group accounts in the same way as if they were those of subsidiary undertakings, following the requirements of the 1985 Act and FRS 2. Exemption from consolidation is, however, only permitted where the interest in the quasi-subsidiary has not previously been consolidated and is held exclusively for resale. Where a company has quasi-subsidiaries but no subsidiary undertakings, it should present consolidated accounts for itself and its quasi-subsidiaries with equal prominence to its own individual accounts.

*FRS 5(8,33)*

Control of another entity in this context means the ability to direct the financial and operating policies of that entity with a view to gaining economic benefit from its activities. The ability to prevent others from directing the financial and operating policies of the vehicle is evidence of control, as is the ability to prevent others from enjoying the benefits arising from the vehicle's net assets.

*FRS 5(32,34)*

Evidence of which party gains the benefits from the net assets of an entity can be obtained from an understanding of which party is exposed to the risks inherent in them. Where the financial and operating policies of a vehicle are in substance predetermined, contractually or otherwise, the party possessing control will be the one that gains the benefits arising from the net assets of the vehicle.

# 5.10 Associates and joint ventures

FRS 9 is effective for accounting periods ending on or after 23 June 1998 and introduces into UK accounting detailed rules for determining *inter alia* whether an interest should be classified as an associate or a joint venture, and for accounting for such interests. The Summary section of FRS 9 notes that there are five broad categories of interests, being:

| | Category | Treatment in consolidated accounts |
|---|---|---|
| (a) | Subsidiary | Consolidation |
| (b) | Joint arrangement that is not an entity (JANE) | Effectively proportional consolidation in both the group's and the investor's accounts |
| (c) | Joint venture | Gross equity method |
| (d) | Associate | Equity method |
| (e) | Simple investment | Cost or valuation |

## 5.10.1 Joint ventures

*FRS 9(4)*  FRS 9 discusses at some length the definitions of a joint venture and a JANE. A joint venture is:

> *'an entity in which the reporting entity holds an interest on a long-term basis and is jointly controlled by the reporting entity and one or more other venturers under a contractual arrangement.'*

*85 4A Sch 19*  This is similar to the definition in company law but FRS 9 provides additional assistance by defining an entity, joint control and an interest held on a long-term basis which is also used in determining associate interests.

The more difficult areas in FRS 9 are identifying:

(a) a JANE; and
(b) a structure with the form but not the substance of a joint venture.

Both of these will account directly for their share of the assets, liabilities and cash flows held within the joint structure. The second form has been developed to cope with particular or even peculiar situations in which the participants hold a long-term interest and exercise joint management, but have extremely limited commonality of interest because, in effect, each venturer operates its own business independently of the other venturers. In such cases, the joint venture structure is merely acting as an agent for each venturer.

A JANE (joint arrangement that is not an entity) is defined as:

*FRS 9(4)*  > *'a contractual arrangement under which the participants engage in joint activities that do not create an entity because it would not be carrying on a trade or business of its own. A contractual arrangement where all significant matters of operating and financial policy are predetermined does not create an entity because the policies are those of its participants, not of a separate entity.'*

Paragraphs 8 and 9 of FRS 9 seek to explain this concept. An example may be the case of three oil companies agreeing to build and share use of a pipeline, each paying according to their usage. That is likely to be a JANE. But if the operators of the pipeline start to run it as a separate business, seeking new customers and so on, then it will become a separate entity and so a joint venture.

*FRS 9(20–23)*  Joint ventures adopt the gross equity method. This is similar to the equity method, described below, except that the share of joint ventures' turnover must be shown as a memorandum figure on the profit and loss account and the share of gross assets and liabilities is shown on the balance sheet.

### 5.10.2 Associates

*FRS 9(4)*

*85 4A Sch 20–22,*
*FRS 9(14–17)*

Associates are defined in FRS 9 as entities, not being subsidiary undertakings, where the investor has a participating interest and exercises significant influence over the financial and operating policies of the investee. This is broadly consistent with the definition of an associated undertaking in company law although FRS 9 provides additional guidance, particularly on determining what constitutes significant influence.

Associates should be accounted for in consolidated accounts using the equity method. This means that the investment should be included as a fixed asset investment at the total of:

*FRS 9(29)*

(a)  the investor's share of the net assets of its associates; and
(b)  the goodwill paid (or negative goodwill) arising on the acquisition, less any amortisation or write-down.

The goodwill number should also be disclosed separately.

*FRS 9(27)*

The other main feature of equity accounting is that the investor's share of the associates' operating results is included immediately after the group operating result in the profit and loss account.

# Chapter 6 Directors' transactions, emoluments and interests

## 6.1 Introduction

This chapter summarises the rules relating to the legality of transactions between a company and its directors, and the disclosure of those transactions, including directors' emoluments and interests in the company's shares. For further information, reference should be made to the legislation, and in cases of doubt it may be necessary to take legal advice. Directors should also have regard to their general fiduciary duty towards the company and take into account any additional restrictions, which may be contained in their company's Memorandum and Articles.

### 6.1.1 Definitions

The following general definitions are relevant in the context of this chapter.

*85 s741(1)*
*Table A Art 69*

A **director** is defined as 'any person occupying the position of director, by whatever name called'. This usually includes those identified as alternate directors, unless the company's Articles provide otherwise.

*85 s741(2)*
*85 s330(5), 6 Sch 27(2)*

A **shadow director** is defined as 'a person in accordance with whose directions or instructions the directors of the company are accustomed to act'. Shadow directors are treated as directors in the context of the legality and disclosure of loans and other transactions with directors, but not for the disclosure of directors' emoluments. In practice, it is rare for a person to be identified as a shadow director.

An **alternate director** is someone appointed by a director, typically, to perform all the functions of his/her appointor as a director whenever the director is absent.

*85 s346*

A **connected person** of a director includes, broadly speaking:

(a) a director's spouse, infant children and step-children;
(b) companies 'associated' with him/her (as defined);
(c) trustees of a trust in which the director or any of the persons mentioned above have a beneficial interest; and
(d) partners of any of the above persons.

Parents, brothers and sisters of a director are not included in this definition, which applies to the disclosure of directors' emoluments and other transactions and, also, in the context of relevant companies only (see below), to the determination of whether loans to directors are legal.

*85 s331*

**Relevant companies** are those which are themselves public or in a group containing a public company. Relevant status may thus be acquired whenever a company:

(a) is incorporated as public;
(b) re-registers as public;

(c)  enters a group already containing a public company; or

(d)  is in a group which admits a public company.

Relevant status will be lost if the reverse applies.

*85 s735*  The statutory definition does not include foreign or associated companies. Consequently, a company does not acquire relevant status solely because it is the parent, subsidiary or fellow subsidiary of a foreign public company or because it acquires an investment in a public company which it accounts for as an associate.

# 6.2  Related party transactions

The requirements of FRS 8 are additional to a number of disclosure requirements concerning transactions which involve directors and connected persons that arise from the 1985 Act and which apply to all companies. The Act requires statutory

*85 6 Sch 1*  accounts to disclose dealings with directors and 'connected persons' (including shadow directors) including:

(a)  remuneration;

(b)  compensation for loss of office;

(c)  holdings and dealing in their company's shares;

(d)  loans and similar transactions; and

(e)  material transactions with the company and its subsidiaries in which a director has a material interest.

*SE 12.43 (r,s)*  The Stock Exchange imposes certain additional requirements on listed companies including the disclosure of 'particulars of any contract of significance' in which a director was materially interested.

In addition to the above, there is always the overriding requirement that statutory accounts should give a true and fair view and therefore should include any additional information which is necessary to meet this requirement.

## 6.2.1  Definition of related parties

*FRS 8(2.5)(a)*  Two or more parties are related parties when at any time during the financial period:

(a)  one party has direct or indirect control of the other party; or

(b)  the parties are subject to common control from the same source; or

(c)  one party has influence over the financial and operating policies of the other party to an extent that that other party might be inhibited from pursuing at all times its own separate interests; or

(d)  the parties, in entering a transaction, are subject to influence from the same source to such an extent that one of the parties to the transaction has subordinated its own separate interests.

## 6.2.2  Deemed related parties

*FRS 8(2.5)(b)*  Certain parties are deemed by the standard to be related parties of the reporting entity. These are:

(a)  its ultimate and intermediate parent undertaking, subsidiary undertakings and fellow subsidiary undertakings;

(b)  its associates and joint ventures;

(c)  investors or venturers in respect of which the reporting entity is an associate or a joint venture;

(d) pension funds for the benefit of employees of the reporting entity or of any entity that is a related party of the reporting entity; and

(e) directors, including shadow directors, of the reporting entity and the directors of its ultimate and intermediate parent undertakings.

### 6.2.3 Presumed related parties

*FRS 8(2.5)(c)* Unless there is evidence to the contrary, the following are presumed to be related parties of a reporting entity:

(a) a person owning or able to exercise control over 20 per cent or more of the voting rights of the entity, whether directly or indirectly (via another entity or close family);

(b) each person acting in concert so as to exercise control or influence over the reporting entity. Persons acting in concert are further defined as persons who, pursuant to an agreement or understanding (whether formal or informal) actively co-operate, whether by the ownership by any of them of shares in an undertaking or otherwise, to exercise control or influence over that undertaking;

(c) entities managing, or managed by, the reporting entity under a management contract; and

(d) key management, i.e., persons having the authority or responsibility for directing or controlling the activities and resources of the reporting entity.

### 6.2.4 Deemed unrelated parties

*FRS 8(4)* Some specific exemptions are highlighted as deemed unrelated parties which would otherwise have required disclosure due to one party being economically dependent on another. These exemptions include providers of finance in the course of their business (e.g., a clearing bank providing normal overdraft facilities), public utilities, government departments and third parties with whom they trade directly as part of their normal trading (e.g., customers, suppliers, franchisers, etc.).

### 6.2.5 Definition of related party transactions

*FRS 8(2.6)* FRS 8 defines a related party transaction as:

(a) the transfer of assets or liabilities or the performance of services;

(b) by, to or for a related party; and

(c) irrespective of whether a price is charged.

## 6.3 Disclosure of a related party transaction

FRS 8 requires:

*FRS 8(6)* (a) the disclosure of material transactions with related parties. The following should be disclosed in respect of such transactions:

(i) names of the transacting related parties and a description of the relationship between them;

(ii) a description of the transactions including the amounts involved and any other elements necessary for an understanding of the financial statements; and

(iii) the amounts due to or from related parties at the balance sheet date and provisions for doubtful debts due from such parties at that date and amounts written off in the period in respect of debts due to or from related parties; and

*FRS 8(5)*   (b)  the disclosure of the reporting entity's controlling party and the ultimate controlling party if different.

### 6.3.1  Materiality

*FRS 8(20)*   Only material transactions need to be disclosed for this purpose. Transactions are deemed material when their disclosure might reasonably be expected to influence decisions made by the users of general purpose financial statements. The question of materiality should be considered in relation to the related party when that party is a director or key employee as well as the significance of the transaction to the reporting entity.

### 6.3.2  Aggregation

*FRS 8(21)*   Similar transactions may be aggregated by type of related party although transactions should not be aggregated in such a way as to obscure the importance of significant transactions. In addition, aggregation should not be used to conceal a transaction with an individual.

### 6.3.3  Exemptions

*FRS 8(3)*   FRS 8 provides a number of exemptions from disclosure in group situations.

# 6.4  Legality of transactions with directors

The objective of the prohibitions against loans to directors in the 1985 Act is to restrict the scope for abuse of a director's position, particularly in a group including a public company, through the control of credit to directors in its widest form.

*85 s330, s331*   Transactions not involving credit are not included within the scope of these rules. To achieve this, various methods of providing credit are identified, including:

(a)  loans;

(b)  quasi-loans (basically, indirect loans via third parties);

(c)  credit transactions (basically, the provision of goods, services or land on deferred credit);

(d)  guarantees and security in connection with loans, quasi-loans and credit transactions;

(e)  assignments or the assumption of obligations from third parties concerning transactions which the company is itself prohibited from concluding; and

(f)  mutual aid or back-to-back transactions, whereby a third party enters into a transaction which the company may not itself conclude, and in return the company provides some benefit to the third party.

The legislation defines not only the type of credit which is restricted, but also the persons to whom credit may or may not be extended and the types of company which may provide credit.

### 6.4.1  General rule on loans

*85 s330*   A company may not make, or agree to make, a loan to a director of the company or its holding company, or provide any guarantee or security in connection with a loan made to such a director by a third party. It is also prohibited from assuming or assigning liabilities or rights attaching to transactions between a director and a third party that the company itself could not conclude (e.g., 'buying' a loan to a director made by someone else) or from providing mutual aid (e.g., placing deposits or business with a bank in return for the bank's making a loan to a director of the company). A company which is not a relevant company may, however, enter into quasi-loans and credit transactions for directors and their connected persons and make loans to their connected persons.

### 6.4.2 Restrictions on relevant companies

In addition to the general restrictions which apply to all companies, relevant companies may not make loans to any persons connected with directors of the company or of its holding company and, in addition, may not enter into any of the following transactions with directors of the company or its holding company or with any of their connected persons:

*85 s330*

(a) quasi-loans;
(b) credit transactions;
(c) guarantees or security concerning loans, quasi-loans and credit transactions by third parties; or
(d) assignments or mutual aid arrangements concerning any prohibited transactions.

### 6.4.3 Scope of restrictions

The restrictions on loans, quasi-loans and other credit transactions only apply where the person to whom they are made was a director of the company or its holding company, or was connected with such a director, at the time of the transaction. A transaction which was not in breach of these restrictions when it was initiated is not invalidated if the beneficiary becomes a director or connected with a director subsequently.

### 6.4.4 Permitted credit transactions

Despite the general prohibition on loans to, and other credit transactions with, directors, there is an extensive list of permitted transactions. These exceptions to the rule fall into three categories:

(a) transactions permitted because of their purpose (e.g., expense advances to directors of non-relevant companies which have been approved by, or can subsequently be ratified by, the company in general meeting);
(b) transactions which fall below specified levels (e.g., loans below £5,000 in aggregate); and
(c) certain transactions with the directors of money-lending companies (i.e., favourable housing loans and normal arm's-length commercial loans).

Appendix 2 contains a table summarising the various purposes for which credit may be given to directors and their connected persons. It distinguishes between non-relevant and relevant companies, and indicates what financial limits (if any) apply. There are normally no restrictions on providing credit to the directors of subsidiary companies if they are not also main board directors.

### 6.4.5 Aggregation

In calculating whether, and to what extent, a loan or other form of credit is subject to the exemptions in (b) and (c) at **6.4.4** above, the company must consider the aggregate impact of other transactions with the same director. In each case, the monetary amounts must take into account not just the value of any proposed transaction but also:

*85 s339*

(a) the amount outstanding in respect of any existing transaction of the same type made under the same exemption by the company or any subsidiary of the company; and

(b) the value of any existing assignments, assumptions of obligations from third parties, mutual aid arrangements or back-to-back transactions made under the same exemption by the company or any subsidiary of the company.

In both cases (except where the exemption relates to a loan to a director of less than £5,000), it is also necessary to include amounts relating to transactions with or for persons connected with the director (or with the director, if the proposed transaction is for a connected person).

*85 s340*  The 1985 Act defines the amounts or values that are to be taken into account when aggregating items to determine whether they are within the specified legal limits. If a value cannot be ascertained, the transaction is automatically deemed to exceed £100,000.

### 6.4.6 Penalties

*85 s341, s342*  Civil remedies, including restitution and, in the case of relevant companies only, criminal penalties, may be enforceable in cases of transactions which exceed the permitted limits.

# 6.5 Disclosure of directors' transactions

*85 6 Sch 19*  The general principle is that any transaction or agreement involving the various types of credit mentioned above is disclosable by any company in respect of a person who was a director of the company or its holding company, or a connected person of such a director at any time during the year:

(a) whether or not it was permitted;

(b) whether or not the person was a director or connected person at the time of the transaction; and

(c) whether or not, in cases involving subsidiaries, the company was a subsidiary at the time of the transaction.

*85 s237*  The auditors are required to report the relevant details, so far as they are able, if the accounts fail to provide them.

Appendix 3 contains a table summarising the various disclosures required and the exemptions available for companies other than banks. The disclosure requirements apply to transactions with directors and shadow directors, and their connected persons.

### 6.5.1 Material interests

*85 6 Sch 15–16*  In addition to disclosing details of loans, quasi-loans and credit transactions, the accounts must also contain particulars of other transactions in which a director has a material interest. The 1985 Act does not, however, define what is meant by a material interest. The most common interpretation is that 'material' should be interpreted as meaning 'relevant to the users of the accounts'. This would require disclosure of any transactions where the director's interest was either material in the context of the company's accounts or material to the director himself. This interpretation is consistent with the interpretation of material in FRS 8 *Related Party Disclosures* and ensures that shareholders are informed of potential conflicts of *FRS 8(20)*  interest.

*85 6 Sch 17*  An interest in a transaction or arrangement is deemed not to be material if a majority of the directors, excluding the director with the interest, agrees that it is not so, although this does not override the requirements of FRS 8.

### 6.5.2 Exemption from disclosure

The following transactions are exempt from disclosure on the basis of specified *de minimis* limits:

*85 6 Sch 24*  (a) credit transactions, or other arrangements relating to credit transactions, where the aggregate value of any such transactions or arrangements for an individual director and his connected persons does not exceed £5,000; and

*85 6 Sch 25*  (b) transactions in which a director has a material interest and which did not exceed in aggregate £1,000 during the financial year or, if more, the lower of £5,000 and 1 per cent of net assets at the year end.

*SE 12.43(r)*  The Stock Exchange requires disclosure by listed companies of any 'contract of significance' in which a director is or was materially interested. A 'contract of significance' is one which represents in amount or value a sum equal to 1 per cent or more

*SE 12.44*  of:

(a) the aggregate of the group's share capital and reserves, in the case of a capital transaction or a transaction of which the principal purpose is the granting of credit; or

(b) in other cases, the total purchases, sales, payments or receipts, as the case may be, of the group.

### 6.5.3 Scope of disclosures

There is a distinction between the disclosure by a holding company and that made by any other company. A holding company is required to disclose details of all transactions carried out by itself or its subsidiaries for its own or its holding com-

*85 6 Sch 15*  pany's directors, shadow directors or their connected persons. This applies even where the holding company is exempted from preparation of consolidated accounts. Any other company is required to disclose transactions which it has entered into with its own or its holding company's directors, shadow directors or

*85 6 Sch 16*  their connected persons. Accordingly, transactions disclosable by a subsidiary in its accounts but not involving a holding company director will not normally be disclosable in the group accounts.

# 6.6 Directors' remuneration

*85 6 Sch*  The 1985 Act requires detailed disclosure of directors' remuneration, as illustrated in the model accounts in Part II. In particular, all listed companies and companies quoted on the Alternative Investment Market are required to show aggregate details of directors' remuneration under four headings:

(a) emoluments;
(b) gains made on the exercise of share options;
(c) amounts receivable under long-term incentive schemes; and
(d) company contributions to money purchase pension schemes.

Where the aggregate of (a) to (c) above of all directors exceeds £200,000, the amount of the aggregate attributable to the highest paid director and the amount of (d) attributable to the highest paid director. (There is no longer any exemption in respect of directors whose services are performed wholly or mainly outside the UK.)

### 6.6.1 Definition of emoluments

*85 6 Sch 1(5)*

Emoluments are defined as amounts in respect of qualifying services. Qualifying services are defined as:

(a) services as a director of the company;
(b) services as director of any subsidiary; and
(c) the management of the company or any subsidiary.

*85 6 Sch 13(2)*

The definition of subsidiary is also wide-ranging. As well as subsidiary undertakings it also includes any other undertaking of which a director of the reporting company was a director by virtue of the company's nomination whether direct or indirect. This would include, for example, directorships of associated undertakings where the director is appointed to safeguard the interests of the reporting company.

*85 6 Sch 10*

The definition of emoluments is wide and includes all emoluments:

(a) paid by or receivable from any person – thus, emoluments are disclosable even if they are not paid by the company or any member of the group;
(b) receivable in respect of a period – thus, the accruals concept applies although, where emoluments are not receivable in respect of any particular period, they should be disclosed in the period in which they are actually paid; and
(c) whether paid to the director personally or to a connected person or body corporate controlled by him (as defined in section 346 of the 1985 Act) – thus, payments made to the spouse of a director or to another company which he owns must be disclosed if they are paid in relation to the director's services to the reporting company or its subsidiaries.

Emoluments include salary, fees and annual bonuses, expense allowances subject to UK tax and benefits in kind. There is no longer any requirement to distinguish between salaries and fees. However, 'emoluments' exclude:

(a) the grant of any share options;
(b) gains on the exercise of share options;
(c) anything received or receivable under a long-term incentive scheme;
(d) any company contributions paid (or treated as paid) in respect of a director under any pension scheme; and
(e) any benefits to which a director is entitled under any pension scheme;

for which there are separate disclosure requirements.

### 6.6.2 Payments to third parties

*85 6 Sch 9*

The accounts of all companies must disclose the aggregate payments to third parties for making available the services of a person as director. This includes benefits in kind (the nature of which must be disclosed). Third parties exclude bodies corporate controlled by any of the directors or persons connected with them, since payments to these parties would be deemed to be payments to the connected director. Typically, this would be relevant where a bank has a non-executive director on a board and invoices the company for the director's fees which are never receivable by the director personally.

### 6.6.3 Compensation for loss of office

*85 6 Sch 8*

The aggregate amount of any compensation for loss of office received or receivable by a director must be disclosed. Disclosable compensation includes consideration for, or in connection with, loss of office as a director, as a director of a subsidiary undertaking or of any office in connection with the management of the company or a subsidiary undertaking. The latter must be disclosed separately. Compensation includes benefits in kind, the nature of which must also be disclosed.

## 6.6.4 Share options

The grant of share options represents a benefit, although currently there is no consensus on how the monetary value of the benefit at the date of the grant of the option should be calculated. UITF Abstract 10 sets out the consensus that all companies should disclose information concerning the option prices applicable to the share options of individual directors, together with information about the market prices of shares at the year end and at the date of exercise. However, because of the legal difficulties, the disclosures proposed by the UITF are only a recommendation, although for listed companies these disclosures are now a requirement of the Listing Rules.

Listed companies are also required to disclose the difference between:

(a)  the market price of the shares on the day on which the option was exercised; and
(b)  the price actually paid for the shares.

Share options are defined as 'a right to acquire shares'. The DTI have stated that a right 'to acquire' also includes options 'to subscribe'.

A company that is neither listed nor quoted on AIM is required instead to disclose the number of directors who have exercised share options in the year.

The requirement to disclose the gains arising on the exercise of share options is not limited to the gains arising in respect of options granted to a director in respect of 'qualifying services' but to any gains on any options to acquire shares in the company or a group company. This therefore includes the amount of gains generated by the exercise of any options acquired in the market, or otherwise, prior to the director's appointment.

## 6.6.5 Long-term incentive schemes

*85 6 Sch 1(c)*  Details of any long-term incentive scheme (excluding share options and SAYE options as discussed above) are required. Detailed disclosure is required for each director in respect of:

*SE 12.43A(c)(iv)*  (a)  the interests in the long-term incentive scheme at the start of the period;
(b)  entitlements or awards granted and commitments made under the schemes during the period;
(c)  the money value and number of shares, cash payments or other benefits received under such schemes during the period; and
(d)  the interests in the long-term incentive scheme at the end of the period.

The definition of a long-term incentive scheme is 'any agreement or arrangement under which money or other assets may become receivable by a director and which includes one or more qualifying conditions with respect to service or performance which cannot be fulfilled within a single financial year'.

## 6.6.6  Pension entitlements

The following disclosures are required in respect of contributions and scheme membership:

(a)  the aggregate amount of company contributions to money purchase schemes in respect of directors' qualifying services;

(b)  the number of directors in respect of whom retirement benefits are accruing under money purchase schemes in respect of qualifying service; and

(c)  the number of directors in respect of whom retirement benefits are accruing under defined benefit schemes in respect of qualifying service.

There are additional disclosures in respect of the highest paid director.

*85 6 Sch 7*  Historically, directors have been able to enjoy an enhancement of their benefits, either through the utilisation of a surplus or through an additional contribution made by the company, without disclosure of the details. Hence, new legislation was introduced which requires disclosure of the aggregate amount of retirement benefits paid to or receivable by directors and former directors which are in excess of the retirement benefits to which they were entitled at the later of either:

(a)  the date when benefits first became payable; or

(b)  31 March 1997.

This paragraph is intended to ensure that companies disclose any discretionary increases to the pensions of directors or former directors. However, there is an exception for increases which are paid:

(a)  where the amounts were or could have been paid without recourse to additional contributions; and

(b)  amounts were paid to or receivable by all pensioner members of the scheme on the same basis.

## 6.6.7  Stock Exchange requirements

The Greenbury study group was set up to review the issues relating to directors' remuneration as a direct result of highly publicised concerns about the pay and other remuneration of company directors. It published its report in July 1995 and the Stock Exchange amended the Listing Rules to implement its recommendations.

*SE 12.43A (c)*  The Stock Exchange requires UK incorporated listed companies to include a report by the board on directors' remuneration setting out detailed disclosures concerning the company's policy on executive directors' remuneration and the analysis of remuneration by individual director. The analysis should show as a minimum details of basic salary and fees, benefits in kind, annual bonuses, compensation for loss of office and other termination payments, information on share options on the basis recommended in UITF 10, and details of any other long-term incentive scheme with an accompanying statement of the company's policies on the granting of these schemes. Details must also be given relating to the establishment and terms of reference of remuneration committees and to remuneration policy, service contracts and compensation.

*SE 12.43A (c)(ix)*  The Listing Rules also require disclosure of individual directors' pension benefits. The detailed disclosures in respect of defined benefit schemes include the increase during the period (excluding inflation), the accumulated total of benefits accruing to each director at the end of the period and the transfer value, excluding director's contributions, of the relevant increase in accrued benefit at the end of the period or

*SE 12.43A (c)(x)* sufficient information in order to make a reasonable assessment of this value. For money purchase schemes details of the contribution or allowance paid or payable by the company in respect of each director during the period are required.

The disclosure requirements in the Listing Rules are illustrated in the model accounts in Part II. Companies with only debt securities or fixed income shares listed, overseas companies and investment entities and venture capital trusts with no executive directors are not required to comply with any of these disclosure requirements.

# 6.7 Directors' interests in shares

The required disclosure in the directors' report or the annual accounts of each individual director's interests in shares of the company, its subsidiaries, and any holding company or fellow subsidiary (see model accounts in Part II) is based upon the inclusion of such information in the company's statutory register of directors' interests. The 1985 Act imposes an obligation on each director to notify the company of the acquisition of, or disposal of, any such interests, including any interests acquired or disposed of by the director's spouse or infant child.

*85 7 Sch 2A*

*85 s324–325*

*85 s328*

## 6.7.1 Disclosable interest

Any interest in shares or debentures is disclosable for this purpose, including any of the following:

*85 13 Sch 1*

*85 13 Sch 2*

*85 13 Sch 3(1)(a)*

*85 13 Sch 3(1)(b)*

*85 13 Sch 4,5*

(a) an interest held by a beneficiary of a trust, the trust property of which includes an interest in the shares or debentures of the company;

(b) an interest in a contract for their purchase;

(c) an entitlement held by any person, not being the registered holder, to exercise any right conferred by the holding of those shares or debentures or to control the exercise of any such right;

(d) an interest held by virtue of a body corporate being interested in the shares or debentures, where:

    (i) either the body corporate or its directors are accustomed to act in accordance with the person's instructions; or

    (ii) the person is entitled to exercise, or control the exercise of, at least one third of the voting power at the body corporate's general meetings (NB where a person is entitled to exercise, or control the exercise of, at least one-third of the voting power in a body corporate and that body corporate in turn is entitled to exercise or control the exercise of any general meeting voting power in the second body, then the general meeting voting power in the second is treated as exercisable by that person);

(e) a right, other than by virtue of an interest under a trust, to call for delivery of, or a right or an obligation to acquire or take an interest in, the shares or debentures (e.g., put and call options); and

*85 13 Sch 6*

*85 13 Sch 7*

(f) a joint interest with another person.

*85 13 Sch 8*

In all cases it is irrelevant whether the interest is in identifiable or unidentifiable shares.

Schedule 13 to the 1985 Act sets out detailed circumstances where interests can be disregarded for the purpose of identifying directors' interests.

# Chapter 7 Approval and publication of accounts

## 7.1 Introduction

This chapter summarises the legal requirements concerning the approval, laying, delivering and publishing of accounts, and the exemptions available to certain types of company or group.

## 7.2 Definitions

The following definitions are relevant in the context of this chapter:

*85 s241* **Laying accounts** means circulating them to shareholders for consideration at a general meeting.

*85 s242* **Delivering accounts** means filing them with the Registrar of Companies at Companies House.

*85 s240(4)* **Publishing accounts** means publishing, issuing, circulating or otherwise making them available for public inspection in a manner calculated to invite the general public, or any class of members of the public, to read them.

*85 s240(5)* **Statutory accounts** are the individual or group accounts which are required to be filed with the Registrar of Companies. These may be either the full accounts submitted by most companies or the abbreviated accounts which qualifying small and medium-sized companies may deliver (as discussed below).

*85 s240(5)* **Non-statutory accounts** are any balance sheet or profit and loss account of a company dealing with a complete financial year, other than as part of its statutory accounts. This includes data in newspaper advertisements and prospectuses, employee accounts, preliminary announcements and, to the extent that they include comparative information relating to a complete financial year, interim accounts.

*85 s246* **Abbreviated accounts** are those accounts where advantage has been taken of the disclosure exemptions available to small and medium-sized companies. This term is used for convenience in this chapter, although it is not used explicitly in the 1985 Act.

## 7.3 Approval by board

*85 s233* The statutory accounts must be formally approved by the board and signed, on the company balance sheet, by a director on its behalf. The name of the signatory must be stated. The board must also approve the individual profit and loss account of a parent company which is required to, and does, prepare group accounts in accordance with the 1985 Act, although this approval does not need to be evidenced by

*85 s230*    a signature on the profit and loss account. This is one of the conditions which must be followed if the company wishes to take advantage of the concession to omit its profit and loss account from the group accounts (the normal practice).

### 7.3.1 Approval of directors' report

*85 s234A*    The directors' report must also be approved by the board and signed on its behalf by a director or the company secretary. The latter may not, however, sign the accounts unless he or she is also a director. The name of the signatory must also be stated.

### 7.3.2 Consequences of non-compliance

*85 s233*    It is an offence for the directors to approve, knowingly or recklessly, accounts which do not comply with the 1985 Act. All directors at the time the accounts are approved are considered to be a party to their approval (if those accounts are defective) unless they show that they took all reasonable steps to prevent the accounts

*85 s233, s234A*    being approved. It is also an offence to lay, circulate, publish or file a copy of the accounts or directors' report which has not been signed or which fails to identify the signatory. A director who is found guilty of such an offence is liable to a fine.

## 7.4 Laying and delivering accounts

*85 s238*    Once they have approved the accounts, the directors must circulate them to members, debenture holders and to all those entitled to receive notice of general meetings.

### 7.4.1 Laying accounts

*85 s241*    The directors must, in respect of each financial year, lay before the company in general meeting a copy of the accounts for that year. For statutory purposes, these accounts comprise the profit and loss account (unless it is not required because group accounts have been prepared), balance sheet, supporting notes, the directors' report, the auditors' report and, if appropriate, group accounts. A listed company will include additional information in the accounts it lays before its members in general meeting (see Chapter 8). The accounts must be circulated to members not less than 21 days before the date of the meeting, although this period can be short-

*85 s238*    ened if all members entitled to attend and vote at the meeting agree to it. While this is the legal requirement, the Combined Code contained within the Listing Rules recommends that a period of 20 working days' notice be given.

### 7.4.2 Private company election

*85 s252, s253*    A private company can elect to dispense with the requirement to lay its accounts before its members in general meeting for the current and subsequent years. Once the elective resolution has been passed and filed at Companies House, the company is required to send a copy of its accounts to each member, debenture holder or other person entitled to receive notice of meetings, not less than 28 days before the time allowed for laying and delivering the accounts. The accounts sent to members must be accompanied by a notice informing them of their right to deposit a notice at the company's registered office within 28 days of the accounts being circulated, requiring that a general meeting be held to lay the accounts before the company. The auditors have similar rights. If the directors fail to comply with this, the requisitioner can call the meeting at the company's expense.

### 7.4.3 Delivering accounts

*85 s242*

*85 s228*
*85 s242*

Except in the case of a qualifying unlimited company (see Chapter 9), the directors must deliver to the Registrar of Companies a copy of the accounts for every financial year. Where the company is an intermediate holding company of an EEA parent and has taken advantage of its right not to prepare group accounts, the consolidated accounts of that parent company must also be delivered to Companies House within the same time limit. Any document not in English must have annexed to it a certified translation into English.

*85 s233(4), s234A(3),*
*s236(3)*

*85 s706(2)*

The accounts delivered to Companies House must contain original signatures on the balance sheet, directors' report and auditors' report. In addition, the Registrar of Companies has specified the following requirements for the physical form of accounts to be filed at Companies House:

(a) documents must be on paper which is white or otherwise of a background density not greater than 0.3;
(b) documents must be on paper with a matt finish;
(c) each page must be on A4 size paper;
(d) each page must have a margin all round not less than 10mm wide and, if the document is bound, the bound edge must have a margin of not less than 20mm;
(e) letters and numbers must be clear, legible and of uniform density;
(f) letters and numbers must be not less than 1.8mm high, with a line width of not less than 0.25mm; and
(g) letters and numbers must be black or otherwise providing reflected line density of not less than 1.0.

### 7.4.4 Time limits for laying and delivering accounts

*85 s244*

The company may lay and deliver audited accounts as soon after the end of its financial year as it chooses. However, it must do so by the end of the filing period, which is seven months after its accounting reference date (ARD) for a public company and ten months for a private company. In each case, provided the directors apply to the Registrar before the end of the normal filing period, an extension of a further three months may be claimed giving a filing period of 10 months and 13 months for public and private companies respectively if the company carries on business or has interests overseas. In special cases, which the 1985 Act does not define, the Secretary of State may grant a further extension. Listed companies must comply with the more restrictive time limits for laying accounts imposed by the Stock Exchange (see Chapter 8).

*85 s244(2)*

Modified rules apply to newly incorporated companies and to companies which have altered their ARD. When a newly incorporated company's first financial year is longer than 12 months, the filing period allowed is seven or ten months (depending on whether the company is public or private) from the first anniversary of incorporation, or three months from the end of the company's ARD if later. An existing company which shortens its financial year is allowed the normal seven or ten month period from its new ARD or three months from the date of the notice of change, whichever is later.

### 7.4.5 Default penalties

*85 s242*
*85 s242A*

It is an offence for the directors to fail to deliver their accounts to the Registrar within the time limits set out above. Legal action is, as a matter of practice, taken against the directors of companies that persistently file their accounts late. In addition, Companies House also exacts a civil penalty for each set of accounts which has been filed late. These fines are automatic. The severity of the fine depends, as shown below, on whether the company is private or public and how long after the due date the accounts were filed at Companies House:

| Length of overdue period | Public company | Private company |
| --- | --- | --- |
| Not more than 3 months | £500 | £100 |
| More than 3 months but not more than 6 months | £1,000 | £250 |
| More than 6 months but not more than 12 months | £2,000 | £500 |
| More than 12 months | £5,000 | £1,000 |

# 7.5  Small and medium-sized companies

Small and medium-sized companies are entitled to a number of exemptions in relation to accounts laid and to those delivered. Exemptions for individual company accounts depend on the company's size and status.

Both small and medium-sized companies are permitted to omit from the accounts prepared for filing certain aspects of the statutory accounts drawn up and sent to members. Such 'abbreviated' accounts for small companies comprise only an abbreviated version of their balance sheets and certain specified notes. These abbreviated accounts therefore do not need to contain a directors' report, a profit and loss account or disclose the auditors' remuneration.

*85 s246(5), 8A Sch*

For medium-sized companies the reductions in the level of disclosure for their abbreviated accounts are far more limited than those available to small companies. The main reduction is that less profit and loss account detail and analysis is required.

*85 s246A(3)*

In addition, small and medium-sized companies are able to take advantage of disclosure exemptions for the financial statements delivered to shareholders. These are usually termed 'modified accounts'. Again, the relief available to medium-sized companies is very modest. They are exempt from disclosing compliance with accounting standards. For small companies, the reliefs are extensive and, indeed, such companies may follow Schedule 8 to the 1985 Act, as opposed to Schedule 4 which other companies must follow. By following Schedule 8, small companies may group numerous sub-headings which are required under the formats in Schedule 4 (see Appendix 1) and omit some of the details required to be given by way of note. Furthermore, small companies may opt to follow the Financial Reporting Standard for Smaller Entities (FRSSE) and so be exempt from all other accounting standards.

*85 s246A(2)*

*85 s246*

As discussed in Chapter 5, small and medium-sized groups are also exempt from the requirement to prepare group accounts.

# 7.6  Non-statutory accounts

If directors publish non-statutory accounts, rules apply to ensure that the reader is made aware of their status. In particular, the directors must:

*85 s240*

(a)  make it clear that these are not 'statutory' accounts (i.e., those filed with the Registrar or sent to shareholders);

(b)  indicate whether statutory accounts have been filed; and

(c)  state whether the statutory accounts have been audited and, if so, whether the auditors' report was qualified or contained a statement concerning accounting records or failure to obtain information.

The statutory auditors' report must not be published with non-statutory accounts.

# 7.7 Correction of defective accounts

The 1985 Act adopts a three-tiered approach to the correction of defective accounts. Firstly, directors may voluntarily prepare corrected accounts or directors' reports. Secondly, directors may have to answer enquiries from the Secretary of State regarding apparent defects in their accounts and, if appropriate, correct them. Finally, directors may be ordered by the court to prepare revised accounts. The rules apply both to defective accounts and to accounts which have already been revised.

## 7.7.1 Voluntary correction

*85 s245*  If the directors consider that the annual accounts or directors' report do not comply with the 1985 Act, they are permitted to prepare a revised version. If the accounts have already been laid before the company in general meeting or delivered to Companies House, the directors are allowed to make only such changes as are necessary to ensure that the accounts or report do comply. The directors are not allowed, for example, to make changes simply because they have come to a different view about something.

*SI 1990 No. 2570*  Regulations have been issued clarifying:

(a)  the position if a revised set of accounts or a supplementary schedule of corrections is filed;
(b)  the auditors' duties in relation to the revised accounts;
(c)  the directors' duties where the defective accounts have already been circulated to shareholders, or laid before the company in general meeting, or delivered to Companies House; and
(d)  the duties of directors where a summary financial statement (see Chapter 8) based on the defective accounts has been sent to shareholders.

## 7.7.2 Enquiries by Secretary of State

*85 s245A*  The Secretary of State may give notice to the directors to the effect that there are, or may be, doubts as to whether their accounts comply, and may require them to respond within one month, either by explaining the apparent defect or by preparing revised accounts. He or she is empowered to apply for a court order if the directors fail to respond satisfactorily within the time allowed.

## 7.7.3 Court orders

*85 s245B, SI 1991 No. 13*  An application to the court can be made by the Secretary of State or someone authorised by him. The Financial Reporting Review Panel has been authorised for this purpose although as yet it has not used this power.

A notice of such an application must be filed, with a summary of the relevant background, at Companies House. The court is empowered to require the company to prepare revised accounts and may also give directions concerning:

(a)  audit of the revised accounts;
(b)  revision of the directors' report or any summary financial statement;

(c) publicity; and

(d) the liability of the directors who approved the accounts to pay personally the costs associated with the application and the preparation of revised accounts.

Companies House must be informed of any eventual court order or of the failure or withdrawal of the application to the court.

# Chapter 8  Listed companies

## 8.1  Introduction

*SE Definitions*

A company is a listed company if any class of its securities has been admitted to the Official List of the London Stock Exchange. The London Stock Exchange's publication 'The Listing Rules', often referred to as the 'Yellow Book', sets out the requirements governing admission to listing and the continuing obligations of listed companies.

A company with a quotation on the Alternative Investment Market (AIM) does not have to comply with the requirements of the Listing Rules. Many such companies, however, meet voluntarily some of the disclosure requirements of the Listing Rules, for example by giving fuller analysis of directors' remuneration than that required by company law.

This chapter addresses the additional accounting and reporting requirements applicable to listed companies registered in the UK. It encompasses annual and half-yearly financial reporting and the reporting requirements associated with corporate governance. The specific requirements for special cases (e.g., overseas companies, investment trusts, unit trusts and issuers of specialist and miscellaneous securities) are not discussed. Reference should be made to Chapters 17 to 26 of the Listing Rules for these.

## 8.2  Annual report and accounts

*SE 12.41, 12.42*

A listed company must issue an annual report and accounts, which, in the case of a UK company, must have been prepared in accordance with the 1985 Act and with UK accounting standards, and which must be independently audited. They must be published as soon as possible after the accounts have been approved, and in any event within six months of the end of the financial year to which they relate.

*SE 12.43, 12.43A*

The annual report and accounts of a listed company must include specific information, in addition to that required by the 1985 Act and accounting standards, on a variety of topics, including:

(a)  a commentary on any published forecasts or estimates, where the results for the period under review differ by 10 per cent or more;

(b)  the amount of interest capitalised in the period;

(c)  shareholders' dividends and directors' emoluments waived;

(d)  changes in directors' share interests after the year end;

(e)  substantial shareholdings;

(f)  a statement by the directors that the business is a going concern with supporting assumptions or qualifications as necessary;

(g)  a report to shareholders by the Board on directors' remuneration which should include, or cross-refer to, extensive details of individual directors' remuneration; and

(h) statements regarding compliance with the 'Code of Best Practice' on corporate governance and the application of the Principles of Good Governance which are contained in the 'Combined Code'.

Most of these additional disclosures are illustrated in the model accounts in Part II. The last three are considered in more detail below.

### 8.2.1 Narrative reporting

It is customary for a listed company's annual report and accounts to include a statement from the chairman. Research has shown that the most widely read part of company reports is the opening statement, normally by the chairman. It is therefore of special importance that it should provide a balanced and understandable summary of the company's performance and prospects and that it should represent the collective view of the Board.

Many listed companies now make more extensive narrative disclosures in the form of an Operating and Financial Review (OFR). The recommended content of the OFR is discussed below.

### 8.2.2 Earnings per share

*FRS 14*   Companies whose shares are, or will be, publicly traded must disclose figures for basic and diluted earnings per share (EPS) on the face of the profit and loss account for both the period under review and the corresponding previous period. Both calculations should be disclosed with equal prominence for all periods. The numerators should be disclosed in the notes to the accounts and reconciled to the net profit or loss for the period and the denominators should also be disclosed and reconciled to each other.

Companies often present additional measures of EPS, for example to exclude the effect of exceptional items or the results of discontinued operations. Such additional measures of EPS, which should be disclosed with no greater prominence than basic EPS, must be presented on a consistent basis over time and reconciled to basic EPS. The reason for disclosing the additional measures of EPS should be given.

In 1993 the Institute of Investment Management and Research (IIMR) published a Statement of Investment Practice defining a measure called 'Headline Earnings' which is used in the financial press for the calculation of price/earnings ratios. The essential thrust of Headline EPS is that it should be a measure of trading performance, excluding profits and losses on capital items.

## 8.3  Corporate governance and financial reporting

The importance of sound corporate governance first came to public attention in 1992 with the publication of the 'Cadbury Report' by the Committee on the Financial Aspects of Corporate Governance which was chaired by Sir Adrian Cadbury. The Committee published a Code of Best Practice (the Cadbury Code) which sought to set a benchmark for good corporate governance practices. The Stock Exchange subsequently required listed companies to make a statement about compliance with the Cadbury Code.

In 1995 another corporate governance committee chaired by Sir Richard Greenbury was set up in response to public and shareholder concerns about the remuneration of directors. The committee issued a report and a Code of Best Practice (the Greenbury Code). Most of the Greenbury Code was subsequently incorporated into the Listing Rules of the London Stock Exchange.

In June 1998 the Hampel Committee and the London Stock Exchange published the 'Combined Code' on corporate governance. This Code combined the existing requirements of the Cadbury and Greenbury Codes and added some new requirements as a result of the findings of the Hampel Committee. The London Stock Exchange amended the Listing Rules to take account of the publication of the Combined Code.

Following these changes, a company's annual report should contain the following corporate-governance-related disclosures:

(a) a narrative statement of how the company has applied the Principles of Good Governance set out in the Combined Code;
(b) a statement of compliance with the Code of Best Practice set out in the Combined Code;
(c) a report to the shareholders by the board on directors' remuneration;
(d) a statement that the directors have conducted a review of the effectiveness of the group's system of internal controls; and
(e) a statement by the directors that the business is a going concern with supporting assumptions or qualifications as necessary.

Each of these requirements is discussed below.

## 8.3.1 The Principles of Good Governance

The Combined Code contains 14 Principles of Good Governance to be applied by companies and a further three Principles to be applied by institutional investors. They are basic principles with which it would be difficult to disagree. For example, the first principle is that 'every listed company should be headed by an effective board which should lead and control the company'.

*SE 12.43A(a)* A listed company is required to make a narrative statement of how it has applied these principles, providing explanation which enables its shareholders to evaluate how the principles have been applied. The statement should be as specific as possible to the company's circumstances and avoid 'boilerplate'. The Hampel Committee decided not to prescribe the form or content of this statement because it wanted companies to have a free hand to explain their governance policies in the light of the principles, including any special circumstances applying to them which had led to a particular approach.

## 8.3.2 The statement of compliance

The 14 Principles of Good Governance are supported by a Code of Best Practice containing 45 Code provisions. Many of these provisions are well established from the Cadbury and Greenbury Codes but some are new.

*SE 12.43A(b)* A listed company must state whether or not it has complied throughout the accounting period with the Code of Best Practice. A company that has not complied in full throughout the period must specify the Code provisions with which it has not complied, for what part of the period non-compliance continued and give reasons for non-compliance.

The statement of compliance with the Combined Code was first required for periods ending on or after 31 December 1998 and should cover the whole period.

As the Code was only published in June 1998, even companies that have implemented its requirements without delay may need to report non-compliance for part of the relevant period.

### 8.3.3 Directors' remuneration

The disclosure of the remuneration of the directors is a well established aspect of company law which applies to all companies, public or private. Traditionally, the disclosures were of the aggregate remuneration of all directors together with a separate figure for the highest paid director and 'bandings' for the other directors.

The Greenbury Committee was established in 1995 in response to public and shareholder concerns about the remuneration of directors. These concerns centred on large pay increases and large gains on exercise of share options, as well as concerns about the amounts of compensation paid to some departing directors. A key recommendation of the Greenbury Committee was that companies should set up remuneration committees comprising non-executive directors to determine the company's policy on executive remuneration and specific remuneration packages for each of the executive directors. A further recommendation was that there should be a report of the remuneration committee setting out the remuneration policies together with comprehensive details of each director's remuneration during the period.

The Listing Rules were amended to reflect the recommendations of the Greenbury Committee and also at that time company law was simplified (for example by removing the bandings). Consequently, there is now a two-tier system for disclosure of directors' remuneration with a much more onerous regime for listed companies.

*SE 12.43A(c)*  In response to the publication of the Combined Code in 1998, the Stock Exchange again amended the Listing Rules. The existing requirements for the content of the remuneration committee report were broadly unchanged but, due to a change of emphasis requested by the Hampel Committee, the report is now from the board rather than from the committee. The requirements regarding references to Sections A and B of the Best Practice Provisions annexed to the Listing Rules have been dropped and are now effectively covered by the statement of compliance with the Code of Best Practice.

### 8.3.4 Internal controls

The Combined Code states that directors should, at least annually, conduct a review of the effectiveness of the group's system of internal controls and should report to shareholders that they have done so. The Code specifies that the review should cover all controls, including financial, operational and compliance controls and risk management.

The original requirement to make such a statement was contained in the Cadbury Code, which required the directors to report on the effectiveness of internal controls. The requirement was, however, watered down by the subsequent authoritative guidance issued in 1994 with the support of the Cadbury Committee. The guidance removed the requirement to report on effectiveness and narrowed the review to internal financial controls. The guidance also specified minimum disclosure requirements for the statement about internal controls and listed useful 'criteria for assessing effectiveness'.

The Hampel Committee agreed that public reporting on effectiveness of internal controls should not be required. But the committee also concluded that the scope of the annual review of internal controls should cover the broader range of internal controls rather than being limited to internal financial controls as was previously the case. A committee has now been formed under the aegis of the ICAEW to update the 1994 guidance. The Stock Exchange has stated that, until that guidance is published, a company's statement of compliance will satisfy the requirements of the Listing Rules if the company complies with the 1994 guidance by reporting on internal financial controls.

### 8.3.5 Going concern

The Cadbury Code contained a requirement that the directors should report that the business is a going concern, with supporting assumptions or qualifications as necessary. Guidance regarding the form of this statement and the procedures to be followed by directors when making it were set out in authoritative guidance issued in 1994 with the support of the Cadbury Committee.

*SE 12.43(v)*   The London Stock Exchange subsequently incorporated the requirement for a going concern statement directly into the Listing Rules. Failure to make such a statement would therefore be a breach of the Listing Rules rather than merely a disclosed departure from a Code of Best Practice.

### 8.3.6 Auditors' reports

The statement of compliance with the Code of Best Practice must be reviewed by the company's auditors insofar as it relates to specified paragraphs of the Code
*SE 12.43A*
*SE 12.43(v)*   where compliance can be objectively verified. This includes the statement on internal controls. The auditors must also review the going concern statement.

The auditors should issue a report to the company regarding their review. Between 1995 and 1998 the APB strongly recommended that this report be included in the annual report and this became generally accepted practice. However, in December 1998 the APB reversed this guidance and instead encouraged the inclusion of a statement of auditors' responsibilities, either as a separate statement or within an
*APB Bulletin 1998/10*   expanded auditors' report. This development was prompted by concerns that the scope of the review carried out by the auditors was so limited that such a report might give a misleading impression.

The scope of the auditors' report on the accounts must cover the numerical disclosures regarding directors' remuneration and pension benefits. If the company has not complied with these requirements the auditors must include in their report, so
*SE 12.43A*   far as they are reasonably able to do so, a statement giving the required particulars.

The numerical disclosures should be made either as part of the audited accounts (as illustrated in the model accounts in Part II) or included within the remuneration
*APB Bulletin 1997/2*   report in such a way that it is clear which elements of it have been audited. In the latter case, the first paragraph of the auditors' report will be expanded to include a reference to the pages which contain this information.

## 8.4 Operating and Financial Review

Listed companies are also recommended to comply with a statement issued by the ASB concerning an Operating and Financial Review (OFR). This provides non-mandatory guidance on how to present an objective discussion of the results and financial position of a company. It is directed at listed companies, but is applicable to other large corporations. It recommends that such a discussion should be provided in two sections, an operating review and a financial review, with a view to enabling readers to understand more fully the accounts.

### 8.4.1 Operating review

*ASB Statement 8–22*

The principal aim of the operating review is to enable the users to understand the dynamics of the various lines of business undertaken (i.e., the main influences on the overall results and how these interrelate). Thus, the OFR should identify and explain the main factors that underlie the business and, in particular, those which either have varied in the past or are expected to change in the future. It would ordinarily cover the following areas:

(a) operating results for the period;
(b) dynamics of the business;
(c) investment for the future;
(d) overall return attributable to shareholders;
(e) a comparison between the profit for the financial year and dividends; and
(f) accounting policies.

### 8.4.2 Financial review

*ASB Statement 23–27*

The principal aim of the financial review is to explain to the users of the annual report the capital structure of the business, its treasury policy and the dynamics of its financial position, its sources of liquidity and their application, including the implications of the financing requirements arising from its capital expenditure plans. It would ordinarily cover the following areas:

(a) capital structure and treasury policy;
(b) taxation;
(c) funds from operating activities and other sources of cash;
(d) current liquidity;
(e) going concern (see above); and
(f) off balance sheet value (e.g., unrecorded intangible assets).

*FRS 13 (11–23)*

FRS 13 *Derivatives and Other Financial Instruments: Disclosures* requires extensive narrative disclosures concerning objectives, policies and strategies for holding or issuing financial instruments (including but not limited to derivatives). The required disclosures should be given either in the accounts or in some other statement, such as the OFR, provided that they are incorporated into the accounts by means of a cross-reference in the notes to the accounts to the exact location of the disclosures. Companies that present an OFR will usually wish to present this information as part of that review.

There is no requirement for a statement by the directors on compliance with the ASB Statement in their OFR, although comment on the extent to which it has been followed may help users. Where it is implied, through the use of the words 'operating and financial review' or otherwise, that the directors have endeavoured to follow the principles of the ASB Statement, they should indicate any fundamental departures from them.

One of the Principles of Good Governance is that boards should present a balanced and understandable assessment of a company's position and prospects. The preparation of an OFR on the basis outlined in the ASB's Statement is clearly consistent with this recommendation.

A more detailed checklist for the contents of an OFR is set out in Appendix 4.

# 8.5 Preliminary announcement

*SE 12.40*

A listed company's preliminary announcement of its annual results must be notified to the Company Announcements Office as soon as possible after board approval.

*ASB Statement
Preliminary
Announcements (9)*

The Listing Rules do not otherwise prescribe the timing of the preliminary announcement except as implied by the requirement that the accounts must be published within six months of the year end. The ASB encourages companies to issue their preliminary announcements within 60 days of the year end, whilst recognising that individual circumstances may make it impracticable for some companies to achieve this. While the target of 60 days does not appear ambitious when judged by practice in the USA, it is currently only achieved by a minority of the larger listed companies in the UK.

## 8.5.1 Auditors' agreement

*SE 12.40(a)(i),(iii)*

The announcement must have been agreed with the company's auditors and must give details of the nature of any likely qualification of the auditors' report. Where the auditors' report does, or will, contain an explanatory paragraph dealing with a fundamental uncertainty (for example, referring to uncertainty over the going concern status of the company), the auditors will not agree to the preliminary announcement unless the directors have explained the fundamental uncertainty in

*APB Bulletin 1998/7 (36)*

the preliminary announcement.

*APB Bulletin 1998/7 (23)*

There is an expectation on the part of users that the information in the preliminary announcement will be consistent with the audited accounts. The only way of achieving absolute certainty of this is for the audit to have been completed and the contents of the preliminary announcement to have been extracted from the audited accounts upon which the auditors have signed their report. However, it is necessary to achieve an appropriate balance between timeliness and reliability in the preliminary announcement and many companies announce unaudited results. Where the preliminary announcement is based on draft accounts, the audit must be at an advanced stage. The auditors will need to be satisfied that any matters outstanding with respect to their audit will be unlikely to result in changes to the information

*APB Bulletin 1998/7 (26)*

contained in the preliminary announcement.

## 8.5.2 Form and content

*SE 12.40(a)(ii),(iv)
SE 12.52*

The preliminary announcement should contain, as a minimum, a summary profit and loss account (consistent with the presentation to be adopted in the accounts), along with any significant additional information necessary for the purpose of assessing the results being announced. The minimum information to be included in the summary profit and loss account is:

(a) net turnover;
(b) profit or loss before taxation and extraordinary items;
(c) taxation on profits (UK taxation and, if material, overseas taxation and share of associated undertakings' taxation must be shown separately);
(d) minority interests;
(e) profit or loss attributable to shareholders, before extraordinary items;
(f) extraordinary items (net of taxation);
(g) profit or loss attributable to shareholders;
(h) rates of dividends paid and proposed and total amounts thereof;
(i) earnings per share expressed as pence per share; and
(j) comparative figures for all the above.

As referred to earlier, in July 1998 the ASB published a 'best practice' Statement on preliminary announcements. Compliance with the Statement is not mandatory but its use is commended by the Financial Reporting Council, the Hundred Group of Finance Directors and the London and Irish Stock Exchanges. The Statement contains some far-reaching recommendations on the timing, distribution and content of companies' preliminary announcements.

*ASB Statement*
*Preliminary*
*Announcements*

Regarding content, the Statement goes far beyond the basic requirements of the Listing Rules which are set out above and recommends the inclusion of a balance sheet, cash flow statement and statement of total recognised gains and losses, together with various notes and a management commentary. Most listed companies already provide more than the basic requirements of the Listing Rules, although they do not generally fully comply with the ASB Statement.

A checklist which combines the requirements of the Listing Rules and those of the ASB Statement is contained in Appendix 5.

### 8.5.3 Non-statutory accounts

A company's preliminary announcement will fall within the definition of 'non-statutory accounts' and, accordingly, the following disclosures will be required (both in respect of the current year and the comparative figures as appropriate):

*85 s240*

(a) that the preliminary announcement is not the company's statutory accounts;
(b) whether statutory accounts dealing with the period in question have been delivered to the Registrar of Companies;
(c) whether the auditors have reported on any such statutory accounts; and
(d) whether any such audit report was qualified or contained a statement under section 237(2) or 237(3) of the 1985 Act (i.e., the accounting records or returns were inadequate, or the accounts did not agree with the records or returns, or there had been a failure to obtain necessary information and explanations).

An example of such a statement might read as follows:

*'The financial information set out above does not comprise the company's statutory accounts. Statutory accounts for the previous financial year ended (date) have been delivered to the Registrar of Companies. The auditors' report on those accounts was unqualified and did not contain any statement under section 237(2) or (3) of the Companies Act 1985. The auditors have not yet reported on accounts for the year ended (date), nor have any such accounts been delivered to the Registrar of Companies.'*

## 8.6 Summary financial statement

As part of the general effort to ensure that useful information is provided to shareholders, the requirement to send the full accounts of listed companies to all those entitled to receive them was relaxed. A company whose shares or debentures are listed may instead send a summary financial statement to those persons entitled to receive the full accounts, provided that the summary complies with the requirements set out below.

*85 s251(1)*

### 8.6.1 Ineligibility

If the company is prohibited by its Memorandum or Articles of Association (or any instrument governing or constituting a listed debenture) from sending a summary

*SI 1995 No. 2092*  financial statement to the persons entitled to receive full accounts, then it must send full accounts to everyone.

## 8.6.2 Ascertaining the wishes of an entitled person

*85 s251(2)*

*SI 1995 No. 2092*

Where the company has decided to issue a summary financial statement and an entitled person specifically requests in writing either full accounts or the summary financial statement, then the company must comply with that request. To ascertain the wishes of other entitled persons, the company may carry out a 'relevant consultation'. This requires the company to send a reply paid card to entitled persons with an address within the European Economic Area (accompanying both the full accounts and the summary financial statement) asking whether the entitled person wishes to receive full accounts in the future and clearly outlining the consequences of a failure to respond. Alternatively, the company may send entitled persons an advance notice describing what the summary financial statement will contain and enclosing a reply paid card on which the entitled person can indicate a preference to receive full accounts. In either case, if no response is received requesting full accounts, the company may send only a summary financial statement to that entitled person in the future.

## 8.6.3 Content of the summary financial statement

*85 s251(3)*

The summary financial statement must be derived from the annual report and accounts of the company and must state that it is only a summary of the full accounts.

*SI 1995 No. 2092 1 Sch*

As a minimum, the summary financial statement should include:

(a) specified summary extracts from the directors' report;

(b) a summary profit and loss account, with a note of the amount of total directors' remuneration;

*SE 12.45*  (c) earnings per share information;

(d) a summary balance sheet;

(e) comparative amounts; and

(f) a statement by the company's auditors of their opinion as to whether the summary financial statement is consistent with the full accounts and complies with

*85 s251(4)*  the 1985 Act and the Regulations.

## 8.6.4 'Health warning'

*SI 1995 No. 2092*

The summary financial statement must also include in a prominent position a statement to the effect that the summary financial statement does not contain sufficient information to allow as full an understanding of the results of the group (or company, if it is not required to prepare group accounts) and the state of affairs of the company and group (if applicable) as would be provided by the full annual accounts and report.

## 8.6.5 The right to receive full accounts

*SI 1995 No. 2092*

There should also be a conspicuous statement of the right of an entitled person to demand, free of charge, a copy of the company's last full accounts and how that copy can be obtained. It should also explain how an entitled person may elect to receive full accounts in future years.

*85 s251(7)*

The requirements of section 240 of the 1985 Act, relating to the publication of non-statutory accounts, do not apply to summary financial statements.

# 8.7 Interim report

*SE 12.46*

Listed companies must prepare a report on activities and profit or loss for the first six months of each financial year.

## 8.7.1 Form and content

*SE 12.51, 12.52*

*SE 12.56*

The interim report must contain, as a minimum, a table of figures containing the same items as those set out above for preliminary announcements. The comparative figures in this case will be those for the corresponding interim period in the preceding financial year. The report must also include:

(a) an explanatory statement including any significant information enabling investors to make an informed assessment of the trend of the group's activities and profit or loss;
(b) an indication of any special factor which has influenced those activities and the profit or loss during the period in question;
(c) enough information to enable a comparison to be made with the corresponding period of the preceding financial year; and
(d) so far as possible, a reference to the group's prospects in the current financial year.

*SE 12.47*

The accounting policies and presentation applied to the interim figures must be consistent with the latest published accounts save where they are to be changed in the subsequent annual accounts. Where this is the case, the new accounting policies and presentation should be followed. The changes and the reasons for them should be disclosed in the half-year report. Changes in other circumstances can only be made with the agreement of the Stock Exchange.

*ASB Statement Interim Reports*

In September 1997 the ASB published a 'best practice' Statement on interim reports. As with the ASB Statement on preliminary announcements, compliance is not mandatory but its use is commended by the Financial Reporting Council, the Hundred Group of Finance Directors and the London and Irish Stock Exchanges. As in the case of preliminary announcements, the recommended content is far more extensive than required by the Listing Rules but many listed companies already comply with the more rigorous requirements of the ASB Statement.

## 8.7.2 Publication

*SE 12.48*

*SE 12.49*

*SE 12.50*

The interim report must be published within four months of the end of the period to which it relates. It must be published by notifying the Company Announcements Office without delay after board approval. It must either be inserted in at least one national newspaper or sent to all the holders of the company's listed securities.

## 8.7.3 Non-statutory accounts

If full-year comparative information is provided in the interim report, it will be classified as non-statutory accounts. Consequently, the report will have to include a statement similar to that referred to in the context of preliminary announcements above.

## 8.7.4 Auditors' role

*ASB Statement Interim Reports (58)*

*SE 12.54*

There is no requirement for interim reports to be reviewed by the company's auditors, although this was recommended by the Cadbury Committee. The ASB Statement recommends that an interim report should disclose the extent to which information it contains has been audited or reviewed. If the figures in the interim report have been audited, the full report of the auditors (including qualifications) must be reproduced in full.

# Chapter 9  Special categories of company

## 9.1  Introduction

As explained in Chapter 1, Part VII of the 1985 Act deals with the accounting and audit requirements of companies in general. However, there are various exemptions and special provisions applicable to particular companies according to the nature of their activity (such as banking or insurance companies) or their status (such as unlimited, dormant or oversea companies). This chapter summarises the rules relating to such special categories of companies.

## 9.2  Companies with special activities

Section 255 of the 1985 Act makes special provision for banking and insurance companies, the accounts of which are subject to a different statutory regime. Also discussed below are investment companies and charities, which are each subject to special legislative requirements in addition to those arising under Part VII of the 1985 Act. The brief summaries in this chapter are designed to identify the sources of the relevant regulatory framework. Reference should be made to those sources for the detailed provisions. Many types of regulated companies (including banks and insurance companies) are subject to additional requirements to report to their respective regulatory authorities. These regulatory requirements are beyond the scope of this book.

## 9.3  Banks

*85 s744*
*85 s255A(4)*

A banking company is defined in the 1985 Act as 'a company which is authorised under the Banking Act 1987'. In addition, the legislation recognises the concept of a banking group, defined as a group where:

(a) the parent company is a banking company; or
(b) the parent company does not carry on any material business apart from the acquisition, management or disposal of interests in subsidiary undertakings and its principal subsidiary undertakings are wholly or mainly credit institutions.

### 9.3.1  Statutory framework for individual companies

*85 s255*

The accounts of a banking company must be prepared in accordance with Part I of Schedule 9 to the 1985 Act rather than Schedule 4. The fact that the accounts are prepared in accordance with the special provisions applicable to banks must be stated. Schedule 9 implements the requirements of the EU Bank Accounts Directive and, while it picks up many of the provisions of Schedule 4 verbatim, it adapts layout, terminology and accounting requirements to reflect the special nature of a bank's activities.

*85 s255B*  There is further provision for modifying the general 1985 Act disclosure requirements in Schedule 5 relating to subsidiaries, associates and other significant shareholdings and in Schedule 6 relating to loans (and similar transactions) with directors. The modifications are set out in Parts III and IV respectively of Schedule 9.

### 9.3.2  Non-statutory requirements

The financial statements must also comply with accounting standards and UITF Abstracts. In addition, there are five Statements of Recommended Practice (SORPs) issued jointly by the British Bankers' Association and the Irish Bankers' Federation with which banks are expected to comply.

### 9.3.3  Banking groups

*85 s255A*  Banking groups must prepare accounts in accordance with the provisions applying to companies generally, in particular the rules in Schedule 4A, but with the modifications made by Part II of Schedule 9. In practice, this means that banking groups prepare group accounts based on the disclosures and presentations applicable to banking companies, since one of the modifications made by Part II of Schedule 9 is to replace the cross-references in Schedule 4A to Schedule 4 by references to Part I of Schedule 9.

### 9.3.4  Banking partnerships

*85 s255D*  The statutory requirements also extend to banking partnerships to reflect the fact that the scope of the Bank Accounts Directive is not limited to companies.

### 9.3.5  Statutory formats

*85 9 Sch 1*  Like other companies, banks are also subject to the requirement to draw up their balance sheet and profit and loss account in strict accordance with prescribed formats, using the specified terminology and order. There is no choice of formats for the balance sheet, but the profit and loss account can follow either a vertical or horizontal layout. In practice, British banks usually adopt the vertical layout. Banks are allowed to change from one format to another only where there are 'special reasons'. These reasons must be explained in a note to the accounts.

A bank may provide more detail on the face of the accounts than the formats require. Any item can be subdivided if the bank so wishes and extra lines may be inserted, in any appropriate position, to cater for items not covered by the formats. The bank can alternatively include such assets or liabilities under the general headings 'other assets' and 'other liabilities'. Although the existence of these general headings appears more lenient than the rules for companies in general, Schedule 9 follows the Schedule 4 rules in prohibiting banks from recognising assets of doubtful value such as preliminary expenses, issue expenses or costs of research.

There are special rules in Schedule 9 relating to the following particular balance sheet items:

*85 9 Sch 11*  (a)  subordinated assets;
*85 9 Sch 12*  (b)  syndicated loans;
*85 9 Sch 13,14*  (c)  sale and repurchase agreements; and
*85 9 Sch 15*  (d)  managed funds.

In addition, there is a requirement to include contingent liabilities and commitments (including off balance sheet financial instruments) as memorandum items on the face of the balance sheet.

# 9.4  Insurance companies

*85 s744, s255A(5)*

An insurance company is defined in the 1985 Act as having the same meaning as in the Insurance Companies Act 1982. An insurance group is one where:

(a)  the parent company is an insurance company; or
(b)  the parent company does not carry on any material business apart from the acquisition, management or disposal of interests in subsidiary undertakings, and its principal subsidiary undertakings are wholly or mainly insurance companies.

## 9.4.1  Statutory framework for individual companies

*85 s255*

An insurance company is required to prepare its individual accounts in accordance with Schedule 9A of the 1985 Act rather than Schedule 4. The fact that the accounts are prepared in accordance with the special provisions applying to insurance companies must be stated. Schedule 9A implements the requirements of the EU Directive relating to the annual accounts and consolidated accounts of insurance undertakings. Its requirements are comparable to those of Schedule 4, which apply to most companies, and Schedule 9, which applies to banking companies, but they reflect the terminology and accounting treatment appropriate to the special nature of an insurance company's business.

## 9.4.2  Insurance groups

*s255A(2)*

An insurance group is required to prepare group accounts in accordance with the requirements of Part II of Schedule 9A.

## 9.4.3  Non-statutory requirements

The accounts of insurance companies must also comply with relevant accounting standards and UITF Abstracts unless they are granted specific exemptions. In addition, the Association of British Insurers issued a SORP 'Accounting for Insurance Business' in December 1998.

# 9.5  Investment companies

*85 s266*

An investment company is a public company which has given notice to the Registrar of Companies in the prescribed form of its intention to carry on business as an investment company and which has, since that time, met the following requirements:

(a)  the business of the company has consisted of investing its funds mainly in securities (with the aim of spreading investment risk and giving members the benefit of the results of its management of funds);
(b)  none of the company's holdings in companies (other than in investment companies) represents more than 15 per cent of the value of its investments;
(c)  the Memorandum or Articles of Association of the company prohibit the distribution of capital; and
(d)  the company has not retained more than 15 per cent of the income it derives from securities.

## 9.5.1  Distributions

*85 s265*
*85 4 Sch 71–73*

As discussed in Chapter 10, an investment company is permitted to make a distribution at any time out of its accumulated, realised revenue profits without taking

*FRS 3(31)* account of capital gains and losses, subject to an overall limit based on its net assets. Consequently, both the 1985 Act and FRS 3 incorporate specific exemptions from the normal rules applying to companies to ensure that an investment company is not required to take capital gains and losses through its profit and loss account.

### 9.5.2  Investment trusts

*Income and Corporation Taxes Act 1988* Investment companies are also able to apply for approved investment trust status, which brings with it significant tax advantages, if they meet a series of strict conditions. Since one of these is a requirement to have each class of shares listed, approved investment trust status will make them subject both to the general requirements imposed on all listed companies by the Stock Exchange (see Chapter 8) and the additional ones specific to investment companies (see below).

### 9.5.3  Financial statements

Investment companies are subject to the requirements of the 1985 Act, including Schedule 4, accounting standards and UITF Abstracts, in the same way as other companies. Consequently, the form and content of the accounts of an investment company or group are essentially based on those of other companies. The importance of the distinction between capital and revenue to investment companies, however, gives rise to a number of differences, including the following:

(a) the term 'revenue account' is frequently used instead of the term 'profit and loss account' in recognition of the fact that capital profits and losses are not dealt with through this account;

(b) profits and losses arising from the revaluation of investments do not have to be taken to a revaluation reserve, and can therefore be taken to an unrealised appreciation/depreciation reserve which is not subject to the same restrictions

*85 4 Sch 71(1)* as those placed by the 1985 Act on the revaluation reserve;

(c) provisions for impairment in value of fixed asset investments do not need to be

*85 4 Sch 71(2)* charged to the profit and loss account.

*85 4A Sch 1(3)* The consolidated accounts prepared by a parent company which is an investment company can also take advantage of these exemptions.

### 9.5.4  Stock Exchange requirements

*SE 21.22* The Stock Exchange requires a listed approved investment trust to give the following information in its accounts:

(a) a statement that the Inland Revenue have approved the company as an investment trust, specifying the last accounting period in respect of which such approval has been given and confirming that the company has conducted its affairs in such a way that it will continue to be approved;

(b) an analysis of the investment portfolio by broad industrial or commercial sector and between equity shares, convertible securities, fixed income securities and other investments;

(c) details of its 10 largest investments by market value and all holdings in excess of 5 per cent of the value of the portfolio, stating the market value for each such investment;

(d) an analysis of income between dividends, interest and other income;

(e) an analysis of realised and unrealised profits and losses, with a separate analysis of aggregate profits and losses split between listed and unlisted investments; and

(f) the name of the group or company that manages the investment portfolio, together with an indication of the terms and duration of its appointment and the basis for its remuneration.

# 9.6 Charities

Incorporated charities, like all companies, are subject to the 1985 Act. They are therefore required to produce accounts in accordance with Schedule 4. In addition, they are subject to the requirements of the Charities Act 1993 (although they are specifically exempted from the accounting requirements of that Act) and must therefore file their accounts with the Charity Commissioners as well as with Companies House. The only recognition of the different nature of incorporated charities in the accounting requirements of the 1985 Act is the acknowledgement that they may use the term 'income and expenditure account' instead of 'profit and *85 s262(2)* loss account'.

## 9.6.1 Unincorporated charities

The Charities Act 1993 imposes similar accounting requirements on unincorporated charities, other than those which are exempt or excepted from registration under the Charities Act. The accounting requirements, and the extent to which the accounts of unincorporated charities are subject to independent review or audit, differ depending on the gross income (or expenditure) of the charity. Certain types of charity, including Friendly Societies, Industrial and Provident Societies and registered housing associations are subject to other, more specific, legislation governing their accounts among other matters.

## 9.6.2 Non-statutory requirements

There is a series of SORPs applicable to different types of charities. The main one, 'Accounting by Charities', issued by the Charity Accounting Review Committee, is intended to apply to all charities in the UK and the Republic of Ireland regardless of their size, constitution or complexity, although less stringent requirements apply to small charities. There are also the following specialised SORPs which are relevant for particular classes of charity:

'Accounting by Registered Housing Associations', issued by the National Federation of Housing Associations;

'Authorised Unit Trust Schemes', issued by the Investment Management Regulating Organisation, which, while not specifically designed for charities, is applicable to common investment funds; and

'Accounting in Higher Education Institutions', issued by the Committee for Vice Chancellors and Principals.

In addition, there is detailed guidance for further education institutions issued by the Further Education Council.

The principal SORP on accounting for charities requires a charity's accounts to comprise the following statements:

(a) a statement of financial activities showing all resources made available to the charity and all expenditure incurred and reconciling all changes in its funds;
(b) where required by legislation (as in the case of an incorporated charity subject to Schedule 4 to the 1985 Act), a summary income and expenditure account;
(c) a balance sheet showing the assets, liabilities and funds of the charity, explaining in general terms how the funds may or must be utilised;
(d) a cash flow statement where required by FRS 1; and
(e) notes explaining the accounting policies adopted and providing further useful information.

# 9.7 Companies with special status

Certain companies are also subject to special accounting provisions because they have special status rather than as a result of the legislative framework in which they operate. The following types of company are discussed below: dormant companies; unlimited companies; partnerships; companies limited by guarantee; oversea companies and very small companies.

# 9.8 Dormant companies

*85 s250* If a company qualifies as dormant it can, by special resolution, agree not to appoint an auditor provided that it is not:

(a) a banking company;
(b) an insurance company; or
(c) a person authorised under the Financial Services Act 1986.

A company is regarded as dormant during any period where no significant accounting transaction occurs which would have to be entered in the company's accounting records by virtue of the requirements of section 221 of the 1985 Act concerning proper accounting records. The one exception to this rule is that transactions relating to a subscriber taking up shares as provided in the Memorandum of Association may be disregarded for this purpose.

*85 s250(1)(a)* If a company has been dormant since incorporation the special resolution not to appoint auditors may be passed at any time. Where the company has not been dormant since its formation, it may pass the resolution either at a general meeting or by written resolution at any time after the annual report and accounts for the previous year have been sent out to shareholders, but before the filing deadline for the current year's accounts.

*85 s250(1)* The company must also meet the following criteria before the special resolution may be passed:

(a) it must have been dormant since the end of the previous financial year;
(b) if it is a parent company, it must not have been required to prepare group accounts in respect of the previous financial year; and
(c) it must have qualified as a small company for the previous financial year, or would have done so if it had not been part of an ineligible group.

## 9.8.1 Form of accounts

*85 s250(4)(c)* Full accounts must still be prepared and laid before the company in general meeting. The accounts must be approved by the board, and the balance sheet should be signed by a director on its behalf. If the company traded in the previous year, a profit and loss account is required to give the comparatives in respect of the prior period. If the accounts are not audited, the directors must add a statement, immediately above the signature on the balance sheet, that the company was dormant throughout the year.

## 9.8.2 Ceasing to qualify as dormant

*85 s250(5)* The special resolution continues to be effective until the company ceases to qualify for dormant status because a significant accounting transaction has occurred or until a resolution is passed relating to the appointment of auditors.

# 9.9  Unlimited companies

*85 s254*
An unlimited company is exempt from the requirement to file accounts with the Registrar of Companies in respect of a financial year provided that during that year:

(a)  it has at no time been a parent or subsidiary of an undertaking with limited liability;

(b)  there have been no rights exercisable at any time by, or on behalf of, two or more undertakings with limited liability which would, if exercisable by one of them, have made the company a subsidiary undertaking of it;

(c)  it has at no time carried on business as the promoter of a trading stamp scheme within the Trading Stamps Act 1964.

The company is also not entitled to the filing exemption if it is a banking company, the parent company of a banking group or a qualifying company within the meaning of the Partnerships and Unlimited Companies (Accounts) Regulations 1993 ('the Partnership Regulations') discussed below.

# 9.10  Partnerships

*SI 1993 No. 1820*
The Partnership Regulations require qualifying partnerships to prepare accounts and a directors' report and to obtain an auditors' report on those accounts unless they are entitled to an exemption. For these purposes, a qualifying partnership is a general or limited partnership each of whose members has limited liability (either by virtue of being itself a limited company or because each of its members is a limited company). The accounts have to be prepared in accordance with Part VII of the 1985 Act, although certain disclosure exemptions are available. A copy must be attached to the accounts of each limited company which is a member of the partnership at the end of its financial year for filing with the Registrar of Companies.

## 9.10.1  Disclosure in member company's accounts

Companies which are members of qualifying partnerships need to state the following in their accounts:

(a)  the name and legal form of the undertaking;

(b)  the address of the undertaking's registered office or, if none, its head office; and

(c)  a statement that a copy of the latest accounts of the undertaking has been, or is to be, attached to the copy of the company's annual accounts sent to the Registrar of Companies, or the name of at least one body corporate (which may be the company) in whose group accounts the undertaking has been or is to be dealt with on a consolidated basis.

## 9.10.2  Exemptions from preparing accounts

The criteria for exemption from the requirement for a qualifying partnership to prepare accounts are very wide-ranging:

(a)  the partnership must be dealt with by full consolidation, proportional consolidation or equity accounting in group accounts;

(b)  those group accounts must be prepared by a member of the partnership that is established under the law of a Member State of the EEA or by an EEA parent undertaking of such a member;

(c)  the group accounts must be prepared and audited under the provisions of the Seventh Company Law Directive; and

(d) the group accounts must disclose that advantage has been taken of this exemption.

Where advantage is taken of this exemption, any member of the qualifying partnership which is a limited company must disclose on request the name of at least one member or parent undertaking in whose group accounts the partnership has been or is to be dealt with on a consolidated basis.

# 9.11 Companies limited by guarantee

The requirements of the 1985 Act relating to the accounts and audit of limited companies apply equally to the accounts of a company limited by guarantee. The principal difference is that paid up share capital does not appear on the latter's balance sheet and there is no legal requirement to disclose the amount of the guarantee in the accounts.

# 9.12 Oversea companies

*85 s744*

An oversea company is defined as a company incorporated other than in Great Britain which has established a place of business in Great Britain. There is no statutory definition of a place of business but guidance notes issued by Companies House suggest that there must be some physical or visible appearance that an oversea company has a connection with particular premises and the location must have a degree of permanence. It is unlikely that companies carrying on business in Great Britain solely through an agent, or carrying on business solely from an occasional location, would be considered to have a place of business.

Oversea companies are subject to complex registration requirements that vary in complexity depending on whether the company is deemed to have established a place of business or a branch in Great Britain. Essentially, the difference is that a place of business exists where an oversea company performs functions in Great Britain that are ancillary or incidental to its business as a whole (e.g., maintaining warehouse facilities, administrative offices, internal data processing or share registration or transfer offices). If an oversea company's operations in Great Britain are more extensive, this is likely to constitute a branch. In either case, the oversea company will have to file accounts at Companies House within 13 months of the end of its financial year, but the nature of those accounts will depend on the regime under which the oversea company is registered.

## 9.12.1 Accounting requirements under place of business regime

*85 s700*

*SI 1990 No. 440*

The 1985 Act requires an oversea company registered under the place of business regime to prepare accounts (and, if the oversea company also has subsidiaries, group accounts) in accordance with the 1985 Act. These accounts should be those of the oversea company itself and should not simply reflect the activities carried out through the place of business in Great Britain. They must either be prepared in English or be accompanied by a certified translation. The Oversea Companies (Accounts) (Modifications and Exemptions) Order 1990, however, sets out a number of significant exemptions that greatly reduce this burden. Oversea companies are required to prepare their accounts in accordance with the old Schedule 9 to the 1985 Act, prior to the amendments introduced by the 1989 Act. That Schedule 9 owed its origins to a grandfathering provision to retain the requirements of the 1948 Act for application to banking and insurance companies on implementation of the EC Fourth Directive through the 1981 Act. Oversea companies are therefore effectively permitted to prepare their accounts in accordance with the 1948 Act and the following exemptions also apply:

(a) the inclusion of an auditors' report;
(b) disclosure of UK tax, turnover, subsidiaries, significant investments, the ultimate holding company, particulars of the chairman's and highest paid director's emoluments;
(c) banding of directors' emoluments;
(d) waiver of directors' emoluments;
(e) particulars of transactions with directors and officers of the company; and
(f) directors' report.

### 9.12.2 Accounting requirements under branch regime

*85 s699AA, 21D Sch*

Where an oversea company registered under the branch regime is required by the law in its state of incorporation (its 'parent law') to prepare, have audited and disclose accounts, it must file these accounts, together with an auditors' report and directors' report, at Companies House. If they are not prepared in English they must be accompanied by a certified translation. Where, however, audited accounts are not required to be disclosed under the parent company's law, it will be subject to the same requirements as apply to companies subject to the place of business regime.

## 9.13 Very small companies

*85 s249A*

A company that qualifies as a small company and has a turnover of not more than £350,000 in a financial year and gross assets of not more than £1.4 million is exempt from the requirement for its accounts to be audited, provided that it was not at any time during the financial year:

(a) a public company;
(b) a banking or insurance company;
(c) a registered insurance broker;
(d) an authorised person or appointed representative under the Financial Services Act 1986;
(e) a trade union or employers' association; or
(f) a parent company or subsidiary undertaking (excluding a member of a group where the group qualifies as small and the aggregate results meet the above conditions).

The accounts must, however, still comply with the 1985 Act and must give a true and fair view.

### 9.13.1 Filing

Accounts are still required to be filed with the Registrar of Companies, although advantage may be taken of the provisions for filing abbreviated accounts where the necessary conditions are met.

# Chapter 10  Distributable and realised profits

## 10.1  Introduction

This chapter summarises the legal requirements concerning the distribution of profits and assets. Part VIII of the 1985 Act regulates the distribution of assets and profits and incorporates elements of the EU Second and Fourth Company Law Directives. There are special rules for public companies, investment companies and insurance companies.

## 10.2  Distributable profits

*85 s263(3)*

A company may not make a distribution except out of profits that are available for that purpose. In general, the profits available for distribution by a company are as follows:

(a)  its accumulated realised profits so far as not previously utilised by distribution or capitalisation; less
(b)  its accumulated realised losses so far as not previously written off in a reduction or reorganisation of capital.

### 10.2.1  Public companies

*85 s264*

Public companies have to comply with an additional test when they intend to make a distribution. The proposed distribution must not reduce the net assets of the company to less than the aggregate of the company's called-up share capital and its undistributable reserves.

For this purpose, undistributable reserves are defined as:

(a)  share premium account;
(b)  capital redemption reserve;
(c)  the amount by which accumulated unrealised profits (so far as not previously capitalised) exceed accumulated unrealised losses (so far as not previously written off in a reduction or reorganisation of capital); and
(d)  any other reserve whose distribution is prohibited by statute or by the company's Memorandum or Articles.

The restrictions on distributions by a public company reflect the 'capital maintenance' principle of the EU Second Directive. They have the effect that a public company must reduce its accumulated realised profits by any excess of unrealised losses over unrealised profits.

### 10.2.2  Group reserves

Distributions are made by companies and not by groups. It follows that the profits of a group are distributable to members of the group's holding company only to the extent of the holding company's distributable reserves. The concept of distributable profit is not, therefore, strictly applicable to groups. Whilst there is no legal requirement for a holding company to take into account its share of the net losses (if any) of its subsidiaries in determining its distributable profits, the holding company may need to make a provision for impairment of the value of its investments in those subsidiaries.

# 10.3  Definition of a distribution

85 s263(2)

A distribution is defined as 'every description of distribution of a company's assets to its members, whether in cash or otherwise'. However, the following are specifically excluded:

(a)  an issue of shares as fully paid or partly paid bonus shares;
(b)  a redemption or purchase of any of the company's own shares out of capital or out of unrealised profits;
(c)  a reduction of share capital; and
(d)  a distribution of assets to members of the company on winding up.

The definition of a distribution is wide-ranging since it refers to 'distributions' of any kind and not just 'dividends' as such. Accordingly, payments to a holding company of a gratuitous nature, such as covenanted payments by a trading subsidiary of a charity to its charitable parent undertaking, would also appear to be caught.

Since the definition refers to distributions in terms of a transfer to members, distributions of assets to persons other than members (e.g., a gratuitous transfer to an ultimate holding company rather than through its intermediate holding company) may appear to be outside its scope. In the case of *Aveling Barford Limited* v *Perion Limited*, however, it was held that a payment to a non-member could also be deemed to be a distribution and, as such, subject to the rules relating to distributions. This has implications for the ability of groups to transfer assets between subsidiaries at an under-value (or over-value), where the transferor (or transferee) company has a deficit of distributable reserves.

## 10.3.1  Distributions *in specie*

The statutory rules apply to all distributions, including distributions *in specie*. These rules generally prohibit the distribution of an unrealised profit. However, any unrealised profit in the accounts in respect of the book value of an asset to be distributed *in specie* is to be regarded as realised for the purpose of the distribution. Thus, there need only be sufficient distributable profits to cover the historical cost of the asset to be distributed.

# 10.4  Relevant accounts

85 s270–s276
85 s270(2)

The question whether, and to what extent, a distribution can be made is determined by reference to the company's 'relevant accounts' and, in particular, to the following items in those accounts:

(a)  profits, losses, assets and liabilities;
(b)  provisions (including provisions for depreciation and diminution in the value of assets); and
(c)  share capital and reserves (including undistributable reserves).

85 s270(3)

The relevant accounts will normally be the last annual audited accounts to have been laid before the members in general meeting.

### 10.4.1 Qualified audit report

*85 s271(4)*

If the audit report is qualified, the auditors will have to provide a further statement in writing (either at the time of the qualified audit report or later) as to whether or not, in their opinion, the cause of the qualification is material in deciding whether the distribution would be in breach of the 1985 Act.

*85 s271(3)*

*APB Practice Note 8*
*(Example 7)*

For this purpose, a qualified audit report is one with a qualification to the effect that, in the auditors' opinion, the accounts have not been properly prepared in accordance with the 1985 Act. A copy of this statement must be put before the company in general meeting before a distribution can be made. An example of suitable wording for the auditors' statement can be found in the APB's Practice Note 8 *Reports by Auditors under Company Legislation in the United Kingdom*. This can either be a separate statement or included in the statutory audit report.

### 10.4.2 Interim accounts

*85 s270(4)*

If the annual audited accounts disclose that there are insufficient distributable profits to make a distribution, the directors will have to refer to 'interim accounts'. These must be prepared to such a standard that they would enable a reasonable judgement to be made as to the relevant amounts (i.e., profits, losses, assets, liabilities, provisions, share capital and reserves).

*85 s272*

The interim accounts prepared by a public company must comply with all the usual rules for preparing annual accounts (i.e., section 226 of and Schedule 4 to the 1985 Act, with such modifications as are necessary because the accounts are not in respect of a complete financial year) and must be filed with the Registrar of Companies. They do not, however, need to be audited. There are no rules concerning the format of interim accounts for a private company, nor is there any filing requirement. Consequently, private companies can use suitable management accounts to support a dividend payment.

### 10.4.3 Initial accounts

*85 s273*

Similar requirements relate to public companies which wish to make a distribution during their first financial year. In such a case, however, the accounts (known as 'initial accounts') must also be accompanied by an auditors' report.

### 10.4.4 Successive distributions

*85 s274*

Where a distribution has already been made out of the distributable profits shown in the relevant accounts, this must be taken into account before any subsequent distribution is made. In addition to items falling within the normal definition of a distribution, account must also be taken of the following items:

(a)   lawful financial assistance for the acquisition of own shares provided out of distributable profits;
(b)   unlawful financial assistance which reduces a company's net assets; and
(c)   payments in respect of the purchase of own shares, other than payments made lawfully otherwise than out of distributable profits.

### 10.4.5 Subsequent losses

The 1985 Act does not specifically require companies to take account of subsequent losses in determining the extent of a distribution, provided that the relevant accounts disclose the existence of sufficient distributable reserves. The 1985 Act does, however, recognise that the statutory distribution rules are without prejudice

85 s281 to any enactment, rule of law or any provision in the company's Memorandum and Articles which might restrict the company's ability to distribute. From the perspective of common law, there are provisions which are still applicable, including the need for the directors to act in the best interests of the company and the prohibition on the payment of dividends out of capital. These appear to prohibit the payment of a dividend without taking account of subsequent losses, the company's solvency and working capital requirements and the recoverability of any ACT on the proposed distribution. If there is any doubt as to whether a dividend can lawfully be made in such circumstances, legal advice should be sought.

# 10.5 Calculation of amount of distributable profits

The following example illustrates the calculation of distributable profits for a private company, a public company and an investment company respectively. The terminology used in the example reflects that used in the 1985 Act. In practice, the reserves of a company will follow the descriptions used in the statutory balance sheet formats and are unlikely to be identified as realised or unrealised revenue or capital profits.

|  |  | £ | £ |
|---|---|---|---|
| 1 | Share capital |  | 100 |
| 2 | Reserves |  |  |
| 3 | Unrealised capital profits | 0 |  |
| 4 | Unrealised capital losses | (80) |  |
| 5 | Unrealised revenue profits | 5 |  |
| 6 | Unrealised revenue losses | (10) |  |
| 7 | Total unrealised reserves |  | (85) |
| 8 | Realised capital profits | 40 |  |
| 9 | Realised capital losses | (5) |  |
| 10 | Realised revenue profits | 100 |  |
| 11 | Realised revenue losses | (40) |  |
| 12 | Total realised reserves |  | 95 |
| 13 | Capital and reserves |  | 110 |
| 14 | Total liabilities |  | 110 |
| 15 | Total assets |  | 220 |

Distributable profit

Private company: realised profits less realised losses (line 12) £95

Public company: as above, less net unrealised losses (line 12 less line 7) £10

Investment company (as defined): realised revenue profits less revenue losses (line 10 less lines 6 and 11) £50

NB: distribution not to cause total assets to equal less than $1\frac{1}{2} \times$ total liabilities

(line 15 = 220; $1\frac{1}{2} \times$ line 14 = 165; 220 − 50 = 170).

Maximum dividend still therefore £50

## 10.5.1 Effect of paying an unlawful dividend

Any member of a company who knows, or who has reasonable grounds for believing, at the time of a distribution that its payment is in contravention of the 1985 85 s277 Act is liable to repay it to the company. The 1985 Act does not impose any specific penalties on the company or its directors where an unlawful distribution has been made.

# 10.6 Realised profits

The definition of realised profits and realised losses is fundamental to the identification of distributable profits. The 1985 Act gives the following guidance on the interpretation of these items:

*85 s262(3)*

*'References in this Part to "realised profits" and "realised losses", in relation to a company's accounts, are to such profits and losses of the company as fall to be treated as realised in accordance with principles generally accepted, at the time when the accounts are prepared, with respect to the determination for accounting purposes of realised profits or losses.'*

Furthermore, the accounting principles section of Schedule 4 notes that:

*85 4 Sch 12(a)*

*'Only profits realised at the balance sheet date shall be included in the profit and loss accounts.'*

## 10.6.1 Professional guidance

*TR 481, TR 482*

The CCAB issued guidance on the interpretation of realised and distributable profits in two Technical Releases published in 1982 after the introduction of the legislation governing distributable profits. The main principles of this guidance are still applicable, although they need to be viewed in the context of the accounting principles generally accepted at the time when the relevant accounts are prepared.

## 10.6.2 Generally accepted accounting principles

'Principles generally accepted' for the determination of realised profits should be construed in the context of the fundamental accounting principles laid down in Schedule 4 and SSAP 2. In particular, the latter states, in the context of the prudence concept, that:

*SSAP 2(14)(d)*

*'[Profits] are recognised by inclusion in the profit and loss account only when realised in the form either of cash or of other assets the ultimate cash realisation of which can be assessed with reasonable certainty.'*

*SSAP 20(65)*

A profit required by an accounting standard to be recognised in the profit and loss account should normally be treated as a realised profit, unless the accounting standard specifically indicates that it should be treated as unrealised. An example of such a case is SSAP 20 which recognises that the application of the requirement to take exchange gains on unsettled long-term monetary items through the profit and loss account may result in unrealised exchange gains being taken to the profit and loss account.

It is also possible that realised gains may not pass through the profit and loss account for the year as, for example, where a previously revalued asset is sold and the revaluation surplus realised. It is therefore important for all companies to keep sufficient records to enable them to distinguish between reserves which are distributable and those which are not.

## 10.6.3 Asset revaluations

Where a company's fixed assets have been revalued upwards and an unrealised profit recognised in the accounts, subsequent annual depreciation provisions will

*85 s275(2)*

inevitably be increased to the extent that the revalued assets are depreciated. Any such increase in depreciation charges is to be treated as a realised profit for the purposes of deciding whether a distribution can be made. Accordingly, it would be desirable to transfer each year the difference between the depreciation charge based on the revalued amount and the depreciation charge that would have arisen on the historical cost, as a movement on reserves, from the revaluation reserve to the profit and loss account.

### 10.6.4  Downward revaluations

*85 s275(1)*

Conversely, where a revaluation has resulted in a provision for a diminution in value, the 1985 Act would normally regard this as a realised loss (together with any other provision for depreciation or diminution in value of an asset). However, where a diminution in value has arisen on an asset in the course of a revaluation of all fixed assets (other than goodwill), the 1985 Act permits it to be treated as an unrealised loss for the purposes of determining distributable profits.

*85 s275(4,5)*

Such a revaluation of all fixed assets need not be an actual revaluation which is then incorporated into the accounts. Where no formal revaluation has been carried out, any consideration by the directors of the value of any fixed asset at any time is regarded as a revaluation, provided that the directors are satisfied that the aggregate value of the fixed assets being considered is not lower than their aggregate carrying value in the company's accounts.

*85 s275(6)*

In such circumstances the accounts must state:

(a)  that the directors have considered the value of those fixed assets which have not been formally valued without actually revaluing the assets in question;

(b)  that the directors are satisfied that the aggregate value of those assets at the time in question is or was not less than the aggregate amount at which those assets are or were stated; and

(c)  that the assets that have diminished in value are recorded at their written-down value.

This note should appear in any financial statements (including those issued subsequent to the 'revaluation') that are relevant accounts used to support a distribution where the diminution is not to be treated as a realised loss.

*85 s264(1)*

Where an actual revaluation of all the fixed assets shows an overall deficit, the provisions for diminution in value can still be treated as an unrealised loss for distribution purposes. However, the overall deficit will reduce a public company's distributable profits (unless there are offsetting unrealised profits elsewhere) because a public company's distribution must not reduce its net assets to less than the sum of its share capital and undistributable reserves.

# Part II – Model accounts and commentary

# Introduction

These model accounts illustrate the typical disclosures which would be required of a listed company with subsidiaries and associates. The treatment of joint ventures is not illustrated because of the complexity of overlayering these disclosures with others which are given in these model accounts. An illustration of the disclosure of joint ventures is given in Appendix IV of FRS 9.

In many cases the wording used in the accounts is purely illustrative and in practice will need to be modified to reflect the circumstances of the group. The customary chairman's statement, notice of AGM, list of financial advisers and summary of financial highlights are not included. Nor do the accounts include an Operating and Financial Review (OFR) which would normally cover the main factors underlying the group's financial performance and condition. The OFR and the ASB's non-mandatory statement on the subject are discussed in Chapter 8. The narrative disclosures about derivatives and other financial instruments required by FRS 13 are not illustrated as they would normally be included in the OFR. However, the FRS 13 disclosures are mandatory and within the scope of the auditors' report. They are illustrated in Appendix III of FRS 13.

A facing page commentary briefly outlines the disclosure requirements, which are principally found in the Companies Act 1985, the Listing Rules of the London Stock Exchange, Statements of Standard Accounting Practice, Financial Reporting Standards and UITF Abstracts. Commentary and text are cross-referenced by numbers printed in red, while square brackets are used to indicate alternative wording. Situations requiring further information are highlighted by the use of italics in square brackets.

The facing page commentary is only a summary of the most commonly encountered disclosure requirements as illustrated in these model accounts. It is not a substitute for using a comprehensive disclosure checklist. Reference to the underlying company law and accounting standards will be required in more complex situations.

## Abbreviations

Examples of the abbreviations used in the commentary and in the marginal references in Part I are:

| | |
|---|---|
| *85 s157* | Section 157 of the Companies Act 1985 |
| *85 4 Sch 15* | Paragraph 15 of Schedule 4 to the Companies Act 1985 |
| *SI 1993 No. 1820* | Statutory Instrument No. 1820 issued in 1993 |
| *SSAP 17(23)* | Paragraph 23 of Statement of Standard Accounting Practice No. 17 |
| *FRS 1(12)* | Paragraph 12 of Financial Reporting Standard No. 1 |
| *UITF 13(9)* | Paragraph 9 of Urgent Issues Task Force Abstract 13 |
| *SE 12.43(n)* | Paragraph 43(n) of Chapter 12 of the Listing Rules of the London Stock Exchange |
| *SAS 600(20)* | Paragraph 20 of Statement of Auditing Standards No. 600 |
| *Code A.2.1* | Paragraph A.2.1 of the Combined Code on Corporate Governance |

## Registered number

**1**   *85 s706(2)(a)*   The company's registered number should be prominently displayed on the copy of the accounts delivered to the Registrar of Companies. It need not appear on other printed copies but this practice ensures the requirement will not be overlooked for the copy which is filed.

# Group plc
## Annual report and accounts
## for the year ended _____ 19XX

**1**

Registered number:_____

# Directors' report

**2**    *85 s238*    The directors' report must be attached to the accounts.

*85 s235(3)*    The auditors are required to comment in their report if any information given in the directors' report is not, in their opinion, consistent with the company's accounts.

## Principal activities

**3**    *85 s234(2)*    Details are required of the principal activities of the company and its subsidiary undertakings and any significant changes in those activities during the year.

## Business review

**4**    *85 s234(1)(a)*    A fair review of the development of the business of the company and its subsidiary undertakings during the year and of their position at the year end is required. This could include significant items such as the development of new products or markets, acquired or discontinued operations, major capital projects, etc.

*SE 12.43(b)*    The Stock Exchange requires listed companies to provide in their annual report and accounts an explanation of differences of 10 per cent or more between published forecasts or estimates and actual results.

**5**    *85 7 Sch 6(b)*    An indication of likely future developments in the business of the company and its subsidiary undertakings is required. This could include significant changes which are either planned or at least envisaged. Statements which may be construed as a forecast should be made with care (see The City Code on Take-overs and Mergers, Rule 28).

**6**    *85 7 Sch 6(c)*    An indication is required of any activities of the company and its subsidiary undertakings in the field of research and development.

**7**    *85 7 Sch 6(a)*    Particulars should be given of any important events affecting the company and its
*SSAP 17(18–25)*    subsidiary undertakings that have occurred since the end of the year. SSAP 17 defines these as either 'adjusting' (requiring changes to the accounts) or 'non-adjusting' (requiring disclosure). The 1985 Act would require disclosure of either type if 'important'. To avoid duplication, the directors' report could include a cross-reference to the relevant note to the accounts.

**8**    A chairman's statement and OFR are not included in the model accounts. In practice, these documents provide an ideal framework within which the directors can discuss performance, future developments and other relevant matters. A checklist of disclosure requirements for the OFR, based on the ASB's non-mandatory statement, is given in Appendix 4.

## Results and dividends

**9**    *85 s234(1)(b)*    The recommended dividend must be disclosed.

**2** # Directors' report

For the year ended 31 December 19XX

The directors present their annual report on the affairs of the group, together with the accounts and auditors' report, for the year ended 31 December 19XX.

## Principal activities

**3** The principal activities of the group comprise [*describe*].

The subsidiary and associated undertakings principally affecting the profits or net assets of the group in the year are listed in note 17 to the accounts.

## Business review

**4** [*Describe, for example, major changes in the business, development of new products or markets, acquired or discontinued operations and other factors materially affecting the business.*]

**5** The directors expect the general level of activity to [*comment on expected future developments*].

**6** The group continues to invest in research and development. This has resulted in a number of new products being launched recently which are expected to make significant contributions to the growth of the business. The directors regard investment in this area as a prerequisite for success in the medium-to long-term future.

**7** Details of significant events since the balance sheet date are contained in note 37 to the accounts.

**8** Further details of the group's performance during the year and expected future developments are contained in the chairman's statement and the Operating and Financial Review.

## Results and dividends

The audited accounts for the year ended 31 December 19XX are set out on pages __ to __. The group profit for the year, after taxation and minority interests, was £ _____ (19YY – £ _____).

**9** The directors recommend a final dividend of __ p per ordinary share to be paid on [*date*] to ordinary shareholders on the register on [*date*] which, together with the interim dividend of __ p paid on [*date*], makes a total of __ p for the year (19YY – __ p). The dividend on the __% redeemable preference shares, amounting to __ p per share, was paid on [*date*].

## Directors

**10**  *85 s234(2)*  The note should show the names of persons who were directors of the company at any time during the year. It is usual to state the dates of appointment or retirement. It would also be helpful to include changes in directors since the end of the year and rotation of directors at the annual general meeting.

**11**  *Code A.2.1, A.3.2*  The chairman, chief executive, senior independent non-executive director and other independent non-executive directors should be identified.

*Code A.5.1, B.2.3, D.3.1*  The chairmen and members of the audit, remuneration and nomination committees should also be identified.

*Code A.6.2*  In respect of the directors proposed for election or re-election, provide sufficient biographical details to enable shareholders to make an informed decision. Details would typically include age, other directorships and experience relevant to the reporting company's affairs.

## Supplier payment policy

**12**  *85 7 Sch 12*  If it is the company's policy to follow any code or standard on payment of suppliers, name the code or standard and the place where information about the standard can be obtained. If it is the company's policy:

(a)  to settle the terms of payment with suppliers when agreeing the terms of each transaction;
(b)  to ensure that suppliers are made aware of the terms of payment; and
(c)  to abide by the terms of payment;

state that fact. Otherwise, state what the company's policy is with respect to the payment of suppliers.

Details should also be given of the year-end trade creditors expressed as a number of days. The method of calculation is specified in detail and is based on the amount invoiced by suppliers in the year.

These disclosures are required in respect of the company rather than the group. But it is common for companies that have no trade creditors to disclose a policy and payment period for the group.

## Fixed assets

**13**  *85 7 Sch 1(2)*  A note should also be included indicating the difference between the book amount and the market value of land and buildings if, in the opinion of the directors, the difference is of such significance that it should be drawn to the attention of the members and debenture holders. SSAP 15 requires disclosure of the tax conse-  *SSAP 15(42)*  quences of a sale at the noted value (although it is not mandatory for disclosures in the directors' report).

## Charitable and political contributions

**14**  *85 7 Sch 3–5*  No information is required if the aggregate political and charitable contributions in the UK do not exceed £200. Where political contributions to an individual or a political party exceed £200 the name of that individual or party must be given. Donations for political or charitable purposes to people or parties outside the UK do not have to be disclosed. None of this information need be given by a company which is the wholly owned subsidiary of another company incorporated in Great Britain.

## Year 2000

**15**  *UITF 20*  The disclosure requirements of UITF 20 are summarised in the model accounts. It is impracticable to provide 'model' wording for this disclosure because of the wide variety of circumstances which may exist. These disclosures may alternatively be given elsewhere in the annual report, for example in the OFR.

# Directors' report (continued)

## Directors

**10**  The directors who served during the year were as follows:

**11**  [*Include full list of directors. Identify the chairman, chief executive, senior independent non-executive director and other independent non-executive directors. The chairmen and members of the audit, remuneration and nomination committees should also be identified.*]

Mr _____ resigned on [*date*]. Mr _____ and Ms _____ retire by rotation at the next annual general meeting and, being eligible, offer themselves for re-election. Mr _____ who was appointed a director on [*date*] retires at the next annual general meeting and, being eligible, offers himself for re-election.

[*Provide sufficient biographical details on the directors proposed for election or re-election to enable shareholders to take an informed decision.*]

## Supplier payment policy

**12**  The company's policy, which is also applied by the group, is to settle terms of payment with suppliers when agreeing the terms of each transaction, ensure that suppliers are made aware of the terms of payment and abide by the terms of payment. Trade creditors of the company at 31 December 19XX were equivalent to _____ (19YY – £ _____) days' purchases, based on the average daily amount invoiced by suppliers during the year.

## Fixed assets

**13**  In the opinion of the directors [the current open market value of the group's interests in land and buildings exceeds the book value by £_____. The group's liability to taxation if land and buildings were sold at that value would approximate £_____ /there is no material difference between the book and the current open market value of interests in land and buildings].

## Charitable and political contributions

**14**  During the year the group made charitable donations of £_____ . [There were no political contributions/Political contributions amounted to £_____, of which £_____ was made to [*name of party*] and £_____ to [*name of individual*].]

## Year 2000

**15**  [*Disclose the risks and uncertainties for the group associated with the year 2000 problem or, if no assessment has been made or its materiality not determined, that fact; the group's general plans to address the year 2000 issues relating to its business and operations and, if material, its relationships with customers, suppliers and other relevant parties; whether the total estimated cost of these plans, including amounts to be spent in future periods, has been quantified; and where applicable an indication of the basis on which the figures are calculated (e.g., the treatment of internal costs and replacement expenditure).*]

## The euro

| | | |
|---|---|---|
| **16** | *UITF 21* | An indication of costs likely to be incurred should be disclosed where the potential impact of the changeover to the euro is likely to be significant. |

## Substantial shareholdings

| | | |
|---|---|---|
| **17** | *85 s198, s199* *SE 12.43(l)* | Most share interests of 3 per cent or more and all share interests of 10 per cent or more in nominal value must be notified to a plc. The Stock Exchange requires listed companies to disclose in their annual report and accounts details of interests notified or, if no one has notified such an interest, to provide a negative statement to that effect. The disclosure relates to any class of capital which may vote in all circumstances at general meetings of the company. |

## Contracts with controlling shareholders

| | | |
|---|---|---|
| **18** | *SE 12.43(r,s)* | 'Contracts of significance' between the company or a subsidiary and a 'controlling shareholder' are to be disclosed. The Stock Exchange also requires particulars of contracts for the provision of services by a 'controlling shareholder' to the company or any of its subsidiaries (except where it is not a significant contract and is of a kind which it is the shareholders' principal business to provide). |
| | *SE 3.12* *SE 12.44* | A 'controlling shareholder' is any person entitled to exercise or control the exercise of 30 per cent or more of the votes or control the appointment of directors with a majority of votes at board meetings, while a 'contract of significance' is one which represents in amount or value a sum equal to 1 per cent or more of: |

(a) in the case of a capital transaction or a transaction of which the principal purpose or effect is the granting of credit, the aggregate of the group's share capital and reserves; or
(b) in other cases, the total annual purchases, sales, payments or receipts, as the case may be, of the group.

Details of such contracts do not necessarily have to be included in the directors' report and may be dealt with elsewhere in the annual report and accounts.

## Acquisition of the company's own shares

| | | |
|---|---|---|
| **19** | *85 7 Sch 7–8* | The 1985 Act requires particulars of own shares purchased or acquired (e.g., by forfeiture, surrender, gift or reduction of capital) or made subject to charges or liens during the year. In respect of purchases by the company, details are required of the number and nominal value of the shares purchased, the percentage of the relevant called-up capital, the aggregate consideration paid and the reasons for the purchase. |
| **20** | *SE 12.43(n)* | Listed companies are required to disclose details of any shareholders' authority for the purchase of own shares still valid at year end. In the case of all purchases made or proposed to be made by the company during the year otherwise than through the market or by tender or partial offer to all shareholders, details are required of the names of the sellers. For purchases, or options or contracts to make purchases, entered into since the year end, equivalent information to that required by Schedule 7 to the 1985 Act in respect of purchases during the year must be given. |

## Disabled employees

| | | |
|---|---|---|
| **21** | *85 7 Sch 9* | The company's policies in respect of applications for employment from disabled persons, the treatment of employees that become disabled and the training, career development and promotion of disabled persons should be described. This information is only required if the parent company employs on average more than 250 persons in the UK. However, many listed companies make this disclosure voluntarily when the parent company is small or non-trading. |

# Directors' report (continued)

## The euro

16    [*Where the potential impact of the introduction of the euro is likely to be significant to the group, the UITF recommends that information and discussion should be given, including an indication of the total costs likely to be incurred.*]

## Substantial shareholdings

17    On [*a date not more than one month prior to the date of notice of the annual general meeting*], the company had been notified, in accordance with sections 198 to 208 of the Companies Act 1985, of the following interests in the ordinary share capital of the company.

| Name of holder | Number | Percentage held |
| --- | --- | --- |
|  | _____ | _____ |

## Contracts with controlling shareholders

18    [*Name of shareholder*], a controlling shareholder, provided the company with [*describe services*] amounting to £ _____ (19YY – £ _____) during the year.

## Acquisition of the company's own shares

19    Further to the shareholders' resolutions of [*date*], the company purchased [*number*] ordinary shares with a nominal value of £ _____ , and representing __% of the company's called-up ordinary share capital, for a consideration of £ _____ .

20    At the end of the year, the directors had authority, under the shareholders' resolutions of [*date*], to purchase through the market [*number*] of the company's ordinary shares at prices ranging between £ _____ and £ _____ per share. This authority expires on [*date*].

## Disabled employees

21    Applications for employment by disabled persons are always fully considered, bearing in mind the aptitudes of the applicant concerned. In the event of members of staff becoming disabled, every effort is made to ensure that their employment with the group continues and that appropriate training is arranged. It is the policy of the group that the training, career development and promotion of disabled persons should, as far as possible, be identical to that of other employees.

## Employee consultation

**22**  *85 7 Sch 11*  A description is needed of the action taken during the year to introduce, maintain or develop arrangements to:

(a) provide employees systematically with information affecting them as employees;
(b) consult them (or their representatives) regularly on decisions likely to affect their interests;
(c) encourage employees' involvement through share schemes or other means; and
(d) achieve a common awareness by all employees of the financial and economic factors affecting the company's performance.

This disclosure applies to any company employing on average more than 250 persons in the UK. However, many listed companies make this disclosure voluntarily when the parent company is small or non-trading.

## Special business

**23**  *SE 14.17*  Whenever shareholders are sent a notice of a meeting which includes any business, other than ordinary business at an annual general meeting, and where the business is to be considered at or on the same day as the annual general meeting, an explanation may be incorporated in the directors' report rather than in an explanatory circular accompanying the notice.

The ordinary business of an annual general meeting is defined for the purposes of the Listing Rules as receiving or adopting the accounts; declaring a dividend; reappointing directors and appointing directors to replace those retiring at the meeting; reappointing auditors and authorising the directors to fix their remuneration; granting, renewing or varying authority under section 80 of the 1985 Act or (within certain limits) disapplying section 89 of the 1985 Act; granting or renewing a general authority for a company to purchase its own shares; and renewing or regranting an existing authority for a scrip dividend alternative.

Chapter 14 of the Listing Rules sets out requirements in relation to the contents of circulars which may be required in other circumstances. Unless the circular is of a 'routine nature' as defined in Chapter 14, it must be approved by the Stock Exchange prior to publication.

## Auditors

**24**  A statement concerning the reappointment of auditors is customary but not required.

## Approval and signature of directors' report

**25**  *85 s234A*  The directors' report should be approved by the board of directors and signed by a director or the company secretary on its behalf. The name of the signatory should be stated. The copy of the directors' report which is delivered to the Registrar of Companies must contain an original signature.

# Directors' report (continued)

## Employee consultation

22    The group places considerable value on the involvement of its employees and has continued to keep them informed on matters affecting them as employees and on the various factors affecting the performance of the group. This is achieved through formal and informal meetings, the company magazine and a special edition for employees of the annual accounts. Employee representatives are consulted regularly on a wide range of matters affecting their current and future interests. The employee share scheme has been running successfully since its inception in 19__. It is open to all employees and [*describe major features of the scheme*]. [In addition, all employees receive an annual bonus related to the overall profitability of the group.]

## Special business

23    A resolution will be placed before the annual general meeting to increase the authorised share capital of the company from £ _____ to £ _____ by the creation of [*number*] new ordinary shares of _____ each.

## Auditors

24    The directors will place a resolution before the annual general meeting to reappoint [*name of auditors*] as auditors for the ensuing year.

25    [Address of registered office]    By order of the Board,


[Signature]

[Director/Secretary]

[Date]                                      [Name of signatory to be stated]

# Corporate governance statements

In June 1998 the Hampel Committee and the London Stock Exchange published the 'Combined Code' on corporate governance. The Code combines the existing requirements of the Cadbury Code on corporate governance with the requirements of the Greenbury Code on directors' remuneration and adds some new requirements as a result of the findings of the Hampel Committee.

*SE 12.43A* For years ending on or after 31 December 1998, the Listing Rules of the London Stock Exchange have been amended to take account of the Combined Code and to require listed companies incorporated in the UK to make certain statements in their annual report.

At the time of writing there were no examples of companies reporting under these new requirements. Furthermore, guidance for internal control reporting under the Combined Code was still being developed. It is therefore particularly important to have regard to any subsequent pronouncements by the Stock Exchange and other interested parties such as the Auditing Practices Board and the ICAEW.

## Compliance with the Code of Best Practice

**26** *SE 12.43A(b)* The company must make a statement as to whether or not it has complied throughout the financial year with the Code provisions set out in section 1 of the Combined Code. A company that has not complied with the Code provisions, or complied with only some of them or complied for only part of the year, must specify the Code provisions with which it has not complied, for what part of the period such non-compliance continued, and give reasons for any non-compliance.

There are 45 Code provisions in section 1 of the Combined Code and many companies will not have complied with all of them throughout the first accounting period to which paragraph 12.43A of the Listing Rules applies. Although the Stock Exchange has made it clear that any such non-compliance must be disclosed, it has also recommended that shareholders and others monitoring compliance with the Combined Code should do so with flexibility, common sense and with regard to the individual companies' circumstances.

## Application of Principles of Good Governance

**27** *SE 12.43A(a)* The company must provide a narrative statement of how it has applied the Principles of Good Governance set out in section 1 of the Combined Code, providing explanation that enables its shareholders to evaluate how the Principles have been applied.

The Preamble to the Combined Code by the Hampel Committee stresses that the form and content of this statement is not prescribed. The Committee intends that companies should have a free hand to explain their governance policies in the light of the Principles, including any special circumstances applying to them which have led to a particular approach.

As noted above, at the time of writing there were no examples of companies reporting under Listing Rule 12.43A, although a few had made general comments about the Code and the Principles. It will be important to monitor developing practice in this area. The model accounts demonstrate one approach to dealing with this statement.

# Corporate governance statements

In June 1998 the Hampel Committee and the London Stock Exchange published the Combined Code on corporate governance. This combines the Cadbury Code on corporate governance, the Greenbury Code on directors' remuneration and new requirements arising from the findings of the Hampel Committee.

## Statement of compliance with the Code of Best Practice

**26**    The company has complied throughout the year with the provisions of the Code of Best Practice set out in section 1 of the Combined Code [except for the following matters: *Specify the relevant provisions of the Code, the period affected and the reason*].

[Where the posts of Chairman and Chief Executive are combined in one person, Code provision A.2.1 requires that a justification be provided. As Chairman and Chief Executive, Mr _____ is responsible for running both the board and the company's business. However, a majority of the board are non-executive directors and under the leadership of Mr _____ they have, in the board's view, the ability and authority to ensure that the combination of roles does not work to the disadvantage of the company and its shareholders.]

**28**    Code provision D.2.1 requires directors, at least annually, to conduct a review of the effectiveness of the group's system of internal control. The directors have performed such a review. [They limited their review to internal financial controls, as permitted by the London Stock Exchange, pending publication of guidance for directors on the broader aspects of internal control.]

Code provision D.3.1 requires the members of the audit committee to be named in the report and accounts. Mr _____, Mr _____ and Mr _____ served on the committee throughout the year.

## Statement about applying the Principles of Good Governance

**27**    The company has applied the Principles of Good Governance set out in section 1 of the Combined Code by complying with the Code of Best Practice as reported above. Further explanation of how the Principles have been applied is set out below and, in connection with directors' remuneration, in the remuneration report.

[*To the extent that the company is able to provide further specific explanations that will enable shareholders to evaluate how the Principles have been applied, provide statements under the headings shown below. To avoid uninformative and excessive disclosures, it is suggested that companies do not reproduce or paraphrase provisions of the Code of Best Practice with which they have complied. However, it is envisaged that all companies will make a statement about applying Principle C.1 on dialogue with institutional shareholders because there are no related Code provisions. All companies should also make a narrative statement on Principle D.2 on internal control, because the existing guidance for directors issued in December 1994 'Internal control and financial reporting' specifies the minimum contents of a directors' statement on the subject. The text below reflects these requirements.*]

# Corporate governance statements (continued)

## [Board effectiveness

*Additional explanation of how Principle A.1 has been applied, e.g.,* The board considers that it has shown its commitment to leading and controlling the company by: launching Project X, a new initiative to explain the group's current strategy to all its employees and to seek their input; meeting on a monthly basis throughout the year and formally considering how and to whom matters covered at each meeting should be communicated beyond the board; arranging for non-executive directors to visit each of the group's principal locations at least once every two years to discuss the operations with local management.]

## [Division of responsibilities between Chairman and Chief Executive

*Additional explanation of how Principle A.2 has been applied, e.g.,* The board has shown its commitment to dividing responsibilities for running the board and running the company's business by: appointing Mr _____ as non-executive Chairman; naming Mr _____ as senior independent director; establishing an Operations Committee of Divisional Managing Directors under the chairmanship of the Chief Executive, Mr _____ , and establishing a procedure whereby the Operations Committee reports formally to the board each month.]

## [Board balance

*Additional explanation of how Principle A.3 has been applied, e.g.,* The company's commitment to achieving a balance of executive and non-executive directors is shown by: the fact that over the past three years the number of independent non-executive directors has risen from one to four while the numbers of executives and other non-executives have remained the same at four and two respectively; the fact that the board has asked the nomination committee to make recommendations for the appointment of two further independent non-executive directors.]

## [Timeliness and quality of board information

*Additional explanation of how Principle A.4 has been applied, e.g.,* The board has sought to ensure that directors are properly briefed on issues arising at board meetings by establishing procedures for: distributing board papers one week in advance of meetings; considering the adequacy of the information provided before making decisions; adjourning meetings or deferring decisions when directors have concerns about the information available to them; having a standing agenda item to consider the timeliness and quality of information; making the company secretary responsible to the board for the timeliness and quality of information.]

## [Transparency of board appointments

*Additional explanation of how Principle A.5 has been applied, e.g.,* In the board's view the appointment in the year of Mr _____ showed how the board follows formal and transparent procedures when appointing directors. In particular, the nomination committee instructed external consultants to identify a shortlist of suitable candidates. All the candidates were interviewed by at least two members of the committee and evaluations of all candidates were circulated to all members of the nomination committee. The nomination committee was unanimous in recommending the appointment to the board.]

# Corporate governance statements (continued)

## [Regular re-election of directors

*Additional explanation of how Principle A.6 is applied, e.g.,* As disclosed in the directors' report, the director who was appointed during the year is offering himself for re-election and all directors are now subject to re-election every two years rather than every three years as required by the Provisions of the Code of Best Practice.]

## Dialogue with institutional shareholders

The directors seek to build on a mutual understanding of objectives between the company and its institutional shareholders by [following suggestions contained in the Myners Report 'Developing a Winning Partnership', namely, making an annual strategic presentation to institutional investors; meeting shareholders to discuss long-term issues and obtain feedback; communicating regularly throughout the year and issuing quarterly trading updates; providing comprehensive training to managers involved in investor relations].

## [Constructive use of AGM

*Additional explanation of how Principle C.2 is applied, e.g.,* The board has sought to use the AGM to communicate with private investors and encourage their participation by: inviting shareholders to submit questions in advance; referring minority interest questions for later response; arranging presentations by operational management. The success of these measures is shown by the fact that last year's AGM was attended by _____ shareholders and _____ questions from shareholders were answered at the meeting or subsequently.]

## [Balanced and understandable assessment of position and prospects

*Additional explanation of how Principle D.1 has been applied, e.g.,* The board has shown its commitment to presenting balanced and understandable assessments of the company's position and prospects by: complying with non-mandatory statements issued by the Accounting Standards Board relating to the Operating and Financial Review included in this Annual Report, its preliminary announcement and its interim report; complying in this year's accounts with the new accounting standard FRS 12 *Provisions, Contingent Liabilities and Contingent Assets* before it becomes mandatory; canvassing the views of investors and analysts on how the company could improve its financial reporting; including a glossary of accounting terms in the Annual Report and seeking wherever possible to use plain English.]

# Internal control

*Code D.2.1*  The directors should, at least annually, conduct a review of the effectiveness of the group's system of internal controls and should report to shareholders that they have done so. The review should cover all controls, including financial, operational and compliance controls and risk management.

The Cadbury Code contained a similar requirement. However, authoritative guidance issued with the backing of the Cadbury Committee confirmed that the scope of the review could be restricted to internal financial control. The Hampel Committee reconsidered this matter and decided that the directors should review the wider range of controls listed above.

Some companies perceive that it is difficult to know that they have complied with the requirement unless the criteria set out in the December 1994 publication 'Internal Control and Financial Reporting' are updated. A working party has been set up by the ICAEW to produce guidance for directors on the scope, extent, nature and review of internal controls to which Code Principle D.2 and provision D.2.1 refer. The objective of this working party is to produce guidance by the summer of 1999.

The Stock Exchange has stated that, until that guidance is published, a company's statement of compliance will satisfy the requirements of the Listing Rules if a company complies with the existing arrangements on internal controls by reporting on their internal financial controls pursuant to the 1994 guidance. A company that has adopted this approach should indicate in its statement of compliance that it has done so and may wish to reflect this approach in their narrative statement about how they have applied Code Principle D.2.

The model accounts have been drafted on the basis that the company has taken advantage of this relaxation by the Stock Exchange. Some companies will, however, feel able to report that they have carried out a review of the wider range of controls as envisaged by the Hampel Committee.

The 1994 guidance requires a company's annual report to include a directors' statement containing, as a minimum, the following four disclosures relating to 'internal financial control':

(a)  acknowledgement that they are responsible for the system of internal financial control;

(b)  explanation that such a system can only provide reasonable and not absolute assurance against material misstatement or loss;

(c)  description of the key procedures the directors have established and which are designed to provide effective internal financial control; and

(d)  confirmation that they or a board committee have reviewed the effectiveness of the system of internal financial control.

The term 'internal financial control' is defined as covering those controls established to provide reasonable assurance of the safeguarding of assets against unauthorised use or disposition, the maintenance of proper accounting records and the reliability of financial information used within the business or for publication.

Where weaknesses in internal control have resulted in material losses, contingencies or uncertainties which require disclosure in the accounts or the auditors' report, the directors should describe what corrective action has been taken or is intended to be taken or explain why no changes are considered necessary.

In all cases, the directors' statement should cover the period of the accounts and should also take account of material developments between the balance sheet date and the date when the accounts are approved.

# Corporate governance statements (continued)

## Maintenance of a sound system of internal control

28 In applying the principle that the board should maintain a sound system of internal control to safeguard shareholders' investment and the company's assets, the directors recognise that they have overall responsibility for ensuring that the group maintains a system of internal control to provide them with reasonable assurance regarding effective and efficient operations, internal financial control and compliance with laws and regulations. However, there are inherent limitations in any system of internal control and, accordingly, even the most effective system can provide only reasonable, and not absolute, assurance.

The key features of the internal [financial] control system that operated throughout the period covered by the accounts are described below. [The directors have limited their comments to internal financial controls, as permitted by the London Stock Exchange, pending publication of guidance for directors on the broader aspects of internal control.]

- Control environment – [*Describe key procedures*]
- Identification and evaluation of business risks and control objectives – [*Describe key procedures*]
- Information systems – [*Describe key procedures*]
- Main control procedures – [*Describe key procedures*]
- Monitoring – [*Describe key procedures and refer to any internal audit function*]

[*The guidance for directors of December 1994 encourages directors to identify major business risks and their financial implications. They might also describe the related control objectives, information systems, control procedures and monitoring.*]

[*Where weaknesses in internal control have resulted in material losses, contingencies or uncertainties which require disclosure in the financial statements or in the auditors' report, the directors should describe what corrective action has been taken or is intended to be taken; or explain why no changes are considered necessary.*]

## [Appropriate audit committee responsibilities and relationships with auditors

*Additional explanation of how the company has applied Principle D.3, e.g.,* The board has shown its commitment to formal and transparent arrangements for financial reporting, internal control and external audit by: informing all employees that any concerns they have in these areas can be raised with the chairman of the audit committee in the strictest confidence; extending the audit committee's terms of reference to cover the group's risk management activities as a whole and not just the financial aspects of internal control; specifying that it would expect each audit committee member to spend at least _____ hours annually on committee business; requiring the audit committee to institute formal measures of external auditor performance.]

# Remuneration report

*SE 12.43A*
*Code B.3.1*

The requirement for a report on directors' remuneration was originally contained in the Cadbury Code. The Hampel Committee decided to retain the requirement but the report is now from the board rather than from the remuneration committee. The contents of the remuneration report are prescribed by the Combined Code and the Listing Rules.

## Remuneration committee

**29**    *Code B.2.3*    The members of the remuneration committee should be listed each year in the board's remuneration report.

## Remuneration policy

**30**    *Code B.3.2*
       *SE 12.43A(c)(i)*

The report should set out the company's policy on executive directors' remuneration. It should draw attention to factors specific to the company. The model accounts list some issues which might typically be discussed. These are derived from paragraph 5.5 of the report of the Greenbury Committee.

## Policy on granting share options

**31**    *SE 12.43A(c)(viii)*    The company's policy on granting of options or awards under its employee share schemes and other long-term incentive schemes should be stated. Any change in the policy or departure from the policy during the year should be explained and justified.

*Code Schedule B Para 3*    If grants under executive share option or other long-term incentive schemes are awarded in one large block rather than phased, the report should explain and justify this.

## Remuneration of non-executive directors

**32**    *Code B.2.4*    The Code requires that the board itself or, where required by the Articles of Association, the shareholders should determine the remuneration of the non-executive directors within the limits set by the Articles of Association. The board may, however, delegate this responsibility to a small sub-committee, which might include the chief executive, where permitted by the Articles. Although there is no disclosure requirement attaching to this Code provision, many companies comment on the

*Greenbury Report 5.7*    method of determining the remuneration of non-executive directors, as was recommended by the Greenbury Committee.

# Remuneration report

As well as complying with the provisions of the Code as disclosed in the company's corporate governance statements, the company has applied the Principles of Good Governance relating to directors' remuneration as described below.

## [The level and composition of directors' remuneration

*Additional explanation of how Principle B.1 is applied, e.g.,* The board has shown that it does not pay more than is necessary to attract and retain the directors needed to run the company successfully in the following ways: executive directors' remuneration, excluding performance-related incentives, has risen on average by _____% per annum over the past three years whereas the company's earnings per shares have risen by _____% over the same period; remuneration is benchmarked against a comparator group of companies comprising _____; the remuneration policy described below provides for _____.]

## Procedures for developing policy and fixing remuneration

29    The members of the remuneration committee are disclosed on page ...

[*Additional explanation of how the company has applied Principle B.2, e.g.,* The board has shown its commitment to formal and transparent procedures for developing remuneration policy, fixing executive remuneration and ensuring that no director is involved in deciding his or her own remuneration by engaging external consultants to report twice yearly to the remuneration committee on executive directors' pay trends.]

## Statement of remuneration policy and details of remuneration

30    The company's policy on executive director remuneration is as follows: [*Describe policy, where applicable, on: the total level of remuneration; the main components and the arrangements for determining them, including the division between basic and performance-related components; the main parameters and rationale for any annual bonus schemes, including caps; how performance is measured, how rewards are related to it, how the performance measures relate to longer-term company objectives and how the company has performed over time relative to comparator companies; the company's policy on allowing executive directors to accept appointments and retain payments from sources outside the company; the company's policy on contracts of service and early termination; and pension schemes for directors, including the type of scheme, the main terms and parameters, what elements of remuneration are pensionable, how the Inland Revenue pensions cap has been accommodated and whether the scheme is part of, or separate from, the main company scheme. Attention should also be drawn to any special arrangements made and any material changes introduced during the year.*]

31    The company's policy on the granting of share options [, awards under its employee share schemes and other long-term incentive schemes] is [*describe policy, explaining and justifying any departure from that policy and any change in that policy*].

32    The remuneration of the non-executive directors is determined by the board as a whole, based on outside advice and review of current practices in other companies.

## Details of remuneration packages

**33**  *SE 12.43A(c)*  The remuneration report should contain details of the emoluments, share options,
*(ii,iii,iv,ix,x)*  long-term incentive scheme benefits and pension benefits for individual directors. In
these model accounts the disclosures have been included in note 8 to the accounts.
This is recommended because the disclosures are required to be within the scope of
the auditors' report.

## Pensionable remuneration

**34**  *SE 12.43A(c)(v)*  If any element of remuneration other than basic salary is pensionable, an explanation and justification should be provided.

## Service contracts

**35**  *SE 12.43A(c)(vi)*  Details of any directors' service contracts with a notice period in excess of one year
or with provision for pre-determined compensation on termination which exceeds
one year's salary and benefits, giving the reasons for such notice periods, should be
included.

**36**  *SE 12.43A(c)(vii)*  The unexpired term of any service contract of a director proposed for election or
re-election at the forthcoming AGM should be stated. If any such director does not
have a service contract, a statement to this effect should be made.

*SE Definitions*  The Listing Rules define a director's service contract as a service contract with a
notice or contract period of one year or more or with provisions for pre-determin-
ing compensation on termination of an amount which equals or exceeds one year's
salary and benefits in kind. As readers of the accounts will not necessarily be aware
of the definition in the Listing Rules, it is advisable to give the notice period even if
it is less than one year.

# Remuneration report (continued)

**33** Full details of the remuneration packages of individual directors and information on share options, long-term incentive schemes and pension benefits are set out in note 8 to the accounts.

**34** [*Explanation and justification of any element of remuneration, other than basic salary, which is pensionable.*]

**35** The service contract of Mr _____ provides for [a notice period of [*number*] years/compensation of £ _____ on termination] because [*state reasons if effective notice period is over one year*].

**36** Mr _____ and Mr _____, who are proposed for re-election at the next annual general meeting, have service contracts which expire on [*date*] and [*date*] respectively. Mr _____ who is also proposed for re-election does not have a service contract.

[*Additional explanation of how the company has applied Principle B.3, e.g.,* The board has shown its commitment to a full statement of remuneration policy and each director's remuneration by disclosing: estimated fair values for executive directors' options at the date of grant; total transfer values of directors' accrued pension benefits.]

# Directors' responsibilities

## Accounts

**37**      *SAS 600(20–23)*    The directors' responsibilities for preparing the accounts should be explained. The
         *Code D.1.1*        statement illustrated reflects the normal responsibilities of company directors and
may need to be adapted for different requirements applicable to certain types of
reporting entity.

The minimum contents for a statement of directors' responsibilities are effectively
prescribed by Statement of Auditing Standards 600. If the statement does not meet
these minimum requirements, the auditors must include similar details in their
report.

## Going concern

**38**      *SE 12.43(v)*     The Listing Rules require the directors to state that 'the business is a going concern
         *Code D.1.3*        with supporting assumptions or qualifications as necessary'. This statement is some-
times found with the 'corporate governance' disclosures as it owes its origins to the
Cadbury Code. It is also often found in the OFR where it can be placed in the context of a discussion of the financing of the group. In these model accounts it has
been included within the statement of directors' responsibilities, because one of the
responsibilities noted in SAS 600 is to prepare the accounts on a going concern
basis unless it is inappropriate to presume that the group will continue in business.

In making the statement, the directors should follow the principles set out in 'Going
Concern and Financial Reporting', published by the Going Concern Working
Group, which requires the statement to reflect one of three basic conclusions based
on what is known to them at the date on which they approve the accounts:

(a) the directors have a reasonable expectation that the company will continue in
operational existence for the foreseeable future; or
(b) they have identified factors which cast doubt on the ability of the company to
continue in operational existence for the foreseeable future but still consider it
appropriate to use the going concern basis in preparing the accounts; or
(c) they consider the company unlikely to continue in operational existence and
therefore the going concern basis is not appropriate.

The guidance notes that it is not possible to specify a minimum period to which the
directors should pay particular attention in assessing going concern. However,
where the period considered by the directors has been limited, for example, to a
period of less than one year from the date of approving the accounts, the guidance
recommends directors to consider disclosing this. In the event of non-disclosure,
SAS 130 requires auditors to refer to the matter in their report.

# Directors' responsibilities

**37**  ## Accounts, including adoption of going concern basis

Company law requires the directors to prepare accounts for each financial year which give a true and fair view of the state of affairs of the company and group and of the profit or loss of the group for that period.

**38**  After making enquiries, the directors have a reasonable expectation that the company and the group have adequate resources to continue in operational existence for the foreseeable future. For this reason, they continue to adopt the going concern basis in preparing the accounts.

In preparing the accounts, the directors are required to: select suitable accounting policies and then apply them consistently; make judgements and estimates that are reasonable and prudent; and state whether applicable accounting standards have been followed, subject to any material departures disclosed and explained in the accounts.

## Other matters

The directors are responsible for keeping proper accounting records which disclose with reasonable accuracy at any time the financial position of the company and group and enable them to ensure that the accounts comply with the Companies Act 1985. They are also responsible for safeguarding the assets of the company and group and hence for taking reasonable steps for the prevention and detection of fraud and other irregularities.

# Auditors' report

## Basic elements

**40**    *SAS 600(14), 85 s240*    The auditors' report should be attached to the accounts and include the following:

**41**    *85 s235(1)*    (a)   a title identifying the persons to whom the report is addressed (for statutory reporting purposes this will be the shareholders);

**42**    (b)   an introductory paragraph identifying the accounts audited;

**43**    (c)   separate sections, appropriately headed, dealing with:

       (i)   the respective responsibilities of the directors and the auditors;

       (ii)   the basis of the auditors' opinion (including a statement as to their compliance or otherwise with auditing standards, together with the reasons for any departure therefrom); and

*85 s235(2)*    (iii)   whether in the auditors' opinion the accounts give a true and fair view and have been properly prepared in accordance with the Companies Act 1985;

**44**    (d)   the manuscript or printed signature of the auditors; and

**45**    (e)   the date of the report.

**46**    *SAS 600(45,46)*    SAS 600 permits but does not require auditors to report explicitly on cash flows. Because the ASB's stated view is that, when required by FRS 1, the inclusion of cash flow information as a separate primary statement is necessary in order for accounts to present a true and fair view, it is preferable that the opinion paragraph in addition to covering the profit and loss and balance sheet should also refer to cash flows.

**47**    *APB Bulletin 1998/10*    The model accounts illustrate an expanded description of auditors' responsibilities which is recommended by the APB for listed companies and is more extensive than that required by SAS 600. This approach enables the auditors to clarify their responsibilities for parts of the annual report other than the audited accounts.

## Other matters

**48**    *Foreword to Accounting Standards 10b SAS 600(47,48)*    The auditors' report should refer to any significant departures from the requirements of applicable accounting standards which are not disclosed or are inadequately disclosed in the accounts or are departures with which the auditors do not concur.

*85 s237(1–3)*    Where relevant the auditors must also state that:

(a)   proper returns have not been received from branches they have not visited;

(b)   proper accounting records have not been kept;

(c)   the accounts are not in agreement with the underlying records and returns;

(d)   they have not obtained all the information and explanations they considered necessary; and

*85 s235(3)*    (e)   the information contained in the directors' report is inconsistent with the accounts.

*85 s237(4)*    In circumstances where the accounts fail to provide the information required by Schedule 6 to the 1985 Act in respect of directors' emoluments and transactions with directors and non-director officers the auditors should, so far as they are reasonably able, provide the relevant details. A similar but additional requirement is *SE 12.43A(c)* imposed on auditors of listed companies where the accounts fail to provide the information required by paragraph 12.43A(c) of the Listing Rules in respect of particulars of directors' remuneration.

## Signature

**49**    *85 s236 Audit Regulations and Guidance (3.06)*    The auditors' report should state the names of the auditors (including their registered status) and be signed by them. The copy of the auditors' report which is delivered to the Registrar of Companies must contain an original signature.

# 40 Auditors' report

## 41 To the Shareholders of Group plc:

42 We have audited the accounts on pages _____ to _____ which have been prepared under the historical cost convention [as modified by the revaluation of certain fixed assets] and the accounting policies set out on pages ___ to ___ .

## Respective responsibilities of directors and auditors

43, 47 The directors are responsible for preparing the Annual Report including, as described on page _____ , the accounts. Our responsibilities, as independent auditors, are established by statute, the Auditing Practices Board, the Listing Rules of the London Stock Exchange, and by our profession's ethical guidance.

We report to you our opinion as to whether the accounts give a true and fair view and are properly prepared in accordance with the Companies Act. We also report to you if, in our opinion, the directors' report is not consistent with the accounts, if the company has not kept proper accounting records, if we have not received all the information and explanations we require for our audit, or if information specified by law or the Listing Rules regarding directors' remuneration and transactions with the company and the group is not disclosed.

We review whether the statement on page _____ reflects the company's compliance with those provisions of the Combined Code specified for our review by the Stock Exchange, and we report if it does not. We are not required to form an opinion on the effectiveness of the company's corporate governance procedures or its internal controls.

We read the other information contained in the Annual Report, including the corporate governance statement, and consider whether it is consistent with the audited accounts. We consider the implications for our report if we become aware of any apparent misstatements or material inconsistencies with the accounts.

## 43 Basis of audit opinion

We conducted our audit in accordance with auditing standards issued by the Auditing Practices Board. An audit includes examination, on a test basis, of evidence relevant to the amounts and disclosures in the accounts. It also includes an assessment of the significant estimates and judgements made by the directors in the preparation of the accounts and of whether the accounting policies are appropriate to the circumstances of the company and of the group, consistently applied and adequately disclosed.

We planned and performed our audit so as to obtain all the information and explanations which we considered necessary in order to provide us with sufficient evidence to give reasonable assurance that the accounts are free from material misstatement, whether caused by fraud or other irregularity or error. In forming our opinion we also evaluated the overall adequacy of the presentation of information in the accounts.

## 43, 46, 48 Opinion

In our opinion, the accounts give a true and fair view of the state of affairs of the company and of the group at 31 December 19XX and of the group's profit and cash flows for the year then ended and have been properly prepared in accordance with the Companies Act 1985.

44, 49 [*Name of auditors*]
Chartered Accountants and Registered Auditors

[*Address*]
45 [*Date*]

# Consolidated profit and loss account

**50**      *85 4 Sch 1,2*      The model profit and loss account illustrates the use of format 1 of the statutory profit and loss account formats. A change in the statutory format adopted is only permitted where, in the directors' opinion, there are special reasons for the change. Particulars of the change and the reasons for it should be disclosed in the accounts in which a new format is first adopted.

## Turnover and operating profit

**51**      *FRS 3(14), FRS 6(28)*      Both turnover and operating profit should be analysed on the face of the profit and loss account between continuing operations, acquisitions (as a component of continuing operations) and discontinued operations (as defined in paragraph 4 of FRS 3).

     *FRS 3(30,64)*      The comparative amounts for continuing operations should include only the results of those operations included in the current year's continuing operations. No reference need be made to the results of acquisitions reported in the previous year.

## Share of associates

**52**      *FRS 9(27)*      The following items should be shown separately on the face of the profit and loss account in respect of the group's share of associates:

(a) operating results – disclosed immediately after group operating results;
(b) exceptional items – for each category;
(c) interest payable; and
(d) any other pre-tax items below operating profit.

For items below profit before tax, the relevant amounts for associates should be included in the group's figures and disclosed in a note.

## Exceptional items reported after operating profit

**53**      *FRS 3(20)*      The following exceptional items, including related provisions, should be shown separately on the face of the profit and loss account after operating profit and before interest, and attributed to continuing or discontinued operations as appropriate:

(a) profits or losses on the sale or termination of an operation;
(b) costs of a fundamental reorganisation or restructuring having a material effect on the nature and focus of the group's operations; and
(c) profits or losses on the disposal of fixed assets.

When the net amount of (a) or (c) is not material, but the gross profits or losses are material, the relevant heading should still appear on the face of the profit and loss account with a reference to a related note analysing the profits and losses.

## Mandatory items

**54**      *85 4 Sch 3(6,7)*      Profit on ordinary activities before taxation, transfers between the profit and loss account and reserves, and the aggregate amount of any dividends paid and proposed must be shown on the face of the profit and loss account.

# Consolidated profit and loss account

For the year ended 31 December 19XX

| | Notes | 19XX £ | 19YY £ |
|---|---|---|---|
| **51** **Turnover** | 1 | | |
| Existing operations | | | |
| Acquisitions | | | |
| | | ——— | ——— |
| Continuing operations | | | |
| Discontinued operations | | | |
| | | ——— | ——— |
| Cost of sales | 2 | | |
| | | ——— | ——— |
| **Gross profit** | 2 | | |
| Other operating expenses (net) | 2 | | |
| | | ——— | ——— |
| **51** **Operating profit** | | | |
| Existing operations | | | |
| Acquisitions | | | |
| | | ——— | ——— |
| Continuing operations | | | |
| Discontinued operations | | | |
| | | ——— | ——— |
| **52** Share of associates' operating profit | 3 | | |
| **53** Profit on sale of discontinued operations | 4 | | |
| **53** Costs of a fundamental restructuring of continuing operations | 4 | | |
| **53** Profit on sale of tangible fixed assets of continuing operations | | | |
| Group | 4 | | |
| **52** Associates | 4 | | |
| | | ——— | ——— |
| **Profit on ordinary activities before finance charges** | | | |
| Finance charges (net) | | | |
| Group | 5 | | |
| Associates | 5 | | |
| | | ——— | ——— |
| **54** **Profit on ordinary activities before taxation** | 6 | | |
| Tax on profit on ordinary activities | 9 | | |
| | | ——— | ——— |
| **Profit on ordinary activities after taxation** | | | |
| Minority interests [(including non-equity interests)] | 28 | | |
| | | ——— | ——— |
| **Profit for the financial year** | 10 | | |

## Dividends and other finance costs

**55**  *FRS 4(59)*  Where the aggregate dividend for each class of share is not given on the face of the profit and loss account and there are amounts relating to non-equity shares, the dividend caption should make it clear that such amounts are included.

**56**  *FRS 4(44)*  In circumstances where the finance costs of non-equity shares are not equal to the dividends, the difference should be reported as an appropriation of profits. This typically arises where non-equity shares are redeemable at a premium, carry stepped dividend rights or carry cumulative dividend rights but because of insufficient distributable reserves a dividend cannot be declared.

## Earnings per share

**57**  *FRS 14*  Companies whose ordinary shares (or potential ordinary shares, as defined in FRS 14) are, or will be, publicly traded are required to provide figures for basic and diluted earnings per share on the face of the profit and loss account in respect of each class of ordinary shares that have a different right to share in the profit or loss of the period. Both basic and diluted EPS should be shown with equal prominence for all periods presented.

## Comparative information

**58**  *85 4 Sch 3(5),4,*  Corresponding amounts must be given for all items in the profit and loss account
*FRS 3(30)*  (unless there is a nil entry for both years). Where the corresponding amounts are not comparable they should be adjusted with particulars of, and the reasons for, any adjustment provided.

# Consolidated profit and loss account (continued)

For the year ended 31 December 19XX

| | | Notes | 19XX £ | 19YY £ |
|---|---|---|---|---|
| **54, 55** | **Dividends paid and proposed [on equity and non-equity shares]** | 11 | | |
| **56** | **Other finance costs of non-equity shares** | 11 | | |
| | Retained profit for the year | 26 | | |
| **57** | **Earnings per share** | | | |
| | Basic | 12 | p | p |
| | Diluted | 12 | p | p |

The accompanying notes are an integral part of this consolidated profit and loss account.

*[Drafting note: Due to the level of detail in the profit and loss account the statement runs to two pages. In practice this is unlikely to arise.]*

# Consolidated statement of total recognised gains and losses

**59**  *FRS 3(27)*  A primary statement should be presented, with the same prominence as the other primary statements, showing the gains and losses recognised in the year insofar as they are attributable to shareholders. Such gains and losses will include, for example, the profit for the financial year, surpluses on the revaluation of fixed assets and currency translation differences on foreign currency net investments.

**60**  *FRS 9(28)*  The investor's share of total recognised gains and losses of its associates should be shown separately under each heading in the statement of total recognised gains and losses, if material. Alternatively, these amounts can be shown in a note that is referred to in the statement.

**61**  *FRS 3(29)*  The cumulative effect of prior year adjustments should be shown at the foot of the statement of total recognised gains and losses of the current year.

**62**  *FRS 3(57)*  Where there are no recognised gains or losses other than the profit for the year, a statement to this effect immediately below the profit and loss account will satisfy the requirement of paragraph 27 of FRS 3. Such a statement could be worded as follows: 'There are no recognised gains or losses in either year other than the profit for that year'.

**63**  *FRS 3(30)*  Corresponding amounts should be given for the previous year.

# Consolidated note of historical cost profits and losses

**64**  *FRS 3(26)*  Where there is a material difference between the result as disclosed in the profit and loss account and the result on an unmodified historical cost basis, a note of the historical cost profit or loss for the year should be presented immediately following the profit and loss account or the statement of total recognised gains and losses. The note should contain a reconciliation of the reported profit on ordinary activities before taxation to the equivalent historical cost amount and also show the retained profit for the financial year reported on an historical cost basis.

This note is comparatively rare in practice as usually the only reconciling item is additional depreciation of revalued properties which is usually immaterial. However, the reconciling items can become much more material when revalued assets are sold.

**65**  *FRS 3(30)*  Corresponding amounts should be given for the previous year.

# Consolidated statement of total recognised gains and losses

For the year ended 31 December 19XX

|  | 19XX £ | 19YY £ |
|---|---|---|
| Profit for the financial year | | |
| Group | | |
| **60** Associates | | |
| | | |
| Unrealised surplus on revaluation of investment properties | | |
| Group | | |
| **60** Associates | | |
| Gain on foreign currency translation | | |
| Loss on overseas borrowing | | |
| **Total recognised gains and losses relating to the year** | | |
| **61** **Prior year adjustment (as explained in note 13)** | | |
| **Total gains and losses recognised since last annual report and accounts** | | |

**62** *[Drafting note: If there are no recognised gains or losses in either period other than the profit (loss) for each period, a statement to this effect immediately below the profit and loss account will satisfy the requirement of paragraph 27 of FRS 3.]*

# Consolidated note of historical cost profits and losses

For the year ended 31 December 19XX

|  | 19XX £ | 19YY £ |
|---|---|---|
| Reported profit on ordinary activities before taxation | | |
| Realisation of property revaluation gains of previous year | | |
| Difference between an historical cost depreciation charge and the actual depreciation charge for the year | | |
| **Historical cost profit on ordinary activities before taxation** | | |
| Historical cost profit for the year retained after taxation, minority interests and dividends | | |

*[Drafting note: This statement is not required if there is no material difference between the profit on ordinary activities before taxation and the retained profit for the period for both periods and their respective historical cost equivalents.]*

The accompanying notes are an integral part of this consolidated statement of total recognised gains and losses and this consolidated note of historical cost profits and losses.

# Balance sheets

**66**  *85 4 Sch 1,2*  The model balance sheets illustrate the use of format 1 of the statutory balance sheet formats. A change in the statutory format adopted is only permitted where, in the directors' opinion, there are special reasons for the change. Particulars of the change and the reasons for it should be disclosed in the accounts in which a new format is first adopted.

In this example, the group and holding company balance sheets are presented separately. They could alternatively be presented on the same page.

## Classification of assets

**67**  *85 s262(1)*  Fixed assets are defined in the 1985 Act as those intended for use on a continuing basis in the group's activities, and any asset which does not qualify as fixed must be shown as current.

## Goodwill

**68**  *FRS 10(7)*  Goodwill should be shown as an asset on the face of the balance sheet.

**69**  *FRS 10(48)*  Negative goodwill should be shown on the face of the balance sheet, immediately below positive goodwill and followed by a subtotal.

## Debtors

**70**  *UITF 4(3)*  Debtors due after more than one year should be disclosed on the face of the balance sheet where the amount is so material in the context of total net current assets that in the absence of such disclosure readers may misinterpret the accounts.

## Creditors

**71**  *Statutory format note 7*
*FRS 4(25,54,100)*  The amount of convertible debt should normally be shown on the face of the balance sheet. However, on grounds of materiality, this information could be given in the notes provided the creditors caption on the face of the balance sheet states that convertible debt is included.

## Shareholders' funds

**72**  *FRS 4(38,40,54,100)*  The total amount of shareholders' funds should be shown on the face of the balance sheet and analysed between amounts attributable to equity and non-equity interests. The analysis may, on grounds of materiality, be given in the notes provided the caption for shareholders' funds states that non-equity interests are included.

*FRS 4 App 1(2)*  FRS 4 does not require any of the individual components of shareholders' funds to be analysed between equity and non-equity interests.

## Minority interests

**73**  *FRS 4(50,54,100)*  A similar analysis to that provided for shareholders' funds is required for minority interests.

## Comparative information

**74**  *85 4 Sch 3(5),4*  Corresponding amounts must be given for all items in the balance sheet (unless there is a nil entry for both years). Where the corresponding amounts are not comparable they should be adjusted with particulars of, and the reasons for, any adjustment provided.

# Consolidated balance sheet

31 December 19XX

| | Notes | 19XX £ | 19YY £ |
|---|---|---|---|
| **67** **Fixed assets** | | | |
| Development costs, patents and trade marks | 14 | | |
| **68** Goodwill | 15 | | |
| **69** Negative goodwill | 15 | | |
| Intangible assets | | | |
| Tangible assets | 16 | | |
| Associates | 17 | | |
| Other investments | 17 | | |
| **Current assets** | | | |
| Stocks | 18 | | |
| Debtors | | | |
| due within one year | 19 | | |
| **70** due after one year | 19 | | |
| Investments | 20 | | |
| Cash at bank and in hand | | | |
| **Creditors:** Amounts falling due within one year | | | |
| **71** Convertible debt | 21 | | |
| Other creditors | 21 | | |
| **Net current assets** | | | |
| **Total assets less current liabilities** | | | |
| **Creditors:** Amounts falling due after more than one year | | | |
| **71** Convertible debt | 22 | | |
| Other creditors | 22 | | |
| **Provisions for liabilities and charges** | 24 | | |
| **Net assets** | | | |

# Consolidated balance sheet (continued)

31 December 19XX

| | Notes | 19XX £ | 19YY £ |
|---|---|---|---|
| **Capital and reserves** | | | |
| Called-up share capital | 25 | | |
| Share premium account | 26 | | |
| Revaluation reserve | 26 | | |
| Other reserves | 26 | | |
| Profit and loss account | 26 | | |
| **72**    **Shareholders' funds** | | | |
| **73**    **Minority interests (including non-equity interests)** | 28 | | |
| **Total capital employed** | | | |
| **72**    **Shareholders' funds may be analysed as:** | | | |
| Equity interests | | | |
| Non-equity interests | | | |

*[Drafting note: Although only the company balance sheet must be signed, some companies adopt the practice of including signatures on the consolidated balance sheet as well.]*

*[Drafting note: Due to the level of detail in the balance sheet the statement runs on to two pages. In practice this is unlikely to arise.]*

The accompanying notes are an integral part of this consolidated balance sheet.

# Company balance sheet

31 December 19XX

| | Notes | 19XX £ | 19YY £ |
|---|---|---|---|
| **67** **Fixed assets** | | | |
| Development costs, patents and trade marks | 14 | | |
| Tangible assets | 16 | | |
| Investments | 17 | | |
| | | _____ | _____ |
| | | _____ | _____ |
| **Current assets** | | | |
| Stocks | 18 | | |
| Debtors | | | |
| due within one year | 19 | | |
| **70** due after one year | 19 | | |
| Investments | 20 | | |
| Cash at bank and in hand | | | |
| | | _____ | _____ |
| **Creditors:** Amounts falling due within one year | | | |
| **71** Convertible debt | 21 | | |
| Other creditors | 21 | | |
| | | _____ | _____ |
| | | _____ | _____ |
| **Net current assets** | | | |
| | | _____ | _____ |
| **Total assets less current liabilities** | | | |
| **Creditors:** Amounts falling due after more than one year | | | |
| **71** Convertible debt | 22 | | |
| Other creditors | 22 | | |
| | | _____ | _____ |
| **Provisions for liabilities and charges** | 24 | | |
| | | _____ | _____ |
| **Net assets** | | | |
| | | ══════ | ══════ |

## Approval and signature

**75**

*85 s233* The company's accounts, including its group accounts, should be approved by the board of directors. The company's balance sheet should be signed by a director on behalf of the board, with the name of the signatory stated. An original signature is required on the copy delivered to the Registrar of Companies. A consolidated balance sheet presented separately from that of the parent company need not be signed (although it often is). SSAP 17 requires the date on which the accounts are

*SSAP 17(26)* approved by the board to be disclosed.

Normal practice for listed companies is for the company's balance sheet to be signed by two or three directors, usually the chairman and/or chief executive and the finance director.

# Company balance sheet (continued)

31 December 19XX

| | Notes | 19XX £ | 19YY £ |
|---|---|---|---|
| **Capital and reserves** | | | |
| Called-up share capital | 25 | | |
| Share premium account | 26 | | |
| Revaluation reserve | 26 | | |
| Other reserves | 26 | | |
| Profit and loss account | 26 | | |

**72**  **Shareholders' funds**

**Shareholders' funds may be analysed as:**
Equity interests
Non-equity interests

**75**  The accounts on pages __ to __ were approved by the board of directors on [*date*] and signed on its behalf by:

[*Name*]  Director

[*Name of signatory to be stated*]

[*Date*]

The accompanying notes are an integral part of this balance sheet.

[*Drafting note: Due to the level of detail in the balance sheet, the statement runs on to two pages. In practice this is unlikely to arise.*]

# Consolidated cash flow statement

**76**     *FRS 1(5)*     FRS 1 (revised 1996) *Cash Flow Statements* applies, with certain exceptions, to all accounts intended to give a true and fair view of the financial position and profit or loss. The main exceptions relate to the accounts of companies which are eligible to take advantage of the small company exemptions in the 1985 Act, similar unincorporated entities, 90 per cent owned subsidiary undertakings, provided the group accounts are publicly available, pension schemes and mutual life assurance companies.

## Standard headings

**77**     *FRS 1(7)*     The cash flow statement should list the cash flows for the period classified under the standard headings shown in the model accounts.

          The first seven headings should be in sequence. The cash flows relating to liquid resources and financing can be combined under a single heading provided the cash flows relating to each are shown separately with subtotals.

*FRS 1(8–32)*     The standard sets out individual categories of cash flows under each of the standard headings and requires these to be disclosed separately in the cash flow statement or in a note. The cash flow classifications may be subdivided further to give a fuller description of the activities of the reporting entity or to provide segmental information.

*FRS 1(39)*     Cash flows should be shown net of VAT or other sales tax unless the tax is irrecoverable.

## Equity dividends

**78**     *FRS 1(25)*     Cash outflows included in 'equity dividends paid' are dividends paid on the company's equity shares, excluding any advance corporation tax. Dividends on non-equity shares and dividends paid to minority shareholders in subsidiaries are included within 'returns on investments and servicing of finance'.

## Exceptional items

*FRS 1(37)*     Cash flows relating to items that are classified as exceptional in the profit and loss account should be shown under the appropriate standard headings, according to the nature of each item. Cash flows relating to exceptional items should be identified in the cash flow statement or a note to it and the relationship between the cash flows and the originating exceptional item should be explained.

*FRS 1(38)*     Where cash flows are exceptional because of their size or incidence but are not related to items that are treated as exceptional in the profit and loss account, sufficient disclosure should be given to explain their cause and nature.

## Reconciliation to net debt

*FRS 1(33)*     A note reconciling the movement in cash in the period with the movement in net debt should be given either adjoining the cash flow statement or in a note. The reconciliation is not part of the cash flow statement and, if presented adjoining the cash flow statement, should be clearly labelled and kept separate. In these model accounts the reconciliation is presented in note 31.

## Comparative information

**79**     *FRS 1(48)*     Comparative figures should be given for all items in the cash flow statement and related notes with the exception of the note which analyses the amounts making up net debt and the note on the material effects of acquisitions and disposals on each of the standard headings.

# Consolidated cash flow statement

For the year ended 31 December 19XX

| | | Notes | 19XX £ | 19YY £ |
|---|---|---|---|---|
| | **Net cash inflow from operating activities** | 29 | | |
| 77 | Dividends from [joint ventures and] associates | | | |
| 77 | Returns on investments and servicing of finance | 30 | | |
| 77 | Taxation | 30 | | |
| 77 | Capital expenditure and financial investment | 30 | | |
| 77 | Acquisitions and disposals | 30 | | |
| 77, 78 | Equity dividends paid | | | |
| | | | | |
| | **Cash outflow before management of liquid resources and financing** | | | |
| 77 | Management of liquid resources | 30 | | |
| 77 | Financing | 30 | | |
| | | | | |
| | **Decrease in cash in the year** | 31 | | |

The accompanying notes are an integral part of this consolidated cash flow statement.

# Statement of accounting policies

**80**  *85 4 Sch 36,*
*SSAP 2(18)*  The accounting policies adopted for dealing with items which are judged material or critical to determining the result for the year and in stating the financial position should be explained. These policies should be applied consistently throughout the year and from one year to the next.

## True and fair view

**81**  *85 s226(2,4), s227(3,5)*  The accounts are required to give a true and fair view of the profit or loss for the financial year and the state of affairs at the end of it. This paramount principle underpins all the accounting requirements of the 1985 Act and accounting standards. If accounts drawn up in compliance with the 1985 Act do not provide sufficient information to give a true and fair view, then the necessary additional information must be given.

*85 s226(5), s227(6)*
*UITF 7*  In special circumstances it is possible that compliance with one or more requirements of the 1985 Act, even when supplemented by additional information, is inconsistent with the requirement for the accounts to show a true and fair view. In these cases the directors must depart from the specific requirements to the extent necessary to show a true and fair view and must disclose the particulars of the departure, the reasons for it and its effect.

## Statutory accounting principles

**82**  *85 4 Sch 9–14,*
*SSAP 2(14)*  All companies are required to comply with the following fundamental accounting principles:

(a)  consistency;
(b)  prudence;
(c)  accruals;
(d)  going concern; and
(e)  separate determination.

*85 4 Sch 15, SSAP 2(17)*
*UITF 7*  If it appears to the directors that there are special reasons for departing from any of these accounting principles they may do so, but particulars of the departure, the reasons for it and its effect should be disclosed.

## Substance over form

**83**  *FRS 5(30,31,67)*  FRS 5 requires accounts to reflect the commercial effect of transactions rather than simply adhere to their legal form and to provide sufficient disclosure to enable the effects to be understood. Where a transaction results in the recognition of assets or liabilities whose nature differs from that of items usually included under the relevant balance sheet heading (e.g., factored debts remaining on balance sheet), the differences should be explained.

## Basis of accounting

**84**  A statement regarding the cost convention adopted is customary, for example, historical cost or modified historical cost (i.e., including asset revaluations).

*85 4 Sch 36A*
*Foreword to Accounting*
*Standards 19, UITF 7*  The directors should state that the accounts have been prepared in accordance with applicable accounting standards. Particulars of any material departure, the reasons for it and its effect should be disclosed.

## Basis of consolidation

**85**  This policy note should cover the basis of consolidation and the treatment of subsidiaries acquired or disposed of during the year.

*85 4A Sch 3,*
*FRS 2(40, 41)*  Uniform group accounting policies should be used for valuing the assets and liabilities to be included in the group accounts, if necessary by adjusting for consolidation the amounts which have been reported by subsidiary undertakings in their individual accounts. Particulars of any departure from this principle, including the different policy used, the reasons for it and its effect should be disclosed.

# Statement of accounting policies

31 December 19XX

The principal accounting policies are summarised below. They have all been applied consistently throughout the year and the preceding year with the exception explained in note 13.

**84** ## Basis of accounting

The accounts have been prepared under the historical cost convention, modified to include the revaluation of certain fixed assets, and in accordance with applicable accounting standards.

**85** ## Basis of consolidation

The group accounts consolidate the accounts of Group plc and its subsidiary undertakings drawn up to 31 December each year. The results of subsidiaries acquired or sold are consolidated for the periods from or to the date on which control passed. Acquisitions are accounted for under the acquisition method.

**86** ## Intangible assets – goodwill

Goodwill arising on the acquisition of subsidiary undertakings and businesses, representing any excess of the fair value of the consideration given over the fair value of the identifiable assets and liabilities acquired, is capitalised and written off on a straight line basis over its useful economic life, which is between seven and a maximum of twenty years. Provision is made for any impairment.

Negative goodwill is similarly included in the balance sheet and is credited to the profit and loss account in the periods in which the acquired non-monetary assets are recovered through depreciation or sale. Negative goodwill in excess of the fair values of the non-monetary assets acquired is credited to the profit and loss account in the periods expected to benefit.

Goodwill arising on acquisitions in the year ended 31 December 1997 and earlier periods was written off to reserves in accordance with the accounting standard then in force. As permitted by the current accounting standard the goodwill previously written off to reserves has not been reinstated in the balance sheet. On disposal or closure of a previously acquired business, the attributable amount of goodwill previously written off to reserves is included in determining the profit or loss on disposal.

**87** ## Intangible assets – research and development

Research expenditure is written off as incurred. Development expenditure is also written off, except where the directors are satisfied as to the technical, commercial and financial viability of individual projects. In such cases, the identifiable expenditure is deferred and amortised over the period during which the group is expected to benefit. This period is between three and five years. Provision is made for any impairment.

**87** ## Intangible assets – patents and trade marks

Patents and trade marks are included at cost and depreciated in equal annual instalments over a period of [*number*] years which is their estimated useful economic life. Provision is made for any impairment.

## Goodwill

**86**    *85 4 Sch 21(4)*    The methods and periods of amortisation of goodwill and the reasons for choosing
     *FRS 10(7,55)*    those periods should be disclosed. Where different periods are chosen for each acquisition, the accounting policy might specify a range with further details given in the goodwill note. Additional disclosure requirements apply where goodwill is amortised over a period longer than 20 years or is not amortised.

     *FRS 10(63–64)*    The periods in which negative goodwill is being written back in the profit and loss account should be disclosed, together with an explanation where the negative goodwill exceeds the fair value of the non-monetary assets acquired.

     *FRS 10(71)*    If goodwill remains eliminated against reserves as permitted by the transitional provisions in FRS 10, the accounts should state the accounting policy followed in respect of that goodwill and the fact that the goodwill had been eliminated as a matter of accounting policy and would be charged or credited in the profit and loss account on subsequent disposal of the business to which it related.

## Intangible assets

**87**    *FRS 10(52,55)*    The accounts should disclose the methods and periods of amortisation of intangible assets and also, where relevant, the methods used to value intangible assets.

     *SSAP 13(30)*    The policy on research and development expenditure should be disclosed. SSAP 13 requires research expenditure to be written off in the year of expenditure, but permits in defined circumstances development expenditure to be deferred and amortised.

## Tangible fixed assets

**88**    *85 4 Sch 36*    For each major class of depreciable asset, disclose:

                       (a)    the basis on which the asset is stated;
*85 Sch 18, SSAP 12(25)*    (b)    the depreciation method used; and
                       (c)    the useful economic lives or depreciation rates.

     *85 Sch 3(4)(a)*    In this example, it is assumed that fixtures, fittings, tools and equipment are not material and they are not, therefore, separately identified.

## Revaluation of property

**89**    *85 Sch 29–34*    An accounting policy for revaluations should cover the frequency of revaluation, the treatment of consequential surpluses or deficits and the use of the revaluation reserve.

## Investment properties

**90**    *SSAP 19(10,11)*    Investment properties should be included in the balance sheet at their open market value and, with the exception of leasehold properties where the unexpired period
  *85 s226(5), s227(6)*    of the lease is 20 years or less, should not be depreciated. This represents a depar-
         *UITF 7*    ture from the statutory accounting rules which is necessary in order to give a true and fair view. Particulars of, the reasons for and the effect of the departure should be disclosed.

## Investments

**91**    *85 4 Sch 19,36*    The policy in respect of any impairment of fixed asset investments should be disclosed.

     *85 s133(1)*    With respect to the balance sheet of the parent company it is helpful to explain whether advantage has been taken of merger relief.

# Statement of accounting policies (continued)

## 88  Tangible fixed assets

Tangible fixed assets are stated at cost or valuation, net of depreciation and any provision for impairment. Depreciation is provided on all tangible fixed assets, other than investment properties and freehold land, at rates calculated to write off the cost or valuation, less estimated residual value, of each asset on a [straight-line/reducing balance] basis over its expected useful life, as follows:

| | |
|---|---|
| Freehold buildings | [ __ years/ __% per annum] |
| Leasehold land and buildings | [ __ years/ __% per annum/term of lease] |
| Plant and machinery | [ __ years/ __% per annum] |

Residual value is calculated on prices prevailing at the date of acquisition or revaluation.

## 89  Revaluation of properties

Individual freehold and leasehold properties [other than investment properties] are revalued every [*number*] years with the surplus or deficit on book value being transferred to the revaluation reserve, except that a deficit which is in excess of any previously recognised surplus over depreciated cost relating to the same property, or the reversal of such a deficit, is charged (or credited) to the profit and loss account. A deficit which represents a clear consumption of economic benefits is charged to the profit and loss account regardless of any such previous surplus. Where depreciation charges are increased following a revaluation, an amount equal to the increase is transferred annually from the revaluation reserve to the profit and loss account as a movement on reserves. On the disposal or recognition of a provision for impairment of a revalued fixed asset, any related balance remaining in the revaluation reserve is also transferred to the profit and loss account as a movement on reserves.

## 90  Investment properties

Investment properties are revalued annually. Surpluses or deficits on individual properties are transferred to the investment revaluation reserve, except that a deficit which is expected to be permanent and which is in excess of any previously recognised surplus over cost relating to the same property, or the reversal of such a deficit, is charged (or credited) to the profit and loss account. Depreciation is not provided in respect of freehold investment properties or of leasehold investment properties where the unexpired term of the lease is more than 20 years. The directors consider that this accounting policy, which represents a departure from the statutory accounting rules, is necessary to provide a true and fair view as required under SSAP 19. The financial effect of the departure from the statutory accounting rules [is shown in the notes to the accounts/cannot reasonably be quantified as *[explain circumstances]*/is not material].

## 91  Investments

Except as stated below, fixed asset investments are shown at cost less provision for impairment. Current asset investments are stated at the lower of cost and net realisable value.

In the company balance sheet, for investments in subsidiaries acquired for consideration including the issue of shares qualifying for merger relief, cost is measured by reference to the nominal value only of the shares issued. Any premium is ignored.

## Associates

**92**   *85 4A Sch 22,*   Investments in associated undertakings should be accounted for using the equity
         *FRS 9(26)*       method.

## Stocks

**93**   *85 Sch 22,23,27*   The basis for determining the balance sheet value of stocks should be disclosed.

## Long-term contracts

**94**   *SSAP 9*   A long-term contract is defined in SSAP 9 as a contract entered into for the design, manufacture or construction of a single substantial asset or the provision of a service (or of a combination of assets and services which together constitute a single project) where the time taken substantially to complete the contract is such that the contract activity falls into different accounting periods. Such contracts will usually extend for a period exceeding one year although this is not an essential feature of a long-term contract.

Where long-term contracts are a material element of the group's activities, the accounts should include a related accounting policy note which should cover, in particular, the method of ascertaining turnover and attributable profit (see also policy for turnover).

## Taxation

**95**   *SSAP 8*    This policy note should cover the treatment of corporation tax and advance corpo-
         *SSAP 15*   ration tax and the basis and method for providing for deferred taxation. Specific disclosure is required of the policy followed in accounting for the deferred taxation implications of pensions and other post-retirement benefits.

## Turnover

**96**   *85 s262(1), SSAP 5(8)*   A description of the basis on which turnover is stated is normally provided. See also above for long-term contracts.

# Statement of accounting policies (continued)

### 92 Associates

In the group accounts, investments in associates are accounted for using the equity method. The consolidated profit and loss account includes the group's share of associates' profits less losses, while the group's share of the net assets of the associates is shown in the consolidated balance sheet. Goodwill arising on the acquisition of associates is accounted for in accordance with the policy set out above. Any unamortised balance of goodwill is included in the carrying value of the investment in associates.

### 93 Stocks

Stocks are stated at the lower of cost and net realisable value. Cost includes materials, direct labour and an attributable proportion of manufacturing overheads based on normal levels of activity. Net realisable value is based on estimated selling price, less further costs expected to be incurred to completion and disposal. Provision is made for obsolete, slow-moving or defective items where appropriate.

### 94 Long-term contracts

Amounts recoverable on long-term contracts, which are included in debtors, are stated at the net sales value of the work done less amounts received as progress payments on account. Excess progress payments are included in creditors as payments on account. Cumulative costs incurred net of amounts transferred to cost of sales, less provision for contingencies and anticipated future losses on contracts, are included as long-term contract balances in stock.

### 95 Taxation

Corporation tax payable is provided on taxable profits at the current rate.

Advance corporation tax payable on dividends paid or provided for in the year is written off, except when recoverability against corporation tax payable is considered to be reasonably assured. Credit is taken for advance corporation tax written off in previous years when it is recovered against corporation tax liabilities.

Deferred taxation is provided using the liability method on all timing differences only to the extent that they are expected to reverse in the future without being replaced, except that the deferred tax effects of timing differences arising from pensions and other post-retirement benefits are always recognised in full.

### 96 Turnover

Turnover represents amounts receivable for goods and services provided in the normal course of business, net of trade discounts, VAT and other sales-related taxes.

Profit is recognised on long-term contracts, if the final outcome can be assessed with reasonable certainty, by including in the profit and loss account turnover and related costs as contract activity progresses. Turnover is calculated as that proportion of the total contract value which costs incurred to date bear to total expected costs for that contract.

## Pension costs and other post-retirement benefits

**97**      *SSAP 24(87,88),*     The basis on which amounts are charged to the profit and loss account and recog-
              *UITF 6*     nised in the balance sheet for both defined benefit and defined contribution schemes
should be disclosed.

## Foreign currency

**98**      *85 4 Sch 58(1)*     The policy should cover:

                                            (a)    the basis of translating amounts denominated in foreign currencies;
     *SSAP 20(59)*     (b)    the method used for translating accounts of foreign enterprises; and
                                            (c)    the treatment of exchange differences.

The policy could also cover the treatment of foreign currency borrowings used to
hedge overseas equity investments.

## Leases

**99**      *SSAP 21(57)*     SSAP 21 requires particulars of the policies adopted for accounting for finance
leases and operating leases, and hire purchase transactions with similar character-
            *UITF 12*     istics to these types of leases. The treatment of reverse premiums and similar incen-
tives to sign operating leases could also be disclosed.

# Statement of accounting policies (continued)

## 97 Pension costs and other post-retirement benefits

For defined benefit schemes the amount charged to the profit and loss account in respect of pension costs and other post-retirement benefits is the estimated regular cost of providing the benefits accrued in the year, adjusted to reflect variations from that cost. The regular cost is calculated so that it represents a substantially level percentage of current and future payroll. Variations from regular cost are charged or credited to the profit and loss account as a constant percentage of payroll over the estimated average remaining working life of scheme members. Defined benefit schemes are funded, with the assets of the scheme held separately from those of the group in separate trustee administered funds. Differences between amounts charged to the profit and loss account and amounts funded are shown as either provisions or prepayments in the balance sheet.

For defined contribution schemes the amount charged to the profit and loss account in respect of pension costs and other post-retirement benefits is the contributions payable in the year. Differences between contributions payable in the year and contributions actually paid are shown as either accruals or prepayments in the balance sheet.

## 98 Foreign currency

Transactions in foreign currencies are recorded at the rate of exchange at the date of the transaction or, if hedged, at the forward contract rate. Monetary assets and liabilities denominated in foreign currencies at the balance sheet date are reported at the rates of exchange prevailing at that date or, if appropriate, at the forward contract rate.

The results of overseas operations are translated at the [closing/average] rates of exchange during the period and their balance sheets at the rates ruling at the balance sheet date. Exchange differences arising on translation of the opening net assets [*average rate only:* and results of overseas operations] and on foreign currency borrowings, to the extent that they hedge the group's investment in such operations, are dealt with through reserves. All other exchange differences are included in the profit and loss account.

## 99 Leases

Assets held under finance leases and other similar contracts, which confer rights and obligations similar to those attached to owned assets, are capitalised as tangible fixed assets and are depreciated over the shorter of the lease terms and their useful lives. The capital elements of future lease obligations are recorded as liabilities, while the interest elements are charged to the profit and loss account over the period of the leases to produce a constant rate of charge on the balance of capital repayments outstanding. Hire purchase transactions are dealt with similarly, except that assets are depreciated over their useful lives.

Rentals under operating leases are charged on a straight-line basis over the lease term, even if the payments are not made on such a basis. Benefits received and receivable as an incentive to sign an operating lease are similarly spread on a straight-line basis over the lease term, except where the period to the review date on which the rent is first expected to be adjusted to the prevailing market rate is shorter than the full lease term, in which case the shorter period is used.

## Finance costs and debt

**100**  *FRS 4(25–31, 42–51)*  Accounting policies for capital instruments should cover the basis of allocation of finance costs of debt, non-equity shares and non-equity minority interests, the calculation of the carrying amount of debt and the treatment of convertible debt.

## Government grants

**101**  *SSAP 4(17,25,28)*  The method of accounting for government grants should be disclosed. The CCAB has received Counsel's opinion that treating government grants as a deduction from the cost of the appropriate asset would contravene the 1985 Act.

## Derivative financial instruments

**102**  *FRS 13(73–76)*  FRS 13 stresses that disclosure of accounting policies used for financial instruments is of particular importance in view of the wide variety of accounting treatments that are adopted. The definition of financial instruments is much wider than just derivatives although the accounting for most other types of financial instruments, such as borrowings and investments, is well established and covered by other accounting policies.

FRS 13 does not include any specific disclosure requirements for accounting policies but indicates that, in order to comply with SSAP 2, the description of accounting policies will usually need to include the following, if the choice of policy applied had a material effect:

(a) the methods used to account for derivative financial instruments, the types of instruments accounted for under each method and the criteria that determine the method used;
(b) the basis for recognising, measuring (both on initial recognition and subsequently) and ceasing to recognise financial assets and financial liabilities;
(c) how income and expenses (and other gains and losses) are recognised and measured;
(d) the treatment of financial assets and financial liabilities not recognised, including an explanation of how provisions for losses are recognised on such assets and liabilities; and
(e) policies on offsetting.

FRS 13 also suggests further policies for financial instruments carried at historical cost and for financial instruments used as hedges.

# Statement of accounting policies (continued)

**100**    ## Finance costs

Finance costs of debt, non-equity shares and non-equity minority interests are recognised in the profit and loss account over the term of such instruments at a constant rate on the carrying amount. Where the finance costs for non-equity shares and non-equity minority interests are not equal to the dividends on these instruments, the difference is also accounted for in the profit and loss account as an appropriation of profits.

**100**    ## Debt

Debt is initially stated at the amount of the net proceeds after deduction of issue costs. The carrying amount is increased by the finance cost in respect of the accounting period and reduced by payments made in the period. Convertible debt is reported as a liability unless conversion actually occurs. No gain or loss is recognised on conversion.

**101**    ## Government grants

Government grants relating to tangible fixed assets are treated as deferred income and released to the profit and loss account over the expected useful lives of the assets concerned. Other grants are credited to the profit and loss account as the related expenditure is incurred.

**102**    ## Derivative financial instruments

The group uses derivative financial instruments to reduce exposure to foreign exchange risk and interest rate movements. The group does not hold or issue derivative financial instruments for speculative purposes.

For a forward foreign exchange contract to be treated as a hedge, the instrument must be related to actual foreign currency assets or liabilities or to a probable commitment. It must involve the same currency or similar currencies as the hedged item and must also reduce the risk of foreign currency exchange movements on the group's operations. Gains and losses arising on these contracts are deferred and recognised in the profit and loss account, or as adjustments to the carrying amount of fixed assets, only when the hedged transaction has itself been reflected in the group's accounts.

For an interest rate swap to be treated as a hedge the instrument must be related to actual assets or liabilities or a probable commitment and must change the nature of the interest rate by converting a fixed rate to a variable rate or vice versa. Interest differentials under these swaps are recognised by adjusting net interest payable over the periods of the contracts.

If an instrument ceases to be accounted for as a hedge, for example, because the underlying hedged position is eliminated, the instrument is marked to market and any resulting profit or loss recognised at that time.

# Notes to the accounts

## Comparative information

**103**    *85 4 Sch 58(2,3),*    Comparative information is required for every item stated in the notes, with the
              *FRS 3(30)*    exception of:

*85 4A Sch 13*    (a)    the accounting treatment of acquisitions;
*85 5 Sch*    (b)    shareholdings in subsidiary and other undertakings;
*85 6 Sch Pts II, III*    (c)    loans, etc. to directors and non-director officers; and
*85 4 Sch 42,46*    (d)    movements on fixed assets, provisions and reserves.

Corresponding amounts should be adjusted if necessary to ensure they are comparable with the figures for the current year. Particulars of the adjustment and the reason for it should be given.

## Segment information

**104**    *85 4 Sch 55*    The 1985 Act contains basic requirements for all companies to analyse their turnover by class of business and geographical segment. SSAP 25 builds on this foundation with more extensive segmental disclosures.

*SSAP 25(41)*    The additional disclosures required by SSAP 25 apply to the following entities:

(a)    plcs or parents with a plc subsidiary; or
(b)    banking or insurance companies or groups; or
(c)    large non-plcs for which purpose the medium-sized company criteria of the 1985 Act are to be multiplied by 10.

However, a subsidiary that is not a plc or a banking or insurance company does not have to comply with SSAP 25 if its parent complies with the standard.

*85 4 Sch 55(5)*    Neither SSAP 25 nor the 1985 Act require disclosure of information that would be
*SSAP 25(43)*    seriously prejudicial to the interests of the group, but the fact that any such information has not been disclosed should be stated.

**105**    *SSAP 25(34)*    For each class of business and geographical segment disclose:

(a)    turnover, distinguishing between third-party and inter-segmental turnover;
(b)    result before taxation and minority interests; and
(c)    net assets.

The company should disclose the geographical segmentation of turnover by origin. It should also disclose turnover to third parties by destination or state where appropriate that this analysis is not materially different from turnover to third parties by origin.

**106**    *SSAP 25(37)*    A reconciliation should be provided where the total of the amounts disclosed by segment does not agree to the related total in the accounts.

**107**    *SSAP 25(36)*    The group's share of the results and net assets of associated undertakings should be disclosed by class of business and geographical segment where associates account for at least 20 per cent of the group's result or net assets. This information need not be disclosed if it is unobtainable or its publication would be prejudicial to the business of the associate. The reasons for non-disclosure should, however, be provided, together with a brief description of the omitted business or businesses.

# Notes to the accounts

31 December 19XX

**104**   ## 1 Segment information

**105**   Classes of business:

| | [Industry A] | | [Industry B] | | [Other industries] | | Group | |
|---|---|---|---|---|---|---|---|---|
| | 19XX £ | 19YY £ | 19XX £ | 19YY £ | 19XX £ | 19YY £ | 19XX £ | 19YY £ |
| **Turnover** | | | | | | | | |
| Total sales | | | | | | | | |
| Inter-segment sales | | | | | | | | |
| **Sales to third parties** | | | | | | | | |
| **Segment profit** | | | | | | | | |
| **106** Common costs | | | | | | | | |
| **Operating profit** | | | | | | | | |
| **107** Share of associates' operating profit | | | | | | | | |
| Exceptional items reported after operating profit | | | | | | | | |
| Finance charges (net) | | | | | | | | |
| **Profit on ordinary activities before taxation** | | | | | | | | |
| **Segment net assets** | | | | | | | | |
| **107** **Share of associates' net assets** | | | | | | | | |
| **106** Unallocated net assets | | | | | | | | |
| **Net assets** | | | | | | | | |

135

# Notes to the accounts (continued)

## 1 Segment information (continued)

**105** Geographical segments:

| | [United Kingdom] | | [Rest of Europe] | | [Other] | | Group | |
|---|---|---|---|---|---|---|---|---|
| | 19XX £ | 19YY £ | 19XX £ | 19YY £ | 19XX £ | 19YY £ | 19XX £ | 19YY £ |
| **Turnover by destination:** | | | | | | | | |
| Sales to third parties | | | | | | | | |
| | ═══ | ═══ | ═══ | ═══ | ═══ | ═══ | ═══ | ═══ |
| **Turnover by origin:** | | | | | | | | |
| Total sales | | | | | | | | |
| Inter-segment sales | | | | | | | | |
| **Sales to third parties** | ─── | ─── | ─── | ─── | ─── | ─── | ─── | ─── |
| | ═══ | ═══ | ═══ | ═══ | ═══ | ═══ | ═══ | ═══ |
| **Segment profit** | | | | | | | | |
| | ═══ | ═══ | ═══ | ═══ | ═══ | ═══ | | |

**106** Common costs

|  |  |  |  |  |  |  | 19XX | 19YY |
|---|---|---|---|---|---|---|---|---|
| | | | | | | | ─── | ─── |

| | [United Kingdom] | | [Rest of Europe] | | [Other] | | Group | |
|---|---|---|---|---|---|---|---|---|
| **Operating profit** | | | | | | | | |
| **107** Share of associates' operating profit | | | | | | | | |
| | ═══ | ═══ | ═══ | ═══ | ═══ | ═══ | | |
| Exceptional items reported after operating profit | | | | | | | | |
| | ═══ | ═══ | ═══ | ═══ | ═══ | ═══ | | |
| Finance charges (net) | | | | | | | | |
| **Profit on ordinary activities before taxation** | | | | | | | ─── | ─── |
| | | | | | | | ═══ | ═══ |
| **Segment net assets** | | | | | | | | |
| | ═══ | ═══ | ═══ | ═══ | ═══ | ═══ | | |
| **107 Share of associates' net assets** | | | | | | | | |
| | ═══ | ═══ | ═══ | ═══ | ═══ | ═══ | | |
| **106** Unallocated net assets | | | | | | | | |
| **Net assets** | | | | | | | ─── | ─── |
| | | | | | | | ═══ | ═══ |

Common costs consist of [describe].

Unallocated net assets consist of [describe].

**108**    *FRS 3(15),*    Where a material acquisition, other acquisitions in aggregate, or a discontinuance
        *FRS 6(23,28)*    has a material effect on a major business segment, this should be disclosed.

# Notes to the accounts (continued)

## 1 Segment information (continued)

108 Acquisitions and disposals:

The analyses presented above include the following amounts in respect of operations acquired and discontinued during the year:

| | Acquisition of [name of undertaking] | | Disposal of [name of undertaking] | |
| | [Industry] | [Geographic area] | [Industry] | [Geographic area] |
|---|---|---|---|---|
| | £ | £ | £ | £ |
| Sales to third parties | | | | |
| by destination | | | | |
| by origin | | | | |
| Segment profit | | | | |
| Segment net assets | | | | |

# Cost of sales, gross profit and other operating expenses (net)

**109** *FRS 3(14), FRS 6(28)*   Each statutory profit and loss account format item between turnover and operating profit should be analysed between continuing operations, acquisitions (as a component of continuing operations) and discontinued operations. In this example, the analysis is given in the notes. It could alternatively be provided on the face of the profit and loss account, for example, by using a columnar layout.

The figures for acquisitions (for which no comparatives are required) have been shown in a footnote but might alternatively be shown as a separate column in the note.

*FRS 3(16), FRS 6(29)*   In cases where the post-acquisition results of an operation cannot be practically determined, an indication should be given of the operation's contribution to turnover and operating profit of continuing operations or a statement, with reasons, that such an indication is not possible.

**110**   The heading 'other operating expenses (net)', which is not a statutory one, illustrates the possibility of grouping statutory items together. Labour and depreciation costs will typically need to be allocated across the various statutory captions. Other items which may need to be allocated to appropriate captions could include hire of plant and machinery, amortisation of deferred development costs and foreign currency differences.

*FRS 11(67)*   The analysis includes the statutory caption 'amounts written off investments'. The 1985 Act requires this caption to appear between 'other interest receivable and similar income' and 'interest payable and similar charges', both of which would normally appear below the operating profit line. However, this is incompatible with FRS 11, which requires impairment losses on fixed assets (including some types of investments) to be included within operating profit and disclosed as exceptional items if appropriate. The treatment required by FRS 11 has been followed in the model accounts.

**111** *85 4 Sch 57(3), FRS 3(5,19)*   Exceptional items are defined in FRS 3 as 'material items which derive from events or transactions that fall within the ordinary activities of the reporting entity and which individually or, if of a similar type, in aggregate, need to be disclosed by virtue of their size or incidence if the financial statements are to give a true and fair view'. All exceptional items, other than those falling under paragraph 20 of FRS 3, should be included under the statutory profit and loss account format headings to which they relate and attributed to continuing or discontinued operations as appropriate. The amount of each exceptional item should be disclosed separately in the notes or, if necessary to give a true and fair view, on the face of the profit and loss account. A description of the nature of each item should also be provided.

*FRS 6(30)*   Any exceptional profit or loss in periods following an acquisition which is determined using the fair values recognised on acquisition should be reported in accordance with paragraphs 19 and 20 of FRS 3 and identified as relating to the acquisition.

**112** *FRS 11(69)*   If an impairment loss is measured by reference to value in use of a fixed asset or income-generating unit, the discount rate applied to the cash flows should be disclosed. If a risk-free discount rate is used, some indication of the risk adjustments made to the cash flows should be given.

**113** *85 4 Sch 19(1,3)*   Provisions for impairment of fixed asset investments and the write-back of provisions no longer required should be disclosed.

# Notes to the accounts (continued)

109

## 2 Cost of sales, gross profit and other operating expenses (net)

| | 19XX | | | 19YY | | |
|---|---|---|---|---|---|---|
| | Continuing operations | Discontinued operations | Total | Continuing operations | Discontinued operations | Total |
| | £ | £ | £ | £ | £ | £ |
| Cost of sales | | | | | | |
| | ═══ | ═══ | ═══ | ═══ | ═══ | ═══ |
| Gross profit | | | | | | |
| | ═══ | ═══ | ═══ | ═══ | ═══ | ═══ |
| Distribution costs | | | | | | |
| Administrative expenses | | | | | | |
| Other operating income | ( ) | ( ) | ( ) | ( ) | ( ) | ( ) |
| Amounts written off investments | | | | | | |
| **Other operating expenses (net)** | | | | | | |
| | ═══ | ═══ | ═══ | ═══ | ═══ | ═══ |

110

In relation to the acquisition of [*name of undertaking*], continuing operations in 19XX include cost of sales £_____, gross profit £_____, distribution costs £_____, administrative expenses £_____ and other operating income £_____.

On [*date*], the group disposed of its interest in the ordinary share capital of [*name of undertaking*]. The results of [*name of undertaking*] up to the date of disposal and the comparatives for the year ended 31 December 19YY are shown under discontinued operations.

111

Administrative expenses include £_____ (19YY – £_____) in respect of an exceptional bad debt charge arising in continuing operations.

112

Cost of sales includes £_____ (19YY – £_____) in respect of an exceptional impairment loss on plant and machinery. The impairment loss was measured by reference to the value in use of the assets using a discount rate of ____% which reflects the risks inherent in the forecast cash flows.

113

Amounts written off investments is in respect of fixed asset investments and is analysed as follows:

| | 19XX | 19YY |
|---|---|---|
| | £ | £ |
| Provision for impairment | | |
| Provisions no longer required and written back | | |
| | ──── | ──── |
| | ═══ | ═══ |

## Share of associates' operating profits

**114** *FRS 9(27)* Separate disclosure is required of the group's share of its associates' operating results. Any amortisation or write-down of goodwill arising on acquiring the associates should be disclosed. The group's share of any exceptional items included in operating profit should be shown separately.

The results of associates should be analysed, where relevant, between existing operations, acquisitions and discontinued operations. FRS 3 requires this analysis for operating profit and for exceptional items below operating profit and it would be consistent to make the disclosures also for the results of associates.

## Exceptional items reported after operating profit

**115** *FRS 10(71)(b)* Goodwill previously written off to reserves on acquisition of a business should be included in the calculation of any profit or loss on disposal and separately disclosed as a component of this profit or loss on the face of the profit and loss account or in a note. However, it is important that the figure described as profit or loss on disposal includes the goodwill rather than showing the goodwill as a separate item.

**116** *FRS 3(20,24)* The effect of the exceptional items reported after operating profit on the taxation charge and minority interests should be disclosed. The tax on these items should be calculated by computing the tax on the profit on ordinary activities as if the items did not exist, and comparing this notional tax charge with the actual tax charge for the year. The difference arising should be attributed to the exceptional items.

# Notes to the accounts (continued)

**114**
## 3 Share of associates' operating profits

|  | 19XX £ | 19YY £ |
|---|---|---|
| Existing operations |  |  |
| Acquisitions |  |  |
|  | ———— | ———— |
| Continuing operations |  |  |
| Discontinued operations |  |  |
|  | ———— | ———— |
| Amortisation of goodwill |  |  |
|  | ———— | ———— |
|  | ════ | ════ |

**115**
## 4 Exceptional items reported after operating profit

The profit on sale of discontinued operations relates to the disposal of the group's interest in the ordinary share capital of [*name of undertaking*] and is after charging £_____ of goodwill previously written off to reserves on acquisition of this business.

The costs of a fundamental restructuring of continuing operations arose in respect of [*describe restructuring*], which has had a material effect on the nature and focus of the group's operations.

**116**
The effects of the exceptional items reported after operating profit on the amounts charged to the profit and loss account for taxation and minority interests were:

|  | Tax on profit on ordinary activities | | Minority interests | |
|---|---|---|---|---|
|  | 19XX £ | 19YY £ | 19XX £ | 19YY £ |
| Profit on sale of discontinued operations |  |  |  |  |
| Costs of a fundamental restructuring of continuing operations |  |  |  |  |
| Profit on sale of tangible fixed assets of continuing operations |  |  |  |  |
| Increase (decrease) in charge to profit and loss account | ———— | ———— | ———— | ———— |
|  | ════ | ════ | ════ | ════ |

## Finance charges (net)

**117**

As for 'other operating expenses (net)', the heading 'finance charges (net)', which is not a statutory one, is used to illustrate the possibility of grouping statutory items together. The general term 'finance charges' has been used to accommodate some of the less common items illustrated here. In many instances 'net interest payable' would be an acceptable alternative.

## Investment income

**118**    *SSAP 8(25)*

Incoming dividends from UK-resident companies should be included at the amount of cash received or receivable plus the tax credit.

*Statutory format note 12*

Income and interest derived from group undertakings (i.e., parent undertakings and fellow subsidiary undertakings where group accounts are prepared) must be shown separately.

**119**    *SSAP 20(60,68)*

The net amount credited or charged to the profit and loss account in respect of exchange gains or losses on foreign currency borrowings less deposits may be disclosed as part of 'other interest receivable and similar income' or as part of 'interest payable and similar charges' as appropriate.

## Interest payable and similar charges

**120**    *85 4 Sch 53(2)*

Disclosure is required of the amount of interest on or any similar charges in respect of:

(a)   bank loans and overdrafts; and
(b)   other loans.

This disclosure does not apply to interest or charges on loans from group undertakings (which would be shown as a separate item in arriving at the total).

**121**    *SSAP 21(35,53)*

Details of finance charges payable under finance leases and similar hire purchase contracts are required.

**122**    *FRS 4(32,64)*

Profits and losses on repurchase or early settlement of debt should be disclosed as separate items either within or adjacent to 'interest payable and similar charges'.

**123**    *FRS 12(48)*

Where provisions are included on a discounted basis in accordance with FRS 12, the unwinding of the discount should be included as a financial item adjacent to interest but should be shown separately from other interest either on the face of the profit and loss account or in a note.

**124**    *SE 12.43(c),*
*FRS 4(76)*

The amount of interest capitalised in the period should be disclosed, with an indication of the amount and treatment of any related tax relief.

# Notes to the accounts (continued)

**117**

## 5 Finance charges (net)

*Investment income*

|  | 19XX £ | 19YY £ |
|---|---|---|
| **118** Income from other fixed asset investments | | |
| Income from current asset investments | | |
| Other interest receivable and similar income | | |

**119** Other interest receivable and similar income includes net exchange gains on foreign currency borrowings less deposits of £_____ (19YY – £_____).

**120** *Interest payable and similar charges*

|  | 19XX £ | 19YY £ |
|---|---|---|
| Bank loans and overdrafts | | |
| **121** Finance leases and hire purchase contracts | | |
| Other loans | | |
| Share of associates' interest payable and similar charges | | |
| **122** Profit on repurchase of debt | | |
| **123** Unwinding of discount on provisions | | |
| **119** Exchange loss on foreign currency borrowings less deposits (net) | | |
| **124** Interest capitalised | ( ) | ( ) |

*Finance charges (net)*

|  |  |  |
|---|---|---|
| Interest payable and similar charges | | |
| Less: investment income | | |

| | | |
|---|---|---|
| Group | | |
| Associates | | |

## Profit on ordinary activities before taxation

This note should cover the following:

| | | |
|---|---|---|
| **125** | *Statutory format note 14*<br>*85 4 Sch 19(2,3)* | (a) *depreciation and amounts written off tangible and intangible fixed assets.* Impairment losses and reversals of past impairment losses have been shown separately in the relevant fixed asset notes; |
| **126** | *FRS 10(53)* | (b) *amortisation of goodwill*; |
| **127** | *SSAP 4(28)* | (c) *government grants*; |
| **128** | *SSAP 21(55)* | (d) *rentals under operating leases and similar hire purchase contracts* distinguishing amounts relating to the hire of plant and machinery from other amounts; |
| **129** | *85 s390A* | (e) *auditors' remuneration for audit services* which should include all such amounts paid to auditors throughout the group, whether or not those auditors are the parent company's auditors; and |
| **130** | *SSAP 13(31)* | (f) *research and development expenditure* analysed between the current year's expenditure and amortisation of deferred expenditure. |

**131**  *85 s390B*
*SI 1991 No. 2128*

The disclosure of auditors' remuneration for non-audit services has been shown separately below the tabulation. In this way, it can be made clear that the amount disclosed is restricted to amounts paid to the parent company's auditors in the UK in respect of services charged to group companies incorporated in the UK. The disclosure includes amounts paid to 'associates' of the auditors. Some companies also disclose the total worldwide non-audit fees as an additional voluntary disclosure.

## Staff costs

**132**  *85 4 Sch 56(1)*

The costs and categorisation of staff cover all those employed in the year (whether overseas or in the UK). Categories may be determined by the directors 'having regard to the manner in which the company's activities are organised'. This could follow the layout of the profit and loss account (e.g., production, distribution, etc.) or by geographical area, or by principal activity or product. Executive directors would normally be included in the analysis.

**133**  *85 4 Sch 56(4),94*

'Social security costs' means contributions by the group to any State social security or pension scheme, fund or arrangement; and 'pension costs' includes any other costs incurred by the group in providing pensions for employees.

**134**  *85 6 Sch Pt III*

In respect of loans, quasi-loans and credit transactions (and related guarantees, etc.) to non-director officers, the 1985 Act requires disclosure of the aggregate amounts outstanding at the year end and the number of persons concerned (in each case separately for loans, quasi-loans and credit transactions). Disclosure is not required for an individual if the aggregate amount outstanding at the year end does not exceed £2,500 for that individual.

# Notes to the accounts (continued)

## 6 Profit on ordinary activities before taxation

Profit on ordinary activities before taxation is stated after charging (crediting):

|  |  | 19XX £ | 19YY £ |
|---|---|---|---|
| **125** | Depreciation and amounts written off tangible fixed assets |  |  |
|  | owned |  |  |
|  | held under finance leases and hire purchase contracts |  |  |
|  | Amortisation of patents and trade marks |  |  |
| **130** | Research and development |  |  |
|  | current year expenditure |  |  |
|  | amortisation of deferred expenditure |  |  |
| **126** | Amortisation of goodwill |  |  |
| **127** | Government grants |  |  |
| **128** | Operating lease rentals |  |  |
|  | plant and machinery |  |  |
|  | other |  |  |
| **129** | Auditors' remuneration for audit services |  |  |

**131** Amounts payable to [*name of auditors*] and their associates by the company and its UK subsidiary undertakings in respect of non-audit services were £_____ (19YY – £_____).

## 7 Staff costs

**132**

The average monthly number of employees (including executive directors) was:

|  | 19XX Number | 19YY Number |
|---|---|---|
| Production |  |  |
| Distribution |  |  |
| Sales |  |  |
| Administration |  |  |

|  | 19XX £ | 19YY £ |
|---|---|---|
| Their aggregate remuneration comprised: |  |  |
| Wages and salaries |  |  |
| Social security costs **133** |  |  |
| Other pension costs (see note 34) |  |  |

## Directors' remuneration

**135**    *85 6 Sch 1(1)*    Aggregated details of directors' remuneration should be disclosed under four headings:

(a) emoluments;
(b) gains made on exercise of share options;
(c) amounts receivable under long-term incentive schemes; and
(d) company contributions to money purchase schemes.

*85 6 Sch 1(2)*    Where the aggregate of (a) to (c) above exceeds £200,000, the total amount attributable to the highest paid director should be separately disclosed along with the amount of (d) above and details of any accrued defined benefit pensions. For a listed company, these disclosures will usually be made as part of tabulations giving details for each director.

*SE 12.43A(c)*    As discussed in the commentary on the remuneration report, listed companies (subject to certain exceptions) are required to provide particulars of individual directors' remuneration packages and incentives.

The particulars required include:

(a) full details of each element in the remuneration package of each director by name;
(b) information on share options for each director in accordance with the recommendations of UITF 10;
(c) details of any long-term incentive schemes, other than share options disclosed under (b) above, including interest of each director by name at the beginning and end of the period and awards made and benefits received during the period; and
(d) details of pension contributions to a money purchase pension scheme or details of accrued benefits under a defined benefit scheme.

**136**    *SE 12.43A(c)(ii)*    The amount of each element of the remuneration package for the year of each director by name should be disclosed. Details should include, but not be restricted to:

(a) basic salaries and fees;
(b) the estimated money value of benefits in kind;
(c) annual bonuses and deferred bonuses; and
(d) compensation for loss of office and other termination payments;

together with a total for each director for the period and for the corresponding prior period.

Any significant payments to former directors should also be disclosed.

## Fees paid to third parties

**137**    *85 6 Sch 9*    Aggregate payments to third parties for making available the services of a person as director should be disclosed. Typically, this would be relevant where a bank has a non-executive director on a board and invoices the company for the director's fees which are never receivable by the director personally.

Amounts paid to or receivable by persons 'connected with' the director or companies controlled by the director are not paid to 'third parties' and should be disclosed in the table of emoluments as if they had been paid to the director.

**138**    The 1985 Act requires only the aggregate amount of such payments but for a listed company it would be appropriate to provide some further explanation, for example, the name of the director for whom the payments are made.

# Notes to the accounts (continued)

## 7 Staff costs (continued)

**134** At 31 December 19XX the following amounts were outstanding from non-director officers:

|  | £ | Number of officers |
|---|---|---|
| Loans |  |  |
| Quasi-loans |  |  |
| Credit transactions |  |  |

## 8 Directors' remuneration, interests and transactions

**135** *Aggregate remuneration*

The total amounts for directors' remuneration and other benefits were as follows:

|  | 19XX £ | 19YY £ |
|---|---|---|
| Emoluments |  |  |
| Gains on exercise of share options |  |  |
| Amounts receivable under long-term incentive schemes |  |  |
| Money purchase contributions |  |  |
| Total |  |  |

**136** *Directors' emoluments*

| Name of director | Fees/Basic salary £ | Taxable benefits £ | Annual bonuses £ | 19XX total £ | 19YY total £ |
|---|---|---|---|---|---|
| Executive [*List directors*] |  |  |  |  |  |
| Non-executive [*List directors*] |  |  |  |  |  |
| Aggregate emoluments |  |  |  |  |  |

**137** Fees to third parties

Annual bonuses are determined by the remuneration committee based on the level of growth in [*describe performance measures*]. Bonuses are capped at ___ % of basic salary.

## Compensation for loss of office

**139**      *85 6 Sch 8*    The aggregate amount of any compensation to directors or past directors in respect
           *SE 12.43A(c)(ii)*    of loss of office should be disclosed. For a listed company, details of the individual
                                         directors should be disclosed.

## Share options

**140**      *UITF 10(10),*    The UITF believes that the grant of share options gives rise to a benefit which
           *Appendix*    should be included as part of directors' remuneration. Because of difficulties in
           *SE 12.43A(c)(iii)*    measuring the value of any benefit and apportioning it over time, the UITF has recommended increased disclosure in respect of share options rather than specifying a valuation method. The additional disclosures, which are mandatory for listed companies and which must be made for each director separately, are as follows:

(a) the number of shares under option at the end of the year and at the beginning of the year (or date of appointment if later);

(b) the number of options granted, exercised and lapsed unexercised during the year;

(c) the exercise prices;

(d) the dates from which options may be exercised and the expiry dates;

(e) the cost of the options (if any);

(f) for options exercised during the year, the market price of the shares at the date of exercise;

(g) where directors have options exercisable at different prices and/or different dates, the above information should be given for each exercise price and/or date combination;

(h) a concise summary of any performance criteria on which the exercise of the options is conditional; and

(i) the market price of shares at the end of the year and the range during the year (high and low).

If the above information would lead to a statement of excessive length, a more concise disclosure, using weighted average exercise prices for each director, would be a satisfactory alternative, although some additional disclosures may be necessary. This more concise approach is explained in UITF 10.

UITF 10 does not require the gain on exercise of options in the period to be quantified for each director but does ensure that sufficient information is made available for the gains to be calculated. The 1985 Act requires the aggregate gains on exercise for all directors to be disclosed, but not individual amounts. It is, however, regarded as good practice to disclose the gains for each director and this is illustrated in these model accounts. If this is not done, the remuneration of the highest paid director must be disclosed including any gains on exercise of share options.

*85 7 Sch 2B*    Where the disclosures in respect of directors' share options recommended by UITF 10 are not given for an unlisted company, details are required of any right to subscribe for shares or debentures granted to or exercised by each director (or his/her immediate family) during the year. This information would usually be disclosed in the directors' report.

## Long-term incentive schemes

**141**      *SE 12.43A(c)(iv)*    In addition to the disclosure of the aggregate amounts receivable under long-term incentive schemes which is required by the 1985 Act, the Listing Rules specify further disclosures of individual directors' entitlements under such schemes. In practice, it may sometimes be difficult to comply with the letter of the Listing Rules because they envisage a particular type of scheme. A narrative description of the nature of the scheme and an indication of how each director's entitlement is calculated would usually be appropriate.

# Notes to the accounts (continued)

## 8 Directors' remuneration, interests and transactions (continued)

**138**  Fees to third parties comprise amounts paid to [*name of third party*] under an agreement to provide the group with the services of Mr _____. The agreement requires [*describe main terms*].

**139**  In addition to his emoluments shown above, Mr _____ was paid £_____ by the company as compensation for loss of office as director following his resignation from the board on [*date*]. This amount includes £ _____ in respect of the estimated cost of providing Mr _____with secretarial services subsequent to his departure.

[*Disclose any significant payments made to former directors during the period.*]

Mr _____ waived emoluments of £ _____ (19YY – £ _____) and has agreed to waive future emoluments totalling £_____ in respect of services to be provided over [*specify period*].

**140**  *Directors' share options*

Aggregate emoluments disclosed above do not include any amounts for the value of options to acquire ordinary shares in the company granted to or held by the directors. Details of the options are as follows:

| Name of director | 1 January 19XX | Granted | Exercised | Lapsed | 31 December 19XX | Exercise price | Gains on exercise 19XX | Gains on exercise 19YY |
|---|---|---|---|---|---|---|---|---|
| Total | | | | | | | | |

The options are exercisable between the following dates:

[*Specify for each director the period over which the options are exercisable.*]

Exercise of options is subject to [*describe relevant performance criteria*]. The market price of the ordinary shares at 31 December 19XX was £_____ and the range during the year was £_____ to £_____.

**141**  *Directors' long-term incentive schemes*

Aggregate emoluments described above do not include any amounts in respect of long-term incentive schemes. The company operates the following schemes [*give details of schemes*].

Details of the directors' interests in the schemes are as follows:

[*List directors and for each describe the interests of each director by name in the long-term incentive schemes at the start of the period under review; entitlements or awards granted and commitments made to each director under such schemes during the period, showing which crystallise either in the same year or subsequent years; the money value and the number of shares; cash payments or other benefits received by each director under such schemes during the period; and the interests of each director in the long-term incentive schemes at the end of the period.*]

## Pension entitlements

**142**  *85 6 Sch 1(1)(d,e)*  The aggregate value of any company contributions paid, or treated as paid, to a money purchase pension scheme in respect of directors' qualifying services should be disclosed. In addition to this, disclose the number of directors to whom retirement benefits are accruing in respect of qualifying services for:

**143**  (a)  money purchase schemes; and
**144**  (b)  defined benefits schemes.

Listed companies must disclose further details for each director by name.

**145**  *SE 12.43A(c)(x)*  For money purchase schemes, disclose the contributions payable in respect of the period.

**146**  *SE 12.43A(c)(ix)*  For defined benefit schemes, give details of the amount of the increase during the period under review (excluding inflation) and of the accumulated total amount at the end of the period in respect of the accrued benefit to which each director would be entitled on leaving service or is entitled having left service during the period under review.

Also give, in respect of each director, the transfer value (less director's contributions) of the relevant increase in accrued benefits (to be calculated in accordance with Actuarial Guidance Note GN11 but making no deduction for any underfunding) as at the end of the period. Disclosure of the transfer value can be avoided by giving extensive further disclosures which are prescribed in the Listing Rules. These alternative disclosures are not illustrated in the model accounts as disclosure of transfer values is regarded as best practice.

## Excess retirement benefits

**147**  *85 6 Sch 7*  Details are required of any excess retirement benefits paid to or receivable by current and past directors to which they were entitled on the date on which the benefits first become payable or 31 March 1997, whichever is the later.

# Notes to the accounts (continued)

## 8 Directors' remuneration, interests and transactions (continued)

The amounts, or value of assets including shares, received or receivable by directors in the period under long-term incentive schemes were as follows:

|  | 19XX £ | 19YY £ |
|---|---|---|
| Name of director |  |  |

**142** *Directors' pension entitlements*

**144, 146** The following directors had accrued entitlements under defined benefit schemes as follows:

|  | Increase in accrued pension excluding inflation £ | Transfer value of increase £ | Accrued pension 31 December XX £ | Accrued pension 31 December YY £ |
|---|---|---|---|---|
| Name of director |  |  |  |  |

The pension entitlement shown is that which would be paid annually on retirement based on service to the end of the year.

The transfer value has been calculated on the basis of actuarial advice in accordance with Actuarial Guidance Note GN 11 and is net of director's contributions.

Members of the scheme have the option to pay additional voluntary contributions; neither the contributions nor the resulting benefits are included in the above table.

## Directors' interest

**148**    *85 7 Sch 2–2A*    This information is based on the interests notified to the company by the directors and recorded in the Register of Directors' Interests, including those of the directors' spouses and minor children. If no interests are held, this must also be stated. The

*SI 1985 No. 802*    principal reliefs from notification, and therefore disclosure in the accounts (or alternatively in the directors' report), apply to:

(a) interests of directors of wholly owned subsidiaries who are also directors of a UK parent which itself maintains the appropriate register;

(b) interests of directors of wholly owned UK subsidiaries of overseas parents in the shares or debentures of that parent or any other overseas company; and

*85 s324(6)*    (c) directors' nominee shareholdings in wholly owned subsidiaries.

**149**    *SE 12.43(k)*    Listed companies should distinguish between beneficial and non-beneficial interests and provide a statement of any changes since the year end in interests in shares, debentures or options, or state that there were no such changes. The statement should be made up to a date not more than one month prior to the date of the notice of the general meeting at which the accounts are to be laid.

It is also normal to disclose the extent of any duplication of interests.

# Notes to the accounts (continued)

## 8 Directors' remuneration, interests and transactions (continued)

**143**   _____ [*Number*] directors are members of money purchase schemes. Contributions paid by the company in respect of such directors were as follows:

|  | 19XX £ | 19YY £ |
|---|---|---|
| **145** Name of director |  |  |

**147**   Retirement benefits amounting to £_____ (19YY – £ _____) were paid to directors and past directors in excess of the benefits to which they were entitled on the later of the date retirement benefits first became payable or 31 March 1997.

**148**   *Directors' interests*

The directors who held office at 31 December 19XX had the following interests in the shares and debentures of group undertakings:

| Name of director | Name of group undertaking and description of shares or debentures | 31 December 19XX | | 1 January 19XX or subsequent date of appointment | |
|---|---|---|---|---|---|
|  |  | *Beneficial* | *Non-beneficial* | *Beneficial* | *Non-beneficial* |

As a result of Mr _____ and Mr _____ being beneficiaries of a family trust, their respective interests in [*name of group undertaking*] contain a duplication of [*number*] shares.

**149**   [No changes/The following changes] took place in the interests of directors between 31 December 19XX and [*a date not more than one month prior to the date of the notice of the annual general meeting*]. [*Describe changes distinguishing between changes in beneficial interests and changes in non-beneficial interests.*]

# Directors' transactions

**150**     *85 6 Sch Pt II*     The following types of transactions with directors, shadow directors and connected persons should be disclosed, irrespective of whether the transaction is permitted by the 1985 Act (see Appendices 2 and 3):

(a)  loans, quasi-loans, credit transactions and any related guarantees or security;

(b)  assignments or assumption by the company of obligations from third parties concerning transactions which the company is itself prohibited from concluding;

(c)  mutual aid or back-to-back transactions, whereby a third party enters into a transaction which the company may not itself conclude, and in return the company provides some benefit to the third party;

(d)  agreements to enter into any such transactions or arrangements; and

(e)  transactions or arrangements in which a director had, directly or indirectly, a material interest.

The disclosures required, which vary depending on the nature of the transaction, and the exemptions from disclosure that are available in certain circumstances, are summarised in Appendix 3.

*FRS 8(6)*     FRS 8 *Related Party Disclosures* is also relevant to the disclosure of transactions with directors and is discussed in relation to note 38 below. FRS 8 may require disclosure of some transactions that would be exempted under the 1985 Act and of transactions with some relatives of directors who would not be 'connected persons' as defined in the 1985 Act.

**151**     *SE 12.43(q)*     The Stock Exchange requires disclosure by listed companies of any 'contract of significance' (as defined in the commentary on the directors' report) in which a director is or was materially interested.

# Notes to the accounts (continued)

## 8 Directors' remuneration, interests and transactions (continued)

**150** *Directors' transactions*

The following transactions have taken place with directors:

Loan to directors:
An unsecured __% loan, repayable on [*date*], made to Mr _____, was outstanding during the year. The amount of his liability including interest to the company at the beginning of the year was £_____ , the maximum during the year was £_____ and at the end of the year was £_____ .

Credit transaction with director:
£_____ is included in debtors in respect of goods and services supplied at favourable rates by a subsidiary undertaking to Mr _____. The total arm's-length value of these transactions was £_____ . The whole amount has been repaid since the balance sheet date.

Quasi-loan to director:
The company made an unsecured non-interest-bearing quasi-loan to Mr _____ amounting to £_____ on [*date*] in respect of personal travel costs incurred by him and initially paid by the company. This was repaid by Mr _____ within [*number*] months.

Security for loan:
During the year the company guaranteed by a floating charge on its fixed assets a housing loan of £_____ taken out by Mr _____. The loan is due to be repaid by Mr _____ in [*number*] instalments by [*date*]. The total liability of Mr _____ at the year end was £_____ , which represents the maximum for which the company would be liable. The loan was guaranteed in order to enable Mr _____ to carry out his duties as a director following his appointment to the Board.

**151** Material interest of director in contracts with the company:
Mr _____ has a controlling interest in [*name of undertaking*], from which the company obtained supplies amounting to £_____ during the year.

# Tax on profit on ordinary activities

**152**     *85 4 Sch 54(3)*     Disclosure is required of:

         *SSAP 8(22,23)*    (a)    the amounts of UK corporation tax (before and after any double taxation relief) and UK income tax and the bases of computation;

                       (b)    the rate of corporation tax (this is conventionally disclosed but is only a requirement if the rate is not known for the whole or part of the period and the latest known rate is used);

**153**                         (c)    the total overseas tax relieved and unrelieved, specifying the amount of unrelieved tax arising from the payment of dividends;

                       (d)    the tax attributable to franked investment income;

                       (e)    the amount of irrecoverable ACT;

         *FRS 9(27)*      (f)    the tax attributable to the group's share of profits less losses of associated undertakings;

**154**     *85 4 Sch 57(1)*      (g)    the effect of including amounts relating to prior years;

**155**       *SSAP 8(22)*      (h)    the transfers to and from deferred tax and the amount of any unprovided deferred tax for the year analysed into its major components; and

   *SSAP 15(33,35,38)*

      *SSAP 15(36)*     (i)    the adjustments to deferred tax arising from changes in tax rates and allowances.

**156**     *85 4 Sch 54(2)*     Any special circumstances affecting the tax charge for the year or future years or

          *FRS 3(23)*     the tax attributable to exceptional items falling within paragraph 20 of FRS 3 should be disclosed and their individual effects quantified. 'Special circumstances' could include significant disallowable expenses, losses brought forward or to be carried forward, recovery of ACT, etc. The effects of a fundamental change in the basis of taxation should be included in the tax charge for the year and disclosed separately on the face of the profit and loss account.

# Notes to the accounts (continued)

**152**    ## 9 Tax on profit on ordinary activities

The tax charge comprises:

|  | 19XX £ | 19YY £ |
|---|---|---|
| Corporation tax at __% (19YY – __%) | | |
| **153** Double taxation relief | | |
| **155** Deferred taxation | | |
| | ———— | ———— |
| Overseas taxation | | |
| Tax credits on franked investment income | | |
| Irrecoverable ACT | | |
| Share of associates' tax | | |
| | ———— | ———— |
| **154** Adjustments in respect of prior years | | |
| current taxation | | |
| deferred taxation | | |
| | ———— | ———— |
| | ═══════ | ═══════ |

**153**    Double taxation relief has been restricted by £_____ (19YY – £_____) due to overseas tax rates exceeding the corporation tax rate of __% and £_____ (19YY – £_____) as a result of the payment of dividends from overseas income.

**155**    If provision were to be made for the full amount of potential deferred taxation the charge for the year would have been increased by:

|  | £ | £ |
|---|---|---|
| Capital allowances | | |
| Future remittances of the accumulated reserves of overseas subsidiary undertakings | | |
| Other timing differences | | |
| | ———— | ———— |
| | ═══════ | ═══════ |

**156**    The tax charge in future periods may be affected by [*describe circumstances*].

159

## Extraordinary items (not illustrated)

*FRS 3(6,22,48)*
*85 4 Sch 57(2)*
For all practical purposes extraordinary items are prohibited by FRS 3 which notes that such items are extremely rare. The ASB has not provided any examples of items that would be treated as extraordinary items.

## Profit attributable to Group plc

**158**
*85 s230*
A parent company may omit its own profit and loss account from the consolidated accounts provided the omission is noted and the parent's profit for the financial year is disclosed.

*SE 12.42(c)*
The London Stock Exchange, however, requires inclusion of the parent's profit and loss account if it contains 'significant additional information'. This disclosure is never seen in practice and it is difficult to envisage circumstances in which it would be relevant.

## Dividends and other finance costs

**159**
*SSAP 8(24)*
Dividends paid and proposed should not include either the related ACT or the attributable tax credit. It is desirable to show the rate of dividend.

**160**
*FRS 4(59)*
Disclosure is required of the aggregate dividends for each class of share. This should include the total amount in respect of each of:

(a) dividends on equity shares;
(b) participating dividends (i.e., dividends on non-equity shares that are always equivalent to a fixed multiple of dividends payable on equity shares);
(c) other dividends on non-equity shares; and
(d) any other appropriations of profit in respect of non-equity shares.

This information could alternatively be given on the face of the profit and loss account.

**161**
*FRS 4(48,99)*
Where shares are issued or proposed to be issued as an alternative to cash dividends (a scrip dividend), the amount of the cash alternative should be shown as an appropriation of profit.

**162**
*SE 12.43(e)*
Listed companies are required to provide particulars of any arrangement by which a shareholder has waived, or agreed to waive, any dividend.

*85 4 Sch 49*
The amount and period of arrears of fixed cumulative dividends should be disclosed for each class of share.

# Notes to the accounts (continued)

**158**

## 10  Profit attributable to Group plc

The profit for the financial year dealt with in the accounts of the parent company, Group plc, was £_____ (19YY – £_____ ).  As permitted by section 230 of the Companies Act 1985, no separate profit and loss account is presented in respect of the parent company.

**159**

## 11  Dividends paid and proposed on equity and non-equity shares and other finance costs of non-equity shares

|  | 19XX £ | 19YY £ |
|---|---|---|

**160**

**Dividends paid and proposed [on equity and non-equity shares]**
Equity shares:
    interim paid of __p (19YY – __p) per ordinary share
    final proposed of __p (19YY – __p) per ordinary share

Non-equity shares:
__% preference dividend paid (19YY – __%)

**Other finance costs of non-equity shares**
[*Describe*]

**161**

During the year, a share alternative was offered in respect of the interim dividend of __p per ordinary share. The alternative comprised the issue of new ordinary shares with a market value of £_____ per existing ordinary share.  Holders of __% of ordinary shares elected for the share alternative.  The total amount of the cash dividend that would otherwise have been paid is included in the above analysis.

**162**

Under an agreement dated [*date*], Mr _____ , who holds [*number*] ordinary shares representing __% of the company's called-up ordinary share capital, has agreed to waive all dividends due to him for a period of [*specify*].

## Earnings per share

*FRS 14(69–70)*    Basic and diluted earnings per share (EPS) should be presented on the face of the profit and loss account for each class of ordinary share that has a different right to share in the net profit for the period. Basic and diluted EPS should be presented with equal prominence for all periods. Basic and diluted EPS should both be presented even if the amounts disclosed are negative (i.e., a loss).

*FRS 14(9)*    Basic EPS should be calculated by dividing the net profit or loss attributable to ordinary shareholders by the weighted average number of ordinary shares outstanding during the period.

*FRS 14(27)*    For the purpose of calculating diluted EPS, the net profit attributable to ordinary shareholders and the weighted average number of shares outstanding should be adjusted for the effect of all dilutive potential ordinary shares.

*FRS 14(71)*    The following information should be disclosed:

**163**    (a)  the numerator used in calculating basic and diluted earnings per share and a reconciliation of those amounts to the net profit or loss for the period; and

**164**    (b)  the denominators used in calculating basic and diluted EPS, and a reconciliation of these denominators to each other.

*FRS 14(73–74)*    Many companies present additional measures of EPS, for example, to exclude the effects of exceptional items and discontinued operations. Following the implementation of FRS 10, it is likely that some companies will wish to highlight the effect of goodwill amortisation in this way. FRS 14 permits disclosure of additional measures of EPS provided that they are presented on a consistent basis over time and are reconciled to the amounts required by the FRS. The EPS required by FRS 14 should be at least as prominent as any additional measure and the reasons for calculating the additional measure should be explained.

Some companies present an additional measure of EPS known as 'IIMR Headline Earnings'. The calculation of this amount is specified by the Institute of Investment Management and Research. It is widely used in the financial press as the basis for calculating price/earnings ratios.

## Prior year adjustment

**165**    *FRS 3(7,29)*    Prior year adjustments are defined in FRS 3 as 'material adjustments applicable to prior periods arising from changes in accounting policies or from the correction of fundamental errors. They do not include normal recurring adjustments or corrections of accounting estimates made in prior periods'. They should be accounted for by restating the comparative figures in the primary statements and notes and adjusting the opening balance of reserves for the cumulative effect. The effect of prior year adjustments on the results for the previous year should be disclosed where practicable.

*85 4 Sch 11,15, FRS 3(62)*    Accounting policies should be applied consistently within the same accounts and from one financial year to the next. Any departure from this statutory principle is only acceptable where a new policy provides a fairer presentation of the result and of the financial position of the reporting entity and details of the change, the reasons for it and the financial effect are disclosed.

*UITF 14(3)*    Where a prior year adjustment arises from a change of accounting policy, UITF Abstract 14 requires disclosure of an indication of the effect on the current year's results, in addition to the effect on the prior year as required by FRS 3. The UITF received legal advice that an indication of the effect on current year's figures is necessary to comply with paragraph 15 of Schedule 4. Before UITF Abstract 14 was issued there had been concern that companies were able to play down the effect of policy changes where the effect on future results was much more material than the effect on past results.

# Notes to the accounts (continued)

## 12 Earnings per share

The calculations of earnings per share are based on the following profits and numbers of shares.

| | Basic | | Diluted | |
|---|---|---|---|---|
| | *19XX* | *19YY* | *19XX* | *19YY* |
| | *£* | *£* | *£* | *£* |
| **163** Profit for the financial year | | | | |
| Preference dividends | | | | |
| Other finance costs of non-equity shares | | | | |
| Interest saved on conversion of debt | | | | |

| | *19XX* Number of shares | *19YY* Number of shares |
|---|---|---|
| **164** Weighted average number of shares: | | |
| For basic earnings per share | | |
| Conversion of preference shares | | |
| Conversion of convertible debt | | |
| Exercise of share options | | |
| For diluted earnings per share | | |

## 165  13 Prior year adjustment

The group policy for calculating the cost of [*describe*] was changed during the year to include [*describe*]. The directors consider that the new policy provides a fairer presentation of the result and of the financial position of the group because [*explain why*]. The comparative figures in the primary statements and notes have been restated to reflect the new policy.

The effects of the change in policy are summarised below:

| | *19XX* | *19YY* |
|---|---|---|
| | *£* | *£* |
| **Profit and loss account** | | |
| [*Describe captions affected.*] | | |
| Increase (decrease) in profit for the financial year | | |
| **Balance sheet** | | |
| [*Describe captions affected.*] | | |
| Increase (decrease) in net assets | | |

## Intangible fixed assets – development costs, patents and trade marks

**166**     *Statutory format note 2*     Concessions, patents, trade marks, licences, etc. may only be included if created (i.e., cost incurred) by the company itself or acquired for valuable consideration.

**167**     *85 4 Sch 42, SSAP 13(32) FRS 10(53)*     Disclose the following separately for each class of intangible assets (and for goodwill):

(a) the cost or revalued amount at the beginning and end of the year;

(b) the cumulative amount of provisions for amortisation or impairment at the beginning and end of the year;

(c) a reconciliation of the movements, separately disclosing:
  (i) additions;
  (ii) disposals;
  (iii) revaluations;
  (iv) transfers;
  (v) amortisation;
  (vi) impairment losses;
  (vii) reversals of past impairment losses; and
  (viii) other movements (e.g., exchange differences); and

(d) the net carrying amount at the balance sheet date.

**168**     *SSAP 13(25) 85 4 Sch 20*     Development costs may only be capitalised in the circumstances specified in SSAP 13. If the costs are deferred then disclosure is required of the reasons and the write-off period.

    *85 s269*     Deferred development expenditure should be treated as a realised loss for dividend calculation purposes, except where the directors decide there are special reasons for not doing so, such as compliance with SSAP 13, and these are disclosed.

# Notes to the accounts (continued)

**166, 167**  ## 14 Intangible fixed assets – development costs, patents and trade marks

| | Group | | | Company | | |
|---|---|---|---|---|---|---|
| | *Development costs* £ | *Patents and trade marks* £ | *Total* £ | *Development costs* £ | *Patents and trade marks* £ | *Total* £ |
| **Cost** | | | | | | |
| At 1 January 19XX | | | | | | |
| Additions | | | | | | |
| Disposals | | | | | | |
| Exchange adjustment | | | | | | |
| At 31 December 19XX | | | | | | |
| | | | | | | |
| **Depreciation** | | | | | | |
| At 1 January 19XX | | | | | | |
| Charge for the year | | | | | | |
| Impairment losses | | | | | | |
| Reversal of past impairment losses | | | | | | |
| Exchange adjustment | | | | | | |
| At 31 December 19XX | | | | | | |
| | | | | | | |
| **Net book value** | | | | | | |
| At 31 December 19XX | | | | | | |
| | | | | | | |
| At 31 December 19YY | | | | | | |

**168**  Development costs have been capitalised in accordance with SSAP 13 and are therefore not treated, for dividend purposes, as a realised loss. The costs related to the development of [*describe*]. Production is expected to commence on [*date*], from which date the related costs will be written off over [*specify period*].

# Intangible fixed assets – goodwill

*FRS 10(7,48)*  Goodwill should be shown as an asset on the face of the balance sheet. Negative goodwill should be shown on the face of the balance sheet, immediately below positive goodwill and followed by a subtotal showing the net amount of the positive and negative goodwill.

**169**  *FRS 10(53)*  A reconciliation of movements in the year should be provided as discussed above for other classes of intangible assets. Movements in positive goodwill should be shown separately from movements in negative goodwill.

*FRS 10(56,57)*  Where an amortisation period is shortened or extended following a review of the remaining useful economic life, or there has been a change in the amortisation method used, the reasons and the effect, if material, should be disclosed in the year of change.

*FRS 10(58)*  Where goodwill (or an intangible asset) is amortised over a period that exceeds 20 years from the date of acquisition or is not amortised, the grounds for rebutting the 20-year presumption in FRS 10 should be disclosed. This should be a reasoned explanation based on the specific factors contributing to the durability of the acquired business (or intangible asset).

*FRS 10(59)*  In addition, where goodwill is not amortised, the accounts should state that they depart from the specific requirements of the 1985 Act to amortise goodwill over a finite period, for the overriding purpose of giving a true and fair view. Particulars of the departure, the reasons for it and its effect should be given in sufficient detail to convey to the reader of the accounts the circumstances justifying the use of the true and fair override.

**170**  *FRS 10(63,64)*  The accounts should disclose the periods in which negative goodwill is being written back to the profit and loss account. Where negative goodwill exceeds the fair value of the non-monetary assets, the amount and source of the 'excess' negative goodwill and the periods in which it is being written back should be explained. This disclosure might be made as part of the accounting policies but is more appropriately made in the goodwill note when it relates to a specific acquisition rather than a general policy.

# Notes to the accounts (continued)

**169** ## 15 Intangible fixed assets — goodwill

| | Positive goodwill £ | Negative goodwill £ | Total £ |
|---|---|---|---|
| **Cost** | | | |
| At 1 January 19XX | | | |
| Additions | | | |
| Disposals | | | |
| Exchange adjustments | | | |
| | | | |
| At 31 December 19XX | | | |
| | | | |
| **Depreciation** | | | |
| At 1 January 19XX | | | |
| Charge for the year | | | |
| Impairment losses | | | |
| Reversal of past impairment losses | | | |
| Negative goodwill written back | | | |
| | | | |
| At 31 December 19XX | | | |
| | | | |
| **Net book value** | | | |
| At 31 December 19XX | | | |
| | | | |
| At 31 December 19YY | | | |

**170** Negative goodwill is being written back on a straight–line basis over a period of [*number*] years which is equal to the period over which the related non-monetary assets of the acquired business are being depreciated.

## Tangible fixed assets

**171**      *85 4 Sch 3,44*      It is assumed in this example that fixtures and fittings are not material in amount and are therefore aggregated with plant and machinery. The 1985 Act requires interests in land and buildings to be split between freehold and long and short leasehold interests. Short leaseholds are those with less than 50 years unexpired.

**172**      *85 4 Sch 42,*    For each major class of depreciable assets disclose the gross amount (cost or valu-
         *SSAP 12 (25,26)*    ation) and the related accumulated depreciation and provide a reconciliation of the opening and closing figures. Where there has been a change in the method of calculating depreciation, the effect, if material, and the reasons should be disclosed.

**173**      *FRS 11(56)*      Any reversal of a previously recognised impairment loss on a tangible fixed asset should be recognised in the current period to the extent that it increases the carrying amount of the fixed asset up to the amount that it would have been had the original impairment not occurred.

**174**      *SSAP 21(49,50)*    SSAP 21 requires either of the following alternative disclosures concerning assets capitalised under finance leases and hire purchase contracts:

(a) either show the gross amounts, the depreciation charge for the year, and the related accumulated depreciation by each major class of asset separately from owned fixed assets; or

(b) integrate leased assets with owned fixed assets and disclose separately the net amount, and the depreciation charge for the year, included in the overall totals.

The note (together with note 6) illustrates the second alternative.

# Notes to the accounts (continued)

171, 172 **16 Tangible fixed assets**

| Group | Investment properties £ | Land and buildings Freehold £ | [Long/Short] leasehold £ | Plant and machinery £ | Payments on account and assets in course of construction £ | Total £ |
|---|---|---|---|---|---|---|
| **Cost or valuation** | | | | | | |
| At 1 January 19XX | | | | | | |
| Additions | | | | | | |
| Acquisition of subsidiary undertaking | | | | | | |
| Revaluations | | | | | | |
| Disposals | | | | | | |
| Transfers | | | | | | |
| Exchange adjustment | | | | | | |
| At 31 December 19XX | | | | | | |
| **Depreciation** | | | | | | |
| At 1 January 19XX | | | | | | |
| Charge for the year | | | | | | |
| Impairment losses | | | | | | |
| Reversal of past impairment losses | | | | | | |
| Adjustments on revaluations | | | | | | |
| Disposals | | | | | | |
| Exchange adjustment | | | | | | |
| At 31 December 19XX | | | | | | |
| **Net book value** | | | | | | |
| At 31 December 19XX | | | | | | |
| At 31 December 19YY | | | | | | |

173

174 Leased assets included above:

**Net book value**
At 31 December 19XX

At 31 December 19YY

169

# Notes to the accounts (continued)

171, 172 **16 Tangible fixed assets (continued)**

| | Land and buildings | | | Plant and machinery | Payments on account and assets in course of construction | Total |
|---|---|---|---|---|---|---|
| **Company** | Investment properties £ | Freehold £ | [Long/Short] leasehold £ | £ | £ | £ |
| **Cost or valuation** | | | | | | |
| At 1 January 19XX | | | | | | |
| Additions | | | | | | |
| Revaluations | | | | | | |
| Disposals | | | | | | |
| Transfers | | | | | | |
| At 31 December 19XX | | | | | | |
| **Depreciation** | | | | | | |
| At 1 January 19XX | | | | | | |
| Charge for the year | | | | | | |
| Impairment losses | | | | | | |
| Reversal of past impairment losses | | | | | | |
| Adjustments on revaluations | | | | | | |
| Disposals | | | | | | |
| At 31 December 19XX | | | | | | |
| **Net book value** | | | | | | |
| At 31 December 19XX | | | | | | |
| At 31 December 19YY | | | | | | |

173 (Depreciation – Reversal of past impairment losses)

174 Leased assets included above:

**Net book value**
At 31 December 19XX

At 31 December 19YY

Freehold land, amounting to £_____ (19YY – £_____) for the group and £_____ (19YY – £_____) for the company, has not been depreciated.

**175**  *85 4 Sch 26(3)*

*SE 12.43(c)*

If interest on capital borrowed to finance production of an asset is included in cost, this treatment and the cumulative amount must be disclosed. Listed companies must also state the amount capitalised during the year and the treatment and amount of the related tax relief. Interest may be capitalised either gross or net of tax relief. The example provided shows the net method.

**176**

The model accounts assume one revaluation of land and buildings with subsequent additions at cost. Where several revaluations have taken place an alternative layout would be:

Freehold and leasehold land and buildings were professionally valued on an open market existing use basis as follows:

|  | Freehold £ | Leasehold £ |
|---|---|---|
| 19.... |  |  |
| 19.... |  |  |
| 19.... |  |  |

*85 4 Sch 33,43*

*SSAP 12(27)*

The item affected, the year and the basis and amount of the valuation must be disclosed and, in the case of assets revalued during the year, the names of the valuers (or particulars of their qualifications). SSAP 12 requires disclosure, if material, of the effects of a revaluation on the depreciation charge for the year.

**177**  *SSAP 19(10–12)*

*85 s226(5), s227(6)*
*UITF 7*

Investment properties should be carried at their open market value and, with the exception of leasehold properties where the unexpired period of the lease is 20 years or less, should not be depreciated. This may, if the effect is material, represent a departure from the statutory accounting rules, which should be disclosed, explained and quantified. It may not be possible to quantify the depreciation which would otherwise have been charged and in such cases the note should make this clear. The names of the valuers (or particulars of their qualifications) and the bases of valuation should be disclosed. In circumstances where a valuation is carried out by an employee or officer of the group, this should also be stated.

*SSAP 19(13)*

Changes in investment property values should be disclosed in the statement of total recognised gains and losses (being a movement on an investment revaluation reserve), unless a deficit (or its reversal) on an individual investment property is expected to be permanent, in which case it should be charged (or credited) to the profit and loss account for the year.

# Notes to the accounts (continued)

## 16 Tangible fixed assets (continued)

Additions to assets in course of construction include interest capitalised, net of tax relief, of:

|  | Group | | Company | |
|---|---|---|---|---|
|  | *19XX* | *19YY* | *19XX* | *19YY* |
|  | £ | £ | £ | £ |
| Interest |  |  |  |  |
| Tax relief |  |  |  |  |

**175** Cumulative interest capitalised, net of tax relief, included in the cost of tangible fixed assets amounts to £_____ (19YY – £_____ ) for the group and £_____ (19YY – £_____ ) for the company.

**176** Freehold and leasehold land and buildings were professionally valued on an open market existing use basis in 19__, with subsequent additions at cost, as follows:

|  | 19XX | | 19YY | |
|---|---|---|---|---|
|  | *Freehold* | *[Long/Short] leasehold* | *Freehold* | *[Long/Short] leasehold* |
|  | £ | £ | £ | £ |
| **Group** |  |  |  |  |
| Valuation 19__ |  |  |  |  |
| Cost |  |  |  |  |
| Cost or revaluation at 31 December 19XX |  |  |  |  |
| **Company** |  |  |  |  |
| Valuation 19__ |  |  |  |  |
| Cost |  |  |  |  |
| Cost or revaluation at 31 December 19XX |  |  |  |  |

**177** Investment properties, which are all freehold, were valued on an open market existing use basis at 31 December 19XX by [*name of surveyors*]. Such properties are not depreciated. [The depreciation which would otherwise have been charged amounts to £_____ (19YY – £_____ ) for the group and £_____ (19YY – £_____ ) for the company.]

**178**  *85 4 Sch 29–34*  Where fixed assets are included at a valuation, the corresponding historical cost amount together with accumulated depreciation on that basis must be shown. Alternatively, the difference between the historical cost and valuation amounts may be shown.

## Fixed asset investments

**179**  The 1985 Act and accounting standards classify fixed asset investments under the following categories:

*85 s258, 10A Sch, FRS 2*  *Subsidiary undertakings* – see Chapter 5.

*FRS 5(7)*  *Quasi-subsidiaries* – companies, trusts, partnerships or other vehicles that, though not fulfilling the definition of a subsidiary, are directly or indirectly controlled by the company and give rise to benefits for the group that are in substance no different from those that would arise were the vehicles subsidiary undertakings. Quasi-subsidiaries are encountered only rarely in practice and are not illustrated in these model accounts.

*FRS 9(4)*
*85 4A Sch 20*  *Associates* – entities, other than subsidiary undertakings, in which the investor has a participating interest and over whose operating and financial policies the investor exercises a significant influence. They are referred to as associated undertakings in the 1985 Act but we have used 'associates' as this is the term used in FRS 9.

*FRS 9(4)*  *Joint ventures* – entities in which the company holds an interest on a long-term basis and which are jointly controlled by the company and one or more other venturers under a contractual arrangement. The treatment of joint ventures is similar to that of associates but with expanded disclosure requirements on the face of the balance sheet and profit and loss account. Joint ventures are not illustrated in these model accounts.

*85 s260*  *Other participating interests* – long-term interests held for the purpose of securing a contribution to the investor's activities by the exercise of control or influence arising from the investments. It is not a requirement (as it is for associates) for the investor to exercise significant influence over the investee's operating and financial policies. A 20 per cent interest is normally assumed to constitute a participating interest. For these purposes an interest includes options and convertible interests. In consolidated accounts most participating interests will be accounted for as associates or joint ventures and so they are not illustrated in these model accounts.

*85 5 Sch 23*  *Other significant investments* – investments held by the company or the group (other than subsidiary undertakings, associates or joint ventures) of 20 per cent or more of the nominal value of any class of share or more than 20 per cent of the investor's assets. Certain additional disclosures are required for such investments.

*85 s262(1)*  Fixed asset investments would normally include trade investments and others held on a long-term basis. Temporary investments of surplus funds should be treated as current asset investments.

**180**  *85 4 Sch 42*  For each class of fixed asset investments, a reconciliation of the opening and closing figures for cost and amounts written off should be provided.

# Notes to the accounts (continued)

## 16 Tangible fixed assets (continued)

178 If land and buildings had not been revalued they would have been included at the following amounts:

| | 19XX | | | 19YY | | |
|---|---|---|---|---|---|---|
| | *Investment properties* £ | *Freehold* £ | *[Long/Short] leasehold* £ | *Investment properties* £ | *Freehold* £ | *[Long/Short] leasehold* £ |
| **Group** | | | | | | |
| Cost | | | | | | |
| Depreciation | | | | | | |
| Net book value | | | | | | |
| **Company** | | | | | | |
| Cost | | | | | | |
| Depreciation | | | | | | |
| Net book value | | | | | | |

## 17 Fixed asset investments

179, 180

| | Group | | Company | |
|---|---|---|---|---|
| | *19XX* £ | *19YY* £ | *19XX* £ | *19YY* £ |
| Subsidiary undertakings | | | | |
| Associates | | | | |
| Other investments and loans | | | | |
| Own shares | | | | |

## Principal group investments

**181**  *85 5 Sch*  The following details are required for each subsidiary undertaking, associate and other significant investment:

*FRS 9(52)*  (a)  the name of the undertaking;
(b)  the country of incorporation (if not incorporated in Great Britain);
(c)  the principal business address (if unincorporated); and
*FRS 2(33)*  (d)  the identity and proportion of shares held, indicating any special rights or constraints attaching to them, distinguishing between parent and group holdings.

*85 s231(3–6)*  Disclosure may be limited to undertakings whose results or financial position principally affect the accounts (provided the limitation is disclosed) and subsidiary undertakings excluded from consolidation. The full information must be annexed to the company's next annual return.

In addition, information relating to undertakings incorporated or carrying on business outside the UK need not be disclosed if the directors consider disclosure would be seriously prejudicial to the undertaking or the group and the Secretary of State for Trade and Industry approves the omission and the omission is disclosed.

*FRS 2(33), FRS 9(52)(c)*  The nature of business of principal subsidiary undertakings and associates should be disclosed.

# Notes to the accounts (continued)

## 17 Fixed asset investments (continued)

*Principal group investments*

The parent company and the group have investments in the following subsidiary undertakings, associates and other investments which principally affected the profits or net assets of the group. To avoid a statement of excessive length, details of investments which are not significant have been omitted.

| | Country of incorporation or principal business address | Principal activity | Holding | % |
|---|---|---|---|---|
| Subsidiary undertakings [*names*] | | | | |
| Associates [*names*] | | | | |
| Other investments [*names*] | | | | |

+ Held directly by Group plc.

## Subsidiary undertakings

The following information should be provided in respect of subsidiary undertakings, where appropriate:

**182**    *85 5 Sch 15(5)*    (a) the reasons for treatment as a subsidiary undertaking (not required if the reason is majority voting rights and the parent holds the same proportion of shares as voting rights);

*FRS 2(34)*    (b) the basis of dominant influence where designation as a subsidiary undertaking is only because of the parent having a participating interest and exercising such influence;

**183**    *85 5 Sch 15(4)*    (c) whether the undertaking has been included in the consolidation or the reasons for exclusion; and

*85 5 Sch 19, FRS 2(44)*    (d) the reason for preparing accounts that are not coterminous with, or are prepared for a different period to, those of the parent together with details of the subsidiary's accounting date or period as appropriate.

**184**    *85 s229, FRS 2(25)*    FRS 2 and the 1985 Act set out the circumstances where a subsidiary undertaking should be excluded from consolidation. In brief, these circumstances arise where:

(a) severe long-term restrictions hinder the exercise of the rights of the parent over the subsidiary's assets or management;

(b) the interest is held exclusively with a view to subsequent resale;

(c) the subsidiary's activities are so different from those of other group undertakings that inclusion would be incompatible with the obligation to give a true and fair view; or

(d) the undertaking is immaterial.

The following particulars are normally required for each excluded subsidiary undertaking:

*FRS 2(26)*    (a) the name of the undertaking and the reasons for exclusion;

*85 5 Sch 17*    (b) the aggregate capital and reserves and the profit or loss for the latest financial year;

*FRS 2(31)*    (c) details of intra-group transactions and balances;

(d) the amounts included in the group profit and loss account in respect of dividends and any write-down in the investment in, or amounts due from, the undertaking, where it is carried other than by the equity method; and

(e) separate accounts for undertakings excluded because of different activities (summarised information may be provided for undertakings that individually or in aggregate do not account for more than 20 per cent of the group's operating profit, turnover or net assets).

*FRS 2(32)*    The disclosures required by paragraph 31 of FRS 2 should be given for each subsidiary undertaking that accounts for more than 20 per cent of the group's operating profit, turnover or net assets and may be given on an aggregate basis for other subsidiary undertakings excluded for the same reason.

## Acquisition of subsidiary undertaking

**185**    The example provided illustrates the typical disclosures required for a business combination accounted for as an acquisition and assumes that the parent company has taken advantage of merger relief in its individual accounts.

**186**    *85 4A Sch 13(2), FRS 6(21)*    The name of the acquired undertaking and the date of the combination should be disclosed for all acquisitions.

**187**    *FRS 6(43)*    In circumstances where advantage is taken of merger relief the difference between the fair value of the shares issued and their nominal value should be shown as a separate reserve in the group accounts. Goodwill should still be calculated by comparing the fair value of the consideration given with the fair value of the net assets acquired.

# Notes to the accounts (continued)

**180**   **17 Fixed asset investments (continued)**

*Subsidiary undertakings*

£

**Cost**
At 1 January 19XX
Additions
Disposals

At 31 December 19XX


**Amounts written off**
At 1 January 19XX
Written off
Written back
Disposals

At 31 December 19XX

**Net book value**


**182**   [*Name of undertaking*] has been treated as a subsidiary undertaking because the group exercises dominant influence over this investment, directing its financial and operating policies.

**183, 184**   All subsidiary undertakings have been included in the consolidation with the exception of [*name of undertaking*] which has been excluded because the group's interest is held exclusively with a view to subsequent resale. [*Name of undertaking*] made a profit of £_____ for the year ended 31 December 19XX and its aggregate capital and reserves at 31 December 19XX amounted to £_____ . During the year no significant transactions took place between [*name of undertaking*] and the group.

**185, 186, 187**   *Acquisition of subsidiary undertaking*

On [*date*] the company acquired __% of the issued share capital of [*name of undertaking*] for consideration comprising the issue of [*number*] ordinary shares of _____ each in the company and [*give details of any other consideration*]. The fair value of the total consideration was £_____ . In accordance with sections 131 and 133 of the Companies Act 1985, the company has taken no account of any premium on the shares issued and has recorded the cost of the investment at the nominal value of the shares issued [plus the fair value of the other consideration]. The resulting difference arising on consolidation has been credited to other reserves.

*FRS 6(23)* For 'material' acquisitions, and other acquisitions in aggregate, the following information should be provided:

**188** *85 4A Sch 13(3),* (a) the composition and fair value of the purchase consideration and details of any *FRS 6(24)* deferred or contingent consideration;

**189** *85 4A Sch 13(5)* (b) a table showing, for each class of assets and liabilities of the acquiree: *FRS 6(25,26)*

(i) the book values immediately before the acquisition, with separate identification of reorganisation or restructuring provisions and related asset write-downs made in the year up to the date of acquisition;

(ii) the fair value adjustments, analysed between revaluations, accounting policy alignments and other significant adjustments, and the reasons for the adjustments;

(iii) the fair values at the date of acquisition; and

(iv) a statement of the amount of purchased goodwill or negative goodwill.

*FRS 6(27)* Where the fair values of the acquiree's asset or liabilities or the purchase consideration can only be determined provisionally, this should be stated and the reasons given. Any subsequent adjustments to these values, with corresponding adjustments to goodwill, should be disclosed and explained;

**190** *FRS 1(23,24),* (c) the amounts of cash included in the consideration or transferred as a result of *FRS 6(33,34)* the acquisition and the effects of the acquisition on the group's cash flows;

**191** *FRS 6(31)* (d) the costs incurred in reorganising, restructuring and integrating the acquisition subsequent to the date of the combination; and

**192** *FRS 6(35)* (e) the profit after tax and minority interests of the acquiree for the period from the beginning of its financial year to the date of acquisition, giving the date on which this period began, and for its previous financial year (this information is only required for material acquisitions).

*85 4A Sch 16* The information required by paragraph 13 of Schedule 4A to the 1985 Act in respect of acquisitions need not be given for an undertaking which is established outside the UK or carries out business outside the UK, if disclosure would be seriously prejudicial and the Secretary of State for Trade and Industry has agreed that the information need not be disclosed.

# Notes to the accounts (continued)

## 17 Fixed asset investments (continued)

**188, 189** *Acquisition of subsidiary undertaking (continued)*

The following table sets out the book values of the identifiable assets and liabilities acquired and their fair value to the group:

| | Book value £ | Revaluation £ | Accounting policy alignment £ | Other significant items £ | Fair value to group £ |
|---|---|---|---|---|---|
| **Fixed assets** | | | | | |
| Intangible | | | | | |
| Tangible | | | | | |
| Investments | | | | | |
| **Current assets** | | | | | |
| Stocks | | | | | |
| Debtors | | | | | |
| Investments | | | | | |
| Cash | | | | | |
| **Total assets** | | | | | |
| **Creditors** | | | | | |
| Debentures | | | | | |
| Bank loans | | | | | |
| Trade creditors | | | | | |
| Other creditors | | | | | |
| Accruals | | | | | |
| **Provisions** | | | | | |
| Pensions | | | | | |
| Taxation | | | | | |
| Reorganisation | | | | | |
| Other | | | | | |
| **Total liabilities** | | | | | |
| **Net assets** | | | | | |
| Minority interest | | | | | |
| Goodwill | | | | | |

**Satisfied by**
Shares issued
[*Describe other consideration*]

*FRS 6(36)*  For 'substantial' acquisitions, summarised profit and loss account information and a statement of total recognised gains and losses for the period to the date of acquisition should be provided in addition to the information in (e) above.

*FRS 6(37)*  'Substantial' acquisitions are where:
*UITF 15*

(a)  for listed companies, any of the percentage ratios set out in Chapter 10 of the Listing Rules exceed 15 per cent;

(b)  for other entities, either:

   (i)   the net assets or operating profits of the acquiree exceed 15 per cent of those of the acquiror; or

   (ii)  the fair value of the consideration given exceeds 15 per cent of the net assets of the acquiror.

   Net assets and profits should be those for the last financial year before acquisition and the net assets should be increased by any goodwill eliminated against reserves; and

(c)  in other exceptional cases where an acquisition is of such significance that disclosure is necessary in order to give a true and fair view.

# Notes to the accounts (continued)

## 17 Fixed asset investments (continued)

*Acquisition of subsidiary undertaking (continued)*

Details of the fair value adjustments are as follows:
[*Describe the reasons for the adjustments.*]

**190**   Net cash outflows in respect of the acquisition comprised:

£

**256**   Cash consideration
Cash at bank and in hand acquired
Bank overdrafts acquired

---

**191**   An amount of £_____ has been charged to the group profit and loss account in respect of costs incurred in reorganising, restructuring and integrating the acquisition in the period from [*date of acquisition*] to 31 December 19XX.

**192, 193**   [*Name of undertaking*] earned a profit after taxation and minority interests of £_____ in the year ended [*date*] 19XX (year ended [*date*] 19YY – £_____), of which £_____ arose in the period from [*date undertaking's financial year began*] to [*date of acquisition*]. The summarised profit and loss account and statement of total recognised gains and losses for the period from [*date acquired undertaking's financial year began*] to [*date of acquisition*], shown on the basis of the accounting policies of [*name of undertaking*] prior to the acquisition, are as follows:

**Profit and loss account**

£

**Turnover**
Cost of sales

**Gross profit**
Other operating expenses (net)

**Operating profit**
[*Describe exceptional items reported after operating profit*]
Finance charges (net)

**Profit on ordinary activities before taxation**
Tax on profit on ordinary activities

**Profit on ordinary activities after taxation**
Minority interests

**Profit for the financial period**

# Sale of subsidiary undertaking

**194**   *85 4A Sch 15*   The following information should be disclosed in respect of the sale of a material
  *FRS 2(48)*   subsidiary undertaking:

(a)   the name of the undertaking;
(b)   any ownership interest retained;
(c)   the extent to which the group's profit is attributable to the undertaking;

**195**   *FRS 2(47)*   (d)   the gain or loss directly arising for the group on an undertaking ceasing to be
  *FRS 10(71)*      its subsidiary undertaking is calculated by comparing the carrying amount of
           the net assets of that subsidiary undertaking attributable to the group's interest
           before the cessation with any remaining carrying amount attributable to
           the group's interest after the cessation together with any proceeds received.
           The net assets compared should include any related goodwill that has not pre-
           viously been either written off through the profit and loss account or attrib-
           uted to prior period amortisation or impairment;

**196**   *FRS 1(23,24)*   (e)   the amounts of cash included in the consideration or transferred as a result of
           the sale and the effects of the sale on the group's cash flows.

*FRS 2(48,49)*   Where an undertaking ceases to be a subsidiary other than by the sale of at least
         part of the group's interest or as a result of the purchase or exchange of shares, the
         relevant particulars should be explained.

# Notes to the accounts (continued)

## 17 Fixed asset investments (continued)

*Acquisition of subsidiary undertaking (continued)*

**Statement of total recognised gains and losses** £

Profit for the financial period
Unrealised surplus on revaluation of investment properties
Gain on foreign currency translation

Total recognised gains and losses relating to the period

**194** *Sale of subsidiary undertaking*

On [*date*] the group sold its___% interest in the ordinary share capital of [*name of undertaking*]. The profit of [*name of undertaking*] up to the date of disposal was £_____, and for its last financial year was £_____.

Net assets disposed of and the related sale proceeds were as follows: £

Fixed assets
Current assets
Creditors
Provisions for liabilities and charges

**Net assets**
Minority interest
Related goodwill

**195** Profit on sale

**Sale proceeds**

Satisfied by:
Cash
Loan notes
[*Describe other consideration*]

**196**
**256** Net cash inflows in respect of the sale comprised:
Cash consideration
Cash at bank and in hand sold
Bank overdrafts sold

# Associates

**197**  *FRS 9(26,29)*  Interest in associates should be accounted for under the equity method and shown in the group's balance sheet as the total of:

(a)  the group's share of net assets; and
(b)  goodwill arising on acquisition, less any amortisation or write-down.

Item (b) should be included in the carrying amount for the associates but separately disclosed.

**198**  *FRS 9(56)*  A note should explain why the facts of any particular case rebut either:

(a)  the presumption that an investor holding 20 per cent or more of the voting rights of another entity exercises significant influence over the operating and financial policies of that entity; or
(b)  the presumption that an investor holding 20 per cent or more of the shares of another entity has a participating interest.

*FRS 9(52)(b)*  Where the accounts used for associates are not coterminous with those of the group and the effect is material, the facts and year-end dates should be disclosed.

**199**  *85 4 Sch 45*  The book value of listed investments should be shown, along with details of the market values (and stock exchange values where these are lower) where they differ from book values. The tax consequences of disposals at market value should be dis-
*SSAP 15(42)*  closed.

**200**  *FRS 9(53)*  Details are required of the group's share of the capital commitments of the associates.

# Notes to the accounts (continued)

## 17 Fixed asset investments (continued)

**197, 198** *Associates*

|  | Group<br>£ | Company<br>£ |
|---|---|---|
| **Cost** | | |
| At 1 January 19XX | | |
| Additions | | |
| Share of retained profit for the year | | |
| Disposals | | |
| At 31 December 19XX | | |
| **Amounts written off** | | |
| At 1 January 19XX | | |
| Written off | | |
| Written back | | |
| Disposals | | |
| At 31 December 19XX | | |
| **Goodwill** | | |
| At 1 January 19XX | | |
| Additions | | |
| Written off | | |
| Disposals | | |
| At 31 December 19XX | | |
| **Net book value** | | |

|  | Group | | Company | |
|---|---|---|---|---|
|  | 19XX<br>£ | 19YY<br>£ | 19XX<br>£ | 19YY<br>£ |
| **199** Listed investments included above | | | | |
| Their aggregate market value was | | | | |
| The tax liability if they were sold at this value would be | | | | |

**200** The group's share of the capital commitments of associates at 31 December 19XX was £_____ (19YY – £ _____).

**201**　　*FRS 9(57)*　Additional disclosures are required where 15 per cent and 25 per cent thresholds are exceeded. The thresholds are applied by comparing the investor's share, for either its associates in aggregate or its individual associates, of gross assets, gross liabilities, turnover and operating results (on a three year average) with the corresponding amounts for the investor group (excluding any amounts included for associates and joint ventures). The note should give the aggregate of the investor's share in its associates of the following:

(a)　turnover;
(b)　fixed assets;
(c)　current assets;
(d)　liabilities due within one year; and
(e)　liabilities due after one year.

**202**　　*FRS 9(58)*　Further information is required in addition to the above where the investor's share in any individual associate exceeds 25 per cent with respect to the investor group. The name of the associate should be given along with the investor's share of the above captions and also:

(a)　profit before tax;
(b)　taxation; and
(c)　profit after tax.

# Notes to the accounts (continued)

## 17 Fixed asset investments (continued)

**201**  The following information is given in respect of the group's share of all associates.

|  | 19XX £ | 19YY £ |
|---|---|---|
| Turnover | | |
| Fixed assets | | |
| Current assets | | |
| Liabilities due within one year | | |
| Liabilities due after one year or more | | |

**202**  Included above is the group's share of [*name of company*] which is detailed individually below.

|  | 19XX £ | 19YY £ |
|---|---|---|
| Turnover | | |
| Profit before tax | | |
| Taxation | | |
| Fixed assets | | |
| Current assets | | |
| Liabilities due within one year | | |
| Liabilities due after one year or more | | |

[*Further analysis should be given where this is necessary to understand the nature of the total amounts disclosed.*]

## Other investments and loans

**203**

*85 5 Sch 23–25,*
*26–28*

The following disclosures are required where the parent company or the group have a significant holding in an undertaking which is not one of its subsidiary undertakings, associates or joint ventures:

(a)  the name of the undertaking;

(b)  the aggregate capital and reserves; and

(c)  the profit for the latest financial year.

This information need not be given if the investment is less than 50 per cent of the nominal value of the shares, and the investee does not have to file accounts at Companies House and does not otherwise publish them in Great Britain or elsewhere, or the investment is immaterial.

*85 4 Sch 33,43*

Where fixed asset investments are carried at a valuation rather than cost a description of the valuation basis, together with comparable historical cost information, is required. In addition, with the exception of listed investments, details are required of the years and amounts of the valuations and in the case of investments valued during the year, the names of the valuers (or particulars of their qualifications).

*85 4 Sch 31(3)*

If any fixed asset investment is carried at a directors' valuation, rather than market value, details are required of the method of valuation adopted and the reasons for adopting it.

# Notes to the accounts (continued)

## 17 Fixed asset investments (continued)

203

*Other investments and loans*

|  | Group | | | Company | | |
|---|---|---|---|---|---|---|
|  | *Other investments* £ | *Loans* £ | *Total* £ | *Other investments* £ | *Loans* £ | *Total* £ |
| **Cost** | | | | | | |
| At 1 January 19XX | | | | | | |
| Additions | | | | | | |
| Disposals | | | | | | |
| At 31 December 19XX | | | | | | |
| **Amounts written off** | | | | | | |
| At 1 January 19XX | | | | | | |
| Written off | | | | | | |
| Written back | | | | | | |
| Disposals | | | | | | |
| At 31 December 19XX | | | | | | |
| **Net book value** | | | | | | |

|  | Group | | Company | |
|---|---|---|---|---|
|  | *19XX* £ | *19YY* £ | *19XX* £ | *19YY* £ |
| Listed investments included above | | | | |
| Their aggregate market value was | | | | |
| The tax liability if they were sold at this value would be | | | | |

## Own shares

**204**     *UITF 13(9)*     Particulars of any employee share ownership plan (ESOP) should be provided, covering:

(a)  the main features of the ESOP and the arrangements for distributing shares;

(b)  the profit and loss account treatment of associated costs;

(c)  the number and market value of shares held by the ESOP and whether dividends on the shares have been waived; and

(d)  the extent to which the shares are under option to employees, or have been conditionally gifted to them.

Following the amendment to UITF 13 by FRS 14, any dividends which have not been waived should be excluded from profit before tax and deducted from the aggregate of dividends paid and proposed. The deduction should be disclosed on the face of the profit and loss account, if material, or in a note.

# Notes to the accounts (continued)

## 17 Fixed asset investments (continued)

*Own shares*

|  | Group £ | Company £ |
|---|---|---|
| **Cost** |  |  |
| At 1 January 19XX |  |  |
| Additions |  |  |
| Transfers to participants |  |  |
| At 31 December 19XX | _____ | _____ |
|  | ======= | ======= |
| **Amounts written off** |  |  |
| At 1 January 19XX |  |  |
| Written off |  |  |
| Transfers to participants |  |  |
| At 31 December 19XX | _____ | _____ |
|  | ======= | ======= |
| **Net book value** |  |  |
|  | ======= | ======= |

The company operates a long-term incentive scheme for senior management of the group. Awards under the scheme are based on appropriate group or business segment profit targets determined by the remuneration committee at the start of each year. Following confirmation of the year's profit performance, the appropriate award is made through an unconditional transfer of ordinary shares in the company to the participants. These shares are transferred out of the Employee Share Ownership Plan (ESOP), a discretionary trust, established to facilitate the operation of the incentive scheme.

The trustees of the ESOP purchase the company's ordinary shares in the open market under a £ _____ facility guaranteed by the company. The company also has an obligation to make regular contributions to the ESOP to enable it to meet its financing costs. Rights to dividends on shares held by the plan have been waived by the trustees.

At 31 December 19XX, £____ (19YY – £____) has been drawn down under the ESOP facility and is shown under long-term creditors in the group's and company's balance sheet. Charges of £____ (19YY – £____) have been reflected in the profit and loss account in respect of the scheme and are included in the analysis of staff costs. The number and market value of the ordinary shares held by the ESOP at 31 December 19XX was [number] (19YY – [number]) and £____ (19YY – £____) respectively.

# Stocks

**205**  *85 4 Sch 23(1)*  Stocks should be shown at the lower of cost and net realisable value on an item-by-
*SSAP 9(26,27)*  item basis and classified in a manner appropriate to the business.

Long-term contracts should be presented in the balance sheet as follows:

**206**  *SSAP 9(30)*  (a) costs incurred less transfers to cost of sales, foreseeable losses and payments on
account in excess of turnover, should be presented under stocks as 'long-term
contract balances' and analysed between 'net cost less foreseeable losses' and
'applicable payments on account';

**207**  (b) turnover less payments on account should be shown under debtors as 'amounts
recoverable on contracts';

**208**  *Statutory format*  (c) payments on account in excess of turnover and long-term contract balances
*note 8*  should be shown under creditors as 'payments on account'; and

(d) provisions for losses in excess of costs incurred (after transfers to cost of sales)
should be shown under provisions for liabilities and charges or creditors.

**209**  *85 4 Sch 27(3)*  Disclosure is required of a material difference between the balance sheet value of
stocks and their replacement cost as at the balance sheet date or their latest pur-
chase price or production cost before then (whichever directors consider the most
appropriate).

*85 4 Sch 26*  The note should indicate, where relevant, that interest on capital borrowed to
finance production has been included (specifying the amount).

# Debtors

**210**  *Statutory format*  The amount due after more than one year should be shown for each debtors cap-
*note 5*  tion.

**211**  *FRS 9(55)*  Details of loans and amounts relating to trading balances due from associates are
required.

*Statutory format*  'Called-up share capital not paid' and 'prepayments and accrued income' may be
*notes 1,6*  included under debtors if they are not shown as separate headings.

**212**  *SSAP 24(86,88)*  For defined benefit pension schemes, differences between amounts charged to the
profit and loss account and amounts funded or paid directly in pensions to mem-
bers of unfunded schemes should be shown as either provisions or prepayments.

**213**  *SSAP 24(87)*  For defined contribution pension schemes differences between contributions
payable in the year and contributions actually paid should be shown as either accruals or prepayments.

*85 4 Sch 51(2)*  The aggregate amount of any outstanding loans to provide financial assistance for
the acquisition of the company's own shares should be disclosed. Such loans should
only exist in limited circumstances which are covered by exemptions from the general prohibition on financial assistance. One exemption is in connection with loans
to ESOPs but, in practice, any loan to an ESOP would be eliminated and replaced
by the underlying investment in own shares as required by UITF Abstract 13 (see
note 17).

# Notes to the accounts (continued)

## 18 Stocks

| | Group | | Company | |
|---|---|---|---|---|
| | 19XX | 19YY | 19XX | 19YY |
| | £ | £ | £ | £ |
| **205** Raw materials and consumables | | | | |
| Work in progress | | | | |
| Finished goods and goods for resale | | | | |
| | ———— | ———— | ———— | ———— |
| | ———— | ———— | ———— | ———— |
| **206** Long-term contract balances | | | | |
| Net cost less foreseeable losses | | | | |
| Less applicable payments on account | ( ) | ( ) | ( ) | ( ) |
| | ———— | ———— | ———— | ———— |
| | ════ | ════ | ════ | ════ |

**209** There is no material difference between the balance sheet value of stocks and their replacement cost.

## 19 Debtors

| | Group | | Company | |
|---|---|---|---|---|
| | 19XX | 19YY | 19XX | 19YY |
| | £ | £ | £ | £ |
| Amounts falling due within one year: | | | | |
| Trade debtors | | | | |
| **207** Amounts recoverable on contracts | | | | |
| Amounts owed by group undertakings | | | | |
| **211** Amounts owed by associates | | | | |
| VAT | | | | |
| ACT recoverable | | | | |
| Other debtors | | | | |
| Prepayments and accrued income | | | | |
| Pension prepayments | | | | |
| **212** defined benefit schemes | | | | |
| **213** defined contribution schemes | | | | |
| | ———— | ———— | ———— | ———— |
| | ———— | ———— | ———— | ———— |

## Current asset investments

**214**  *85 4 Sch 31(4), 33*  Current asset investments may alternatively be carried at current cost (which for practical purposes would normally be market value). In such circumstances, the items concerned, the comparable historical cost amount and details of the valuation basis would all have to be disclosed.

*85 4 Sch 23*  Net realisable value (NRV) must be used if it is lower than cost. Where the reasons for making a NRV provision no longer apply, the provision should be written back to the extent that it is no longer necessary.

*85 4 Sch 27*  Certain investments may be treated as 'fungible' (i.e., indistinguishable from each other) where, for example, investments of the same type are acquired on different occasions. Shares of a particular class with identical rights would normally qualify as fungible. Such assets may be valued using LIFO, FIFO, weighted average or other similar methods, which match acquisitions and disposals on an estimated basis. However, where they are so valued, disclosure is required if their balance sheet value differs materially from their replacement cost as at the balance sheet date, or from the latest invoice price before then (whichever the directors consider more appropriate).

*85 4 Sch 41(3)*  If the company's debentures are held by a nominee or trustee of the company, their nominal amount and book value must be shown.

# Notes to the accounts (continued)

## 19 Debtors (continued)

| | Group | | Company | |
|---|---|---|---|---|
| | *19XX* | *19YY* | *19XX* | *19YY* |
| | *£* | *£* | *£* | *£* |

**210** Amounts falling due after more than one year:

Trade debtors
Amounts recoverable on contracts
Amounts owed by group undertakings
**211** Amounts owed by associates
VAT
ACT recoverable
Other debtors
Prepayments and accrued income
Pension prepayments
    defined benefit schemes
    defined contribution schemes

**214**

## 20 Current asset investments

| | Group | | Company | |
|---|---|---|---|---|
| | *19XX* | *19YY* | *19XX* | *19YY* |
| | *£* | *£* | *£* | *£* |

Listed investments
Unlisted investments

Aggregate market value of listed investments

The tax liability if listed investments were
sold at market value would be

The market value of listed investments includes certain investments for which the market value is considered to be higher than the Stock Exchange value.  The market value of these investments is £____ (19YY – £____) and their Stock Exchange value is  £____ (19YY – £____).

# Creditors

**215**      'Trade creditors' would include invoiced amounts for goods, etc. for production or resale. 'Other creditors' would include overhead items, while 'accruals' would comprise unbilled amounts for known liabilities – these would often be those accruing over time, such as electricity, telephone charges, etc.

**216**    *Statutory format note 7*    *FRS 4(62,65)*    Convertible debt should be shown separately and details provided of its principal features including:

(a) the dates and amounts payable on redemption;
(b) the number and class of shares into which the debt may be converted; and
(c) the timing of conversion and whether it is at the option of the issuer or the holder.

Where the above information cannot adequately explain the commercial effect of convertible debt instruments, particulars of where the relevant information may be obtained should be disclosed.

*85 4 Sch 41(1)*    The following details are required in respect of debentures issued during the year:

(a) the classes of debenture issued; and
(b) for each class, the amount issued and the consideration received.

**217**    *SSAP 21(51)*    Details of obligations (net of finance charges allocated to future periods) under finance leases are required.

**218**    *FRS 9(55)*    Details of loans and amounts relating to trading balances from associates should be disclosed.

**219**    *Statutory format note 9*    *SSAP 8(14)*    Tax, including UK corporation tax payable, and social security creditors should be shown separately. The due date of payment of UK corporation tax is required, except where the amount is shown as a current liability (as will usually be the case).

**220**    *SSAP 8(26,27)*    *SSAP 15(29)*    ACT on proposed dividends (whether recoverable or not) should be included as a current tax liability. If the ACT is regarded as recoverable it should be deducted, to the extent applicable, from the deferred tax liability, or the related asset shown as a deferred asset.

**221**    *Statutory format note 10*    Accruals and deferred income may be shown here or as a separate heading.

**222**    *SSAP 8(26)*    The recommended dividend must be stated (without the addition of related ACT).

# Notes to the accounts (continued)

215

## 21 Creditors: amounts falling due within one year

| | Group | | Company | |
|---|---|---|---|---|
| | *19XX* | *19YY* | *19XX* | *19YY* |
| | £ | £ | £ | £ |

**Convertible debt**

216

[_%] convertible unsecured loan stock 19__

**Other creditors**

217

Obligations under finance leases and hire purchase contracts

Bank loans and overdrafts

Other loans

208

Payments received on account

Trade creditors

Bills of exchange payable

Amounts owed to group undertakings

218
219
219, 220

Amounts owed to associates

Taxation and social security

ACT on proposed dividends

Other creditors

221

Accruals and deferred income

Accrued pension contributions

222

Proposed dividends

   minority shareholders

   equity shareholders

The company has granted a floating charge on its assets to secure bank overdrafts of £_____ (19YY – £____).

# Notes to the accounts (continued)

**215**   **22 Creditors: amounts falling due after more than one year**

|  | Group | | Company | |
|---|---|---|---|---|
|  | *19XX* | *19YY* | *19XX* | *19YY* |
|  | *£* | *£* | *£* | *£* |

**216**   **Convertible debt**
[_%] convertible unsecured loan stock 19__
[_%] guaranteed redeemable convertible
preference shares issued by [*name of
subsidiary undertaking*]

**Other creditors**
**217**   Obligations under finance leases and hire
purchase contracts
Bank loans
Other loans
**208**   Payments received on account
Trade creditors
Bills of exchange payable
Amounts owed to group undertakings
**218**   Amounts owed to associates
**219**   UK corporation tax payable on [*date*]
Other creditors
Government grants
**221**   Accruals and deferred income

201

**223**     *85 4 Sch 48(4)*     For each item under creditors for which security has been given, particulars are required of the nature of the security and the amount secured.

**224**     *85 4 Sch 48(2,3)*     The terms (repayment and interest rates) of each item shown under creditors falling due for repayment wholly or in part after five years must be disclosed. However, a general indication of them may be given if the note would otherwise be excessively long.

**225**     *FRS 4(63)*     The principal features of debt instruments should be disclosed, including:

(a) any unusual obligations or legal arrangements (e.g., subordinated debt and shares issued by subsidiaries that are classified as debt); and
(b) any significant differences between the amounts at which debt is shown in the accounts and the amount payable on the debt or claimable on a winding-up.

*FRS 4(65)*     Where the details provided cannot adequately explain the commercial effect of debt instruments, particulars of where the relevant information may be obtained should be disclosed.

*FRS 4(102)*     Although FRS 4 does not require the disclosure of the market values of capital instruments, it notes that such information may be useful to users of accounts as it provides an insight into the economic burden represented by debt. Disclosure of fair values for financial assets and liabilities is now required by FRS 13 (see note 23).

# Notes to the accounts (continued)

## 22 Creditors: amounts falling due after more than one year (continued)

**223**

The bank loans are secured on freehold properties of certain subsidiary undertakings.

**224**

The [_%] convertible unsecured loan stock 19__ is convertible at the option of the holder into fully paid ordinary shares of the company at £__ per ordinary share up to and including _____ 19__ and may be redeemed at the option of the issuer during the period from _____ 19__ to _____ 19__ at par. Unless previously redeemed or converted, it will be redeemed at par on _____ 19__.

**225**

On _____ 19__, [*name of subsidiary undertaking*], a subsidiary undertaking incorporated in [*name of country*], issued [*number*] [_%] guaranteed redeemable convertible preference shares with a paid up value of __ per share under terms which require them to be classified as debt in the group accounts. The company has guaranteed the shares on a subordinated basis and they are convertible at the option of the holder into fully paid ordinary shares of the company at £__ per ordinary share at any time prior to _____ 19__. The shares outstanding at that date will be redeemed on _____ 19__ at a redemption premium of __% of the paid up value. Systematic annual provision is being made for the premium on redemption and included within the carrying amount of the shares. At 31 December 19XX the amount accrued was £_____ (19YY – £_____).

**224**

[*The terms of repayment and interest rates of each item shown under creditors falling due for repayment wholly or partly after five years must be disclosed. A general indication may be given if the note would otherwise be excessively long.*]

**226** *FRS 4(33)* The maturity of debt should be analysed between amounts falling due:
*85 4 Sch 48(1)*

(a) in one year or less, or on demand;
(b) in more than one year but not more than two years;
(c) in more than two years but not more than five years; and
(d) in more than five years.

*FRS 4(36)* Where the maturity of debt has been assessed by reference to committed back-up facilities, the amounts of debt affected, analysed by the earliest date on which the lender could demand repayment in the absence of the facilities, should be disclosed.

**227** *SSAP 21(52)* Obligations (net of finance charges allocated to future periods) under finance leases should be analysed between amounts payable in the next year, amounts payable in the second to fifth years inclusive, and the aggregate amounts payable thereafter as follows:

(a) either as a separate heading for finance leases; or
(b) combined with a sub-heading of creditors, and analysed as above.

Alternatively, analyse gross obligations with future finance charges deducted from the total.

The categories for the maturity of debt in the model accounts are taken from FRS 4 as amended by FRS 13 and do not correspond exactly with the categories for the maturity of finance leases specified in SSAP 21. For convenience, the same categories have been used in the model accounts for debt and finance leases. The description of each category has been abbreviated rather than following the precise wording in FRS 4 as amended.

# Notes to the accounts (continued)

## 22 Creditors: amounts falling due after more than one year (continued)

Borrowings are repayable as follows:

| | Group | | Company | |
|---|---|---|---|---|
| | *19XX* | *19YY* | *19XX* | *19YY* |
| | *£* | *£* | *£* | *£* |

**Convertible debt**
Between one and two years
Between two and five years
After five years

On demand or within one year

**Bank loans**
Between one and two years
Between two and five years
After five years

On demand or within one year

**Finance leases**
Between one and two years
Between two and five years
After five years

On demand or within one year

**Total borrowings including finance leases**
Between one and two years
Between two and five years
After five years

On demand or within one year

## Derivatives and other financial instruments

FRS 13 requires disclosures about derivatives and other financial instruments. It applies to all entities that have one or more of their capital instruments listed or publicly traded on a stock exchange or market, other than insurance companies, and to all banks and similar institutions. The disclosure requirements for banks and other financial institutions are different from those for other companies.

The objective of these disclosures is to provide information about the impact of financial instruments on the reporting entity's risk profile, how the risks arising from financial instruments might affect the entity's financial performance and condition, and how these risks are managed.

The FRS requires both narrative and numerical disclosures. The narrative disclosures describe the role that financial instruments have in creating or changing the risks that the entity faces, including its objectives and policies in using financial instruments to manage these risks. The numerical disclosures show how these objectives and policies were implemented in the period and provide supplementary information for evaluating significant or potentially significant exposures. Together, these disclosures provide a broad overview of the entity's financial instruments and of the risk positions created by them, focusing on those risks and instruments that are of greatest significance.

**228**    There are complex definitions and exemptions in FRS 13 concerning the financial instruments that are to be included within these disclosures. Non-equity shares issued by the company are dealt with in the same way as the group's financial liabilities but separately disclosed.

**229**    *FRS 13(6)*    Short-term debtors and creditors may be excluded from the disclosures, other than currency disclosures, provided that this is explained.

## Narrative disclosures

**230**    The narrative disclosures may be given either in the accounts or some other statement such as an OFR which is made available with the accounts. If the disclosures are not included in the audited accounts pages of the annual report, there should be a specific cross-reference in the notes to the accounts to the exact location of these disclosures.

The narrative disclosures are not illustrated in the model accounts because they would normally be found in the OFR which is not illustrated. The disclosures also need to be very specific in relation to the group's particular circumstances and policies. However, it must be remembered that these disclosures are mandatory and subject to audit. Examples of the narrative disclosures are given in Appendix III of FRS 13.

The principal requirements for the narrative disclosures are as follows:

*FRS 13(13)*    (a)    an explanation of the role that financial instruments have had during the period in creating or changing the risks the group faces. This should include an explanation of the objectives and policies for holding or issuing financial instruments and the strategies for achieving those objectives that have been followed during the period;

*FRS 13(16)*    (b)    if this explanation reflects a significant change from the previous period, this should be disclosed and the reasons for the change explained;

*FRS 13(18)*    (c)    an explanation of any significant change in the role that financial instruments will have that has been agreed by the directors before the date of approval of the accounts;

*FRS 13(20)*    (d)    an explanation of how the year-end numerical disclosures reflect the objectives, policies and strategies that have been outlined. If the period-end position is materially unrepresentative of the group's position during the period, an explanation should be provided; and

# Notes to the accounts (continued)

## 23 Derivatives and other financial instruments

**230** Pages ___ to ___ of the Operating and Financial Review provide an explanation of the role that financial instruments have had during the period in creating or changing the risks the group faces in its activities. The explanation summarises the objectives and policies for holding or issuing financial instruments and similar contracts, and the strategies for achieving those objectives that have been followed during the period.

**228** The numerical disclosures in this note deal with financial assets and financial liabilities as defined in Financial Reporting Standard 13 *Derivatives and Other Financial Instruments: Disclosures* (FRS 13). For this purpose non-equity shares issued by the company are dealt with in the disclosures in the same way as the group's financial liabilities but separately disclosed. Certain financial assets such as investments in subsidiary and associated companies are also excluded from the scope of these disclosures.

**229** As permitted by FRS 13, short-term debtors and creditors have been excluded from the disclosures, other than the currency disclosures.

### Interest rate profile

**231** The group has no financial assets other than sterling cash deposits of £_____ (19YY – £_____) which are part of the financing arrangements of the group. The sterling cash deposits comprise deposits placed on money market at call, seven-day and monthly rates.

**232** After taking into account interest rate swaps and forward foreign currency contracts entered into by the group, the interest rate profile of the group's financial liabilities at 31 December 19XX was as follows.

| Currency | Total 19XX £ | Floating rate 19XX £ | Fixed rate 19XX £ | Interest-free 19XX £ |
|---|---|---|---|---|
| Sterling | | | | |
| borrowings | | | | |
| non-equity shares | | | | |
| US dollar | | | | |
| Total | | | | |

The profile at 31 December 19YY for comparison purposes was as follows.

| Currency | Total 19YY £ | Floating rate 19YY £ | Fixed rate 19YY £ | Interest-free 19YY £ |
|---|---|---|---|---|
| Sterling | | | | |
| borrowings | | | | |
| non-equity shares | | | | |
| US dollar | | | | |
| Total | | | | |

(e) if the group uses financial instruments as hedges, it should describe the transactions and risks that have been hedged, including the period of time until they are expected to occur, and the instruments used for hedging purposes, distinguishing between those that have been accounted for using hedge accounting and those that have not.

Further guidance on these requirements is given in FRS 13. A checklist of disclosure requirements for the narrative disclosures is given in Appendix 4.

## Interest rate profile

**231**     *FRS 13(32–33)*     If the group has material holdings of financial assets, the same information as that required for financial liabilities should be given as illustrated below. In this example it has been assumed that the group has no financial assets other than sterling cash deposits.

**232**     *FRS 13(26–29)*     The aggregate carrying amount of financial liabilities should be analysed, by principal currency, to show separately those liabilities at fixed rates, those at floating interest rates and those on which no interest is paid.

Interest rate swaps, currency swaps, forward contracts and other derivative financial instruments, whose effect is to alter the interest or currency basis of the financial liabilities, should, as far as possible, be taken into account. So, for example, if the group has taken out a floating rate borrowing and has also entered into an interest rate swap that has the economic effect of fixing the rate, the borrowings should be shown as fixed rate.

Any financial liabilities and derivatives that cannot be adequately reflected in the analysis should be excluded and a summary of their main effects provided instead. This information will need to be sufficient to enable the reader to understand their significance without providing excessive detail. Disclosures might include the notional amount of principal involved, the rates of interest, the period for which the contracts are operative and the terms of any options contained within the instrument.

**233**     *FRS 13(30–31)*     The following should be disclosed for each principal currency:

(a) the weighted average interest rate of the fixed rate financial liabilities;
(b) the weighted average period for which interest rates are fixed;
(c) the weighted average period until maturity for financial liabilities on which no interest is paid; and
(d) the benchmark rate for determining interest payments for the floating rate liabilities.

As noted above, similar disclosures are required for any material holdings of financial assets. These disclosures should be made on a gross basis separately for assets and liabilities. However, some groups manage interest rate risk on a net basis, netting off cash and other liquid resources. The figures may be shown on a net basis where the difference is not material. Where the difference is material, and a group wishes to show the position on a net basis, this may be disclosed as additional information provided that the gross position is also shown.

# Notes to the accounts (continued)

## 23 Derivatives and other financial instruments (continued)

Further analysis of the interest rate profile at 31 December 19XX and at 31 December 19YY is as follows.

| Currency | 19XX | | Interest-free |
|---|---|---|---|
| | Fixed rate | | |
| | *Weighted average interest rate* | *Weighted average period for which rate is fixed* | *Weighted average period to maturity* |
| | *(%)* | *Years* | *Years* |
| Sterling | | | |
| borrowings | | | |
| non-equity shares | | | |
| US dollar | | | |
| Total | | | |

| Currency | 19YY | | Interest-free |
|---|---|---|---|
| | Fixed rate | | |
| | *Weighted average interest rate* | *Weighted average period for which rate is fixed* | *Weighted average period to maturity* |
| | *(%)* | *Years* | *Years* |
| Sterling | | | |
| borrowings | | | |
| non-equity shares | | | |
| US dollar | | | |
| Total | | | |

The interest rate on floating rate financial liabilities is linked to six-month LIBOR in the case of sterling liabilities and US prime rate for US dollar liabilities. Further details of interest rates on long-term borrowings are given in note 22.

## Currency exposures

**234**    *FRS 13(34–37)*    An analysis should be provided of the net amount of monetary assets and liabilities, showing the amount denominated in each currency, analysed by reference to the functional currencies of the operations involved.

The purpose of this analysis is to show the currency exposures that give rise to gains and losses recognised in the profit and loss account. The analysis will therefore need to be constructed to reflect the group's application of SSAP 20. Consequently, assets and liabilities denominated in the same currency as the functional currency of the operations involved should not be included in the analysis. For example, US dollar assets of a US-based subsidiary would be excluded from the analysis but sterling assets of that same subsidiary would be included. The exchange differences on the structural currency exposures, such as the net investment in the US-based subsidiary, are taken to reserves in accordance with SSAP 20. It is for this reason that they are not dealt with in the analysis required by FRS 13.

Following the same principle, if the group has used foreign currency borrowings to finance or provide a hedge against foreign net investments, and the exchange gains and losses on those borrowings are taken to reserves, those borrowings should be excluded from the analysis.

The focus should be on the principal functional currencies and on the principal currencies in which the monetary items are denominated. Excessive detail should be avoided.

The effect of currency swaps, forward contracts and other derivatives that contribute to the matching of currency exposures should be taken into account as far as possible. A summary should be provided of the main effect of any such instruments that have not been taken into account.

# Notes to the accounts (continued)

## 23 Derivatives and other financial instruments (continued)

*Currency exposures*

As explained on page ____ of the Operating and Financial Review, the group's objectives in managing the currency exposures arising from its net investment overseas (in other words, its structural currency exposures) are to maintain a low cost of borrowings and to retain some potential for currency-related appreciation while partially hedging against currency depreciation. Gains and losses arising from these structural currency exposures are recognised in the statement of total recognised gains and losses.

The table below shows the group's currency exposures; in other words, those transactional (or non-structural) exposures that give rise to the net currency gains and losses recognised in the profit and loss account. Such exposures comprise the monetary assets and monetary liabilities of the group that are not denominated in the operating (or 'functional') currency of the operating unit involved, other than certain non-sterling borrowings treated as hedges of net investments in overseas operations. As at 31 December 19XX these exposures were as follows:

| Functional currency of group operation | Net foreign currency monetary assets (liabilities) | | | |
|---|---|---|---|---|
| | *Sterling* £ | *US dollar* £ | *Yen* £ | *Total* £ |
| Sterling | | | | |
| US dollar | | | | |
| Total | | | | |

The exposures at 31 December 19YY for comparison purposes were as follows:

| Functional currency of group operation | Net foreign currency monetary assets (liabilities) | | | |
|---|---|---|---|---|
| | *Sterling* £ | *US dollar* £ | *Yen* £ | *Total* £ |
| Sterling | | | | |
| US dollar | | | | |
| Total | | | | |

The amounts shown in the tables above take into account the effect of any currency swaps, forward contracts and other derivatives entered into to manage these currency exposures.

As at 31 December 19XX, the group also held open various currency swaps and forward contracts that the group had taken out to hedge expected future foreign currency sales.

## Maturity of financial liabilities

**235**    *FRS 13(38–39)*    A maturity profile of the carrying amount of financial liabilities should be presented showing amounts falling due:

(a) in one year or less, or on demand;
(b) in more than one year but not more than two years;
(c) in more than two years but not more than five years; and
(d) in more than five years.

The maturity profile should be determined by reference to the earliest date on which payment can be required or on which the liability falls due.

Where a group has no financial liabilities other than debt, the requirements of FRS 13 will not extend the existing requirements of the 1985 Act and FRS 4. In the case of finance leases it will be necessary to extend the maturity analysis required by SSAP 21 to split the second to fifth year band into two component parts. These disclosures are illustrated in note 22.

However, the definition of financial liabilities is wider than just debt and finance leases. For example, it could include creditors due in more than one year which are not covered by the exemption for short-term debtors and creditors. Also, all non-equity shares issued by the reporting entity should be dealt with in the disclosures in the same way as financial liabilities and separately disclosed. The model accounts illustrate how the disclosures might look where the company has issued non-equity shares. It would be possible to combine these disclosures with those in note 22.

## Borrowing facilities

**236**    *FRS 13(40–43)*    An analysis should be provided of the maturity of any material undrawn committed borrowing facilities showing separately those amounts expiring:

(a) in one year or less;
(b) in more than one year but not more than two years; and
(c) in more than two years.

If conditions precedent are attached to a committed facility, it should be included in the analysis only if all the conditions were satisfied at the balance sheet date.

It will often be useful to provide details of the purpose and period for which material facilities are committed and the extent to which the facilities are subject to annual review by the provider of finance.

## Fair values

**237**    *FRS 13(44–47)*    Financial assets and liabilities (whether recognised or unrecognised in the balance sheet) should be grouped into appropriate categories. For each category the aggregate fair value and the aggregate carrying amount should be disclosed. This treatment is illustrated in the model accounts. Alternatively, the aggregate fair value of items with a positive fair value may be shown separately from the aggregate fair value of items with a negative fair value, again for each category. Companies can choose whether to disclose a single net figure for each category or to disclose two 'gross' figures.

The categories should take into account the purpose for which each asset or liability is held or issued and the type of asset or liability involved. The categories will typically follow the same structure as, but be in more detail than, that used in discussing the objectives, policies and strategies for holding or issuing financial instruments. For example, interest rate derivatives would usually be shown separately from currency derivatives. Financial assets would not usually be included in a category that also included financial liabilities, except that derivatives held or issued for the same purpose would be grouped together, regardless of whether their fair value was positive or negative.

## 23 Derivatives and other financial instruments (continued)

**235** *Maturity of financial liabilities*

The maturity profile of the group's financial liabilities at 31 December 19XX was as follows:

| | Non-equity shares 19XX £ | Borrowings (Note 22) 19XX £ | Total 19XX £ | Total 19YY £ |
|---|---|---|---|---|
| In one year or less | | | | |
| In more than one year but not more than two years | | | | |
| In more than two years but not more than five years | | | | |
| In more than five years | | | | |
| Total | | | | |

**236** *Borrowing facilities*

The group had undrawn committed borrowing facilities at 31 December 19XX, in respect of which all conditions precedent had been met, as follows:

| | 19XX £ | 19YY £ |
|---|---|---|
| Expiring in one year or less | | |
| Expiring in more than one year but not more than two years | | |
| Expiring in more than two years | | |
| Total | | |

**237** *Fair values*

Set out below is a comparison by category of book values and fair values of the group's financial assets and liabilities at 31 December 19XX.

| | 19XX | | 19YY | |
|---|---|---|---|---|
| | Book value £ | Fair value £ | Book value £ | Fair value £ |
| **Primary financial instruments held or issued to finance the group's operations** | | | | |
| Short-term financial liabilities and current portion of long-term borrowings | | | | |
| Long-term borrowings | | | | |
| Financial assets | | | | |
| **Derivative financial instruments held to manage the interest rate and currency profile** | | | | |
| Interest rate swaps | | | | |
| Forward foreign currency contracts | | | | |

FRS 13(48–50)  If the estimated difference between the carrying amount of a financial asset or liability (or of a category of them) and its fair value is not material, the carrying amount may be used as the fair value. For example, this would apply to floating rate debt where payments are reset to market rates at frequent intervals.

However, not all debtors and creditors will have historical cost carrying amounts that approximate to fair value. For example, the fair value of long-term fixed rate debt may be materially greater or lower than its carrying amount depending on changes in interest rates since the debt was issued.

**238**  *FRS 13(51–52)*  The methods and any significant assumptions used in determining fair values should be disclosed. Guidance on procedures for estimating fair values is set out in Appendix IV of FRS 13.

## Gains and losses on hedges

**239**  *FRS 13(58–61)*  Many companies use financial assets and liabilities as hedges to manage their risk profile. When instruments are used in this way they are usually accounted for using hedge accounting whereby changes in the fair value of the hedge are not usually recognised in the profit and loss account immediately they arise. They are either not recognised at all or are recognised and carried forward in the balance sheet. When the hedged transaction occurs, the gain or loss on the hedge is either used to adjust the amount at which the hedged item is dealt with or recognised in the profit and loss account at the same time as the hedged item.

When hedge accounting has been used, the following information should be disclosed:

(a) the cumulative aggregate gains and losses that are unrecognised at the balance sheet date;
(b) the cumulative aggregate gains and losses carried forward in the balance sheet pending their recognition in the profit and loss account (there are no such gains and losses in the example illustrated in these model accounts);
(c) the extent to which these gains and losses are expected to be recognised in the profit and loss account in the next accounting period; and
(d) the amount of gains and losses included in the period's profit and loss account that arose in previous years and were either unrecognised or carried forward in the balance sheet at the start of the reporting period.

The disclosures described at (b), (c) and (d) above should not include gains and losses on hedges that have been accounted for by adjusting the carrying amount of a fixed asset recognised on the balance sheet.

## Market price risk

**240**  *FRS 13 (66–72)*  Companies are encouraged, but not required, to provide numerical disclosures that show the magnitude of market price risk arising over the period for all financial instruments and cash settled commodity contracts and, if significant, all other items carrying market price risk. This information should be provided using a technique or other basis that is consistent with the way the company manages its risk exposures. Companies that use one approach to manage market price risk in one part of their business and a different approach in another part are encouraged to provide separate disclosures for each part.

If these disclosures are provided they should be supplemented by explanations about the method used and any limitations in that method, together with reasons for any material changes in the amount of reported market price risk compared with the previous period.

FRS 13 describes five possible methods of measuring market price risk but it is beyond the scope of this book to discuss them.

# Notes to the accounts (continued)

## 23 Derivatives and other financial instruments (continued)

*Fair values (continued)*

**238**    The fair values of the interest rate swaps, forward foreign currency contracts and sterling denominated long-term fixed rate debt with a carrying amount of £ _____ have been determined by reference to prices available from the markets on which the instruments involved are traded. All the other fair values shown above have been calculated by discounting cash flows at prevailing interest rates.

**239**    *Gains and losses on hedges*

The group enters into forward foreign currency contracts to eliminate the currency exposures that arise on sales denominated in foreign currencies immediately those sales are transacted. It also uses interest rate swaps to manage its interest rate profile. Changes in the fair value of instruments used as hedges are not recognised in the financial statements until the hedged position matures. An analysis of these unrecognised gains and losses is as follows:

| | 19XX | | | 19YY | | |
|---|---|---|---|---|---|---|
| | *Gains*<br>£ | *Losses*<br>£ | *Net*<br>£ | *Gains*<br>£ | *Losses*<br>£ | *Net*<br>£ |
| **Unrecognised gains and losses on hedges at 1 January 19XX**<br>Gains and losses arising in previous years that were recognised in 19XX | | | | | | |
| **Gains and losses arising before 1 January 19XX that were not recognised in 19XX**<br>Gains and losses arising in 19XX that were not recognised in 19XX | | | | | | |
| **Unrecognised gains and losses on hedges at 31 December 19XX** | | | | | | |
| Of which:<br>Gains and losses expected to be recognised in 19WW | | | | | | |
| Gains and losses expected to be recognised in 19VV or later | | | | | | |

**240**    *Market price risk*

*[Companies are encouraged, but not required, to provide numerical disclosures that show the magnitude of market price risk arising over the period for all financial instruments. This information should be provided using a technique or other basis that is consistent with the way the company manages its risk exposures.]*

## Provisions for liabilities and charges

*FRS 12(2,11)*
*85 4 Sch 89*

A provision is defined in FRS 12 as a liability of uncertain timing or amount. This is consistent with the definition in the 1985 Act but briefer. Provisions can be distinguished from other liabilities such as trade creditors and accruals because there is uncertainty about the timing or amount of the future expenditure required in settlement. Although it is sometimes necessary to estimate the amount or timing of accruals, the uncertainty is generally much less than for provisions. All provisions should be dealt with here and not in creditors.

**241**

*FRS 12(89)*
*85 4 Sch 46(1,2)*

Disclose movements for each class of provisions showing separately:

(a)  the carrying amount at the beginning and end of the period;

(b)  additional provisions made in the period, including increases to existing provisions;

(c)  amounts used (i.e., incurred and charged against the provision) during the period;

(d)  unused amounts reversed during the period; and

(e)  the increase during the period in the discounted amount arising from the passage of time and the effect of any change in the discount rate.

Comparative information is not required.

# Notes to the accounts (continued)

## 24 Provisions for liabilities and charges

| | Deferred taxation £ | Deferred consideration £ | Pensions £ | Product warranties £ | Total £ |
|---|---|---|---|---|---|
| **241 Group** | | | | | |
| At 1 January 19XX | | | | | |
| Charged to profit and loss account | | | | | |
| Released unused | | | | | |
| Acquisition of subsidiary undertaking | | | | | |
| Sale of subsidiary undertaking | | | | | |
| ACT recoverable | | | | | |
| Utilised in year | | | | | |
| Adjustment arising from discounting | | | | | |
| Exchange adjustment | | | | | |
| At 31 December 19XX | | | | | |

| | Deferred taxation £ | Deferred consideration £ | Pensions £ | Product warranties £ | Total £ |
|---|---|---|---|---|---|
| **241 Company** | | | | | |
| At 1 January 19XX | | | | | |
| Charged to profit and loss account | | | | | |
| Released unused | | | | | |
| ACT recoverable | | | | | |
| Utilised in year | | | | | |
| Adjustment arising from discounting | | | | | |
| Exchange adjustment | | | | | |
| At 31 December 19XX | | | | | |

*FRS 12(90)*  The following should be disclosed for each class of provision:

    (a) a brief description of the nature of the obligation and the expected timing of payments;

    (b) an indication of the uncertainties about the amount or timing of those payments (including, where relevant, major assumptions); and

    (c) the amount of any expected reimbursement, stating the amount of any asset that has been recognised for that expected reimbursement.

*FRS 6(23,32)*  Movements on, and usage of, provisions or accruals for costs related to an acquisition should be disclosed. This information should be provided for each 'material' acquisition and for other acquisitions in aggregate.

*UITF 6(9)*  Provisions for post-retirement benefits other than pensions should be shown separately.

# Notes to the accounts (continued)

## 24 Provisions for liabilities and charges (continued)

The provision for deferred consideration is in respect of the acquisition of [*name of undertaking*], is payable in 19X_ and is an estimate. The actual amount payable will depend on the profits of the acquired company in the three years to 19X_ but is limited to a maximum of £____.

The pension provision arises from unfunded pension obligations to former employees and is expected to be payable over approximately 15 years.

The provision for product warranties relates to expected warranty claims on products sold in the last three years. It is expected that most of this expenditure will be incurred in the next financial year and that all will be incurred within three years of the balance sheet date.

Details of pensions and other post-retirement benefits are set out in notes 34 and 35 respectively.

**243**     *85 4 Sch 47*    Deferred taxation provisions should be stated separately from other tax provisions
         *SSAP 15(37,40)*   and the amounts provided for and unprovided for disclosed (analysed into their
major components).

         *SSAP 15(41)*     Where the potential amount of deferred taxation on a revalued asset is not shown
because the revaluation does not constitute a timing difference, the particulars
should be explained.

**244**     *FRS 2(54)*      The extent to which deferred taxation has been accounted for in respect of future
         *SSAP 15(44)*    remittances of the accumulated reserves of overseas subsidiary and associated
undertakings and other overseas earnings should be disclosed. Where full provision
has not been made, the reasons should be stated.

# Notes to the accounts (continued)

## 24 Provisions for liabilities and charges (continued)

**243** Deferred taxation provided and deferred taxation not provided are as follows:

| | Provided | | Not provided | |
|---|---|---|---|---|
| | *19XX* | *19YY* | *19XX* | *19YY* |
| | £ | £ | £ | £ |
| **Group** | | | | |
| Accelerated capital allowances | | | | |
| Other timing differences | | | | |
| Accumulated reserves of overseas subsidiary undertakings | | | | |
| Tax losses available | | | | |
| ACT recoverable | | | | |
| | ___ | ___ | ___ | ___ |
| Taxation on revaluation surpluses | | | | |
| Rollover relief | | | | |
| | ___ | ___ | ___ | ___ |
| | === | === | === | === |
| **Company** | | | | |
| Accelerated capital allowances | | | | |
| Other timing differences | | | | |
| Tax losses available | | | | |
| ACT recoverable | | | | |
| | ___ | ___ | ___ | ___ |
| Taxation on revaluation surpluses | | | | |
| Rollover relief | | | | |
| | ___ | ___ | ___ | ___ |
| | === | === | === | === |

**244** The accumulated reserves of certain overseas subsidiary undertakings would be subject to additional taxation if remitted. In the opinion of the directors, these accumulated reserves are required to finance the continuing operations of these undertakings and, accordingly, no provision for additional taxation has been made.

# Called-up share capital

**245** *85 4 Sch 38(1)*
*Statutory format note 12*
The authorised share capital and, for each different class of share, the number and nominal value of shares allotted should be disclosed. Allotted and paid up capital should be shown separately (in this example it is assumed that both amounts are the same).

**246** *FRS 4(56,58,65,85)*
A summary is required of the rights and principal features of each class of share (including classes that are not currently in issue but may be in the future, for example, as a result of the exercise of warrants). This should cover:

*85 4 Sch 38(2)*
(a)  the rights to dividends;
(b)  the dates of and the amounts payable on redemption and whether redemption is required either at the company's or the shareholder's option;
(c)  their priority and amounts receivable on a winding-up;
(d)  their voting rights;
(e)  any variations in rights according to circumstances; and
(f)  any other information necessary to explain why a class of share has been treated as equity or non-equity (as defined in paragraphs 7 and 12 of FRS 4).

*FRS 4(57)*
This information need not be given for equity shares that have one vote per share and have no preferential dividend rights, no redemption rights and an unlimited right to share in a surplus remaining on a winding-up.

*FRS 4(65)*
Where the summary of the rights and principal features of each class of share discussed above cannot adequately explain the commercial effect of the shares, particulars of where the relevant information may be obtained should be disclosed.

*FRS 4(55)*
For each class of non-equity shares (and warrants for non-equity shares) details are required of the attributable amount of non-equity shareholders' funds.

**247** *85 4 Sch 39*
*SE 12.43(o)*
Where shares have been allotted during the year, the class, number and nominal value of the shares should be disclosed. The Stock Exchange requires similar information to be provided in respect of share issues by any unlisted 'major' subsidiary undertaking (a 'major' subsidiary undertaking is one which represents 25 per cent or more of the aggregate of the share capital and reserves or profits before taxation of the group).

*SE 12.43(o)*
In circumstances where listed companies (or their unlisted 'major' subsidiary undertakings) have allotted shares for cash otherwise than to existing shareholders in proportion to their shareholdings and the allotment has not specifically been authorised by the shareholders, details are required of:

(a)  the names of the allottees, if fewer than six in number, and in the case of six or more allottees a brief generic description of them; and
(b)  the market price of the shares on the date of which the terms of issue were fixed.

*SE 12.43(p)*
If the company is a listed subsidiary, the Stock Exchange requires details of participation by the company's parent in any placing made during the year.

**248** *85 4 Sch 40*
Where contingent rights to the allotment of shares exist (e.g., through share options or convertible debt), disclosure is required of the number, description and amount of shares over which the rights may be exercised, the period during which they are exercisable and the price to be paid for the shares allotted.

# Notes to the accounts (continued)

**245**    ## 25 Called-up share capital

|  | 19XX £ | 19YY £ |
|---|---|---|

Authorised
[*Number*] ordinary shares of _____ each
[*Number*] __% redeemable preference shares of _____ each

Allotted, called-up and fully paid
[*number*] ordinary shares of _____ each
[*number*] __% redeemable preference shares of _____ each

**246**    Non-equity shareholders' funds relate entirely to the __% redeemable preference shares. These shares carry an entitlement to dividend at the rate of __p per share per annum and may be redeemed at £_____ per share at any time after _____ 19__ at the option of the company and, in any event, will be redeemed at £_____ per share on _____ 19__. Provision is made for the premium on redemption and is included within non-equity shareholders' funds. At _____ 19XX the amount accrued was £_____ (19YY – £_____). Holders of the redeemable preference shares have [*number*] vote[s] for every [*number*] shares held but only on a resolution for the winding-up of the company or on a resolution affecting the rights attached to the shares or if the preference dividend has remained unpaid for [*number*] months. Holders of the redeemable preference shares have the right on a winding-up to receive, in priority to any other classes of shares, the sum of £_____ per share together with any arrears of dividend.

**247**    During the year the company allotted [*number*] ordinary shares with a nominal value of £_____ in connection with the acquisition of [*name of undertaking*]. In addition, in order to finance [*describe*], the directors exercised their powers, granted at the last annual general meeting, to allot [*number*] ordinary shares with a nominal value of £_____ and at a premium of £_____ for cash to [*identify allottees if no more than 5*]/[*number*] private individuals, being clients of the company's broker]. The market price of these shares on [*date*], the date on which the terms of the issue were fixed, was £_____. [*Number*] ordinary shares were issued further to the share alternative offered in respect of the interim dividend.

**248**    Options have been granted under the [*describe share option schemes*] to subscribe for ordinary shares of the company as follows:

| *Number of shares under option* | *Subscription price per share* | *Exercise period* |
|---|---|---|

# Reserves

**249**     *SSAP 19(15)*     SSAP 19 requires the investment property revaluation reserve to be displayed prominently. 'Other reserves' could include a foreign currency translation reserve, a capital redemption reserve, consolidation reserves, merger reserve or reserves restricted by the Articles.

**250**     *85 4 Sch 46(1,2)*     Movements on reserves must be shown, reconciling beginning and end of year figures. For illustrative purposes this example assumes the following transactions have taken place during the year:

(a) allotments of shares;

(b) a revaluation of investment properties and the release of that element of the revaluation reserve which has been realised as a result of the depreciation, or disposal, of a revalued asset;

*SSAP 20(60), UITF 19(7)*    (c) the offset in reserves of gains on translation of the accounts of foreign subsidiaries and losses on foreign currency borrowings used to hedge the group's investment in such operations;

*FRS 4(41,44)*    (d) an increase in non-equity shareholders' funds due to the appropriation of finance costs, other than dividends, of non-equity shares;

*FRS 4(48)*    (e) a share alternative to a cash dividend; and

*FRS 10(71)*    (f) the inclusion of goodwill previously written off to reserves in the calculation of a profit on sale of a subsidiary undertaking.

# Notes to the accounts (continued)

249, 250 **26 Reserves**

| Group | Share premium account £ | Revaluation reserve Investment properties £ | Other £ | Other reserves £ | Profit and loss account £ | Total £ |
|---|---|---|---|---|---|---|
| At 31 December 19YY as previously stated | | | | | | |
| Prior year adjustment | | | | | | |
| At 1 January 19XX as restated | | | | | | |
| Share issues | | | | | | |
| Expenses of equity share issues | | | | | | |
| Revaluation surplus | | | | | | |
| Realised revaluation surplus | | | | | | |
| Gain on foreign currency translation | | | | | | |
| Loss on foreign currency borrowing | | | | | | |
| Retained profit for the year | | | | | | |
| [*Describe other finance costs of non-equity shares*] | | | | | | |
| Share dividend alternative | | | | | | |
| Goodwill previously written off included in retained profit for the year | | | | | | |
| At 31 December 19XX | | | | | | |

| 251 | *85 4A Sch 14*<br>*FRS 10(71)* | The cumulative amount of goodwill resulting from acquisitions in previous years which has been written off (prior to implementation of FRS 10) should be disclosed, net of any goodwill attributable to disposals. |
|---|---|---|
| 252 | *85 4 Sch 34(4)* | Disclosure is required of the tax treatment of items transferred to the revaluation reserve. |
| 253 | *FRS 2(53)*<br>*FRS 9(54)* | If there are significant statutory, contractual or exchange control restrictions on the ability of subsidiaries, associates or joint ventures to distribute their reserves (other than those shown as non-distributable), the nature and extent of the restrictions should be disclosed. |
| 254 | *UITF 19(9)* | The amount of tax charges and credits arising in respect of exchange differences on foreign currency borrowings should be disclosed separately in addition to the gross amount of the exchange differences. |

# Notes to the accounts (continued)

## 26 Reserves (continued)

|  | Share premium account £ | Revaluation reserve Investment properties £ | Other £ | Other reserves £ | Profit and loss account £ | Total £ |
|---|---|---|---|---|---|---|
| **249, 250**   **Company** | | | | | | |
| At 1 January 19XX | | | | | | |
| Share issues | | | | | | |
| Expenses of equity share issues | | | | | | |
| Revaluation surplus | | | | | | |
| Realised revaluation surplus | | | | | | |
| Gain on overseas equity investment | | | | | | |
| Loss on foreign currency borrowings | | | | | | |
| Retained profit for the year | | | | | | |
| [Describe other finance costs of non-equity shares] | | | | | | |
| Share dividend alternative | | | | | | |
| At 31 December 19XX | | | | | | |

**251**    The cumulative amount of goodwill written off against the group's reserves, net of goodwill relating to undertakings disposed of, is £_____ (19YY – £_____). This amount is net of negative goodwill added to reserves of £_____ (19YY – £_____).

**252**    No deferred tax has been provided by the group or the company in respect of the revaluation reserve since the directors consider that no liability to taxation will arise in the foreseeable future.

**253**    The profit for the year retained in group undertakings includes £_____ (19YY – £_____) retained in countries from which remittances are restricted because of exchange control regulations. The total at 31 December 19XX, subject to these restrictions, is £_____ (19YY – £_____).

**254**    The loss on overseas borrowings shown above is net of £_____ of attributable tax.

# Reconciliation of movements in group shareholders' funds

**255**    *FRS 3(28,59)*    A note reconciling the opening and closing totals of shareholders' funds should be provided. If included as a primary statement, the reconciliation should be shown separately from the statement of total recognised gains and losses.

# Minority interests

**256**    *FRS 4(49)*    Shares issued by subsidiaries to third parties should be accounted for as liabilities if the group taken as a whole has an obligation to transfer economic benefits in connection with them (e.g., by guaranteeing their dividends or redemption). In all other cases they should be reported as minority interests.

**257**    *FRS 4(50,60)*    Minority interests in the profit and loss account and balance sheet should be analysed between equity and non-equity interests.

**258**    Where there are minority interests in a subsidiary undertaking whose assets have been revalued, part of the revaluation surplus will need to be reflected in the 'minority interests' caption in the balance sheet. A reconciliation in the notes may be helpful.

**259**    *FRS 4(61,65)*    A description is required of the principal features of non-equity shares within minority interests and the rights of the holders of these shares against other group companies. Where the description does not adequately explain the commercial effect of such instruments, particulars of where the relevant information may be obtained should be disclosed.

# Notes to the accounts (continued)

255 ## 27 Reconciliation of movements in group shareholders' funds

| | 19XX £ | 19YY £ |
|---|---|---|
| Profit for the financial year | | |
| Other recognised gains and losses relating to the year (net) | | |
| | ——— | ——— |
| Dividends paid and proposed on equity and non-equity shares | | |
| New shares issued | | |
| Goodwill previously written off included in retained profit for the year | | |
| | ——— | ——— |
| Net addition to shareholders' funds | | |
| | ——— | ——— |
| Opening shareholders' funds as previously stated | | |
| Prior year adjustment | | |
| | ——— | ——— |
| Opening shareholders' funds as restated | | |
| | ——— | ——— |
| Closing shareholders' funds | | |
| | ═══ | ═══ |

256, 257 ## 28 Minority interests

| | Equity £ | Non-equity £ | Total £ |
|---|---|---|---|
| At 1 January 19XX | | | |
| Profit on ordinary activities after taxation | | | |
| Dividends paid and proposed | | | |
| 258 Revaluation of subsidiary undertakings' net assets | | | |
| Acquisition of subsidiary undertaking | | | |
| Sale of subsidiary undertakings | | | |
| | ——— | ——— | ——— |
| At 31 December 19XX | | | |
| | ═══ | ═══ | ═══ |

259 Non-equity minority interests comprise [*number*] _% cumulative redeemable preference shares of ___ each in [*name of subsidiary undertaking*]. The shares do not entitle the holders to any rights against other group companies and are redeemable on _____ 19__ at par.

# Reconciliation of operating profit to net cash flows

**260**    *FRS 1(12)*    A reconciliation between operating profit and net cash flow from operating activities should be provided. The reconciliation should disclose separately movements in stocks, debtors and creditors related to operating activities and other differences between cash flows and profit.

**261**    It is desirable that the net cash flow from operating activities be analysed between continuing and discontinued operations.

# Notes to the accounts (continued)

260 ## 29 Reconciliation of operating profit to operating cash flows

|  | 19XX £ | 19YY £ |
|---|---|---|
| Operating profit |  |  |
| Depreciation charges |  |  |
| Profit on sale of tangible fixed assets |  |  |
| Increase in stocks |  |  |
| Decrease in debtors |  |  |
| Increase in creditors |  |  |
| Decrease in provisions |  |  |
| Cash impact of fundamental restructuring |  |  |
| Other |  |  |
| **Net cash inflow from operating activities** |  |  |

261

| | 19XX | 19YY |
|---|---|---|
| Net cash inflow from operating activities comprises: |  |  |
| Continuing operating activities |  |  |
| Discontinued operating activities |  |  |

The operating cash flows include under discontinued activities an outflow of £ _____ which relates to the £_____ exceptional provision for fundamental restructuring made in the 19YY accounts.

## Returns on investments and servicing of finance

**262**    *FRS 1(13)*    'Returns on investments and servicing of finance' are receipts resulting from the ownership of an investment and payments to providers of finance, non-equity shareholders and minority interest.

## Taxation

**263**    *FRS 1(16)*    Cash flows included under 'taxation' are those to or from taxation authorities in respect of the entity's revenue and capital profits. For a subsidiary undertaking, cash flows relating to group relief should be included within this heading.

## Capital expenditure and financial investment

**264**    *FRS 1(19)*    'Capital expenditure and financial investment' includes cash flows relating to the acquisition or disposal of any fixed asset other than one required to be classified under 'acquisitions and disposals' and any current asset investment not included in 'liquid resources'.

## Acquisitions and disposals

**265**    *FRS 1(22)*    Disclosure of cash flows arising from the acquisition or disposal of any trade or business, or of an investment in an entity that becomes or ceases to be an associate, a joint venture or a subsidiary undertaking.

**266**    *FRS 1(45)*    A summary of the effects of acquisitions and disposals of subsidiary undertakings, indicating how much of the consideration comprised cash, should be disclosed in a note.

**267**    Material effects on amounts reported under each of the standard headings reflecting the cash flows of a subsidiary undertaking acquired or disposed of in the period should be disclosed.

# Notes to the accounts (continued)

## 30 Analysis of cash flows

|  |  | 19XX<br>£ | 19YY<br>£ |
|---|---|---|---|
| **262** | *Returns on investments and servicing of finance* | | |
| | Interest received | | |
| | Interest paid | | |
| | Interest element of finance lease rentals | | |
| | Dividends received | | |
| | Preference dividends paid | | |
| | Dividends paid to minority interests | | |
| | **Net cash outflow** | | |
| **263** | *Taxation* | | |
| | UK corporation tax paid | | |
| | Overseas tax paid | | |
| | **Net cash outflow** | | |
| **264** | *Capital expenditure and financial investment* | | |
| | Purchase of intangible fixed assets | | |
| | Purchase of tangible fixed assets | | |
| | Purchase of trade investments | | |
| | Sale of tangible fixed assets | | |
| | **Net cash outflow** | | |
| **265** | *Acquisitions and disposals* | | |
| | Purchase of subsidiary undertaking | | |
| **266** | Net overdrafts acquired with subsidiary undertaking | | |
| | Sale of business | | |
| | Investment in associates | | |
| | **Net cash outflow** | | |

233

## Management of liquid resources

**268**    *FRS 1(26)*    The 'management of liquid resources' section includes cash flows arising from current asset investments held as readily disposable stores of value (e.g., are disposable without disrupting the reporting entity's business and are convertible into cash or can be readily traded).

## Financing

**269**    *FRS 1(29)*    'Financing' cash flows comprise receipts or repayments of principal from or to external providers of finance.

# Notes to the accounts (continued)

## 30 Analysis of cash flows (continued)

**268**    *Management of liquid resources\**

|  | 19XX £ | 19YY £ |
|---|---|---|
| Cash withdrawn from seven day deposit | | |
| Purchase of government securities | | |
| Sale of government securities | | |
| Sale of corporate bonds | | |
| **Net cash inflow** | | |

\* Group plc includes term deposits, government securities and AA rated corporate bonds as liquid resources.

**269**    *Financing*

|  | | |
|---|---|---|
| Issue of ordinary share capital | | |
| Redemption of shares | | |
| Issue of shares of subsidiary undertaking to minority interests | | |
| Increase in short-term borrowings | | |
| Repayment of secured loan | | |
| New unsecured loan | | |
| Capital element of finance lease rental payments | | |
| **Net cash inflow** | | |

**267**    Companies acquired in the year contributed £ ____ to the group's net operating cash flows, paid £ ____ in respect of net returns on investment and servicing of finance, paid £ _____ in respect of taxation and utilised £ _____ for capital expenditure.

**267**    Companies sold in the year contributed £_____ to the group's net operating cash flows, paid £ ___ in respect of net returns on investment and servicing of finance, paid £ ____ in respect of taxation and utilised £ _____ for capital expenditure.

# Analysis and reconciliation of net debt

**270**   *FRS 1(33)*   A reconciliation of the movement of cash in the period with the movement in the net debt should be given in a note.

**271**   The changes in net debt should be analysed from the opening to the closing component amounts.

In simple cases, for example, where the company has net funds comprising cash balances, these two statements could be combined. Some companies present the reconciliation adjacent to the cash flow statement rather than in the notes.

*FRS 1(48)*   Where several balance sheet amounts are combined to form the components of opening and closing net debt, sufficient detail should be shown to enable the cash and other components of net debt to be respectively traced back to the amounts shown under the equivalent captions in the balance sheet.

Comparatives are not required for the statement analysing changes in the balance sheet amounts making up the net debt.

# Major non-cash transactions

**272**   *FRS 1(46)*   Material transactions that do not result in movements of cash should be explained.

# Notes to the accounts (continued)

## 31 Analysis and reconciliation of net debt

271

| | 1 January 19XX £ | Cash flow £ | Acquisitions and disposals* £ | Other non-cash changes £ | Exchange movement £ | 31 December 19XX £ |
|---|---|---|---|---|---|---|
| Cash in hand, at bank | | | | | | |
| Overdrafts | | | | | | |
| | | ——— | | | | |
| | | ——— | | | | |
| Debt due after one year | | | | | | |
| Debt due within one year | | | | | | |
| Finance leases | | | | | | |
| | | ——— | | | | |
| | | ——— | | | | |
| Current asset investments | | | | | | |
| Net debt | | | | | | |

\* Excluding cash and overdrafts.

| | 19XX £ | 19YY £ |
|---|---|---|
| Decrease in cash in the year | | |
| Cash inflow from increase in debt and lease financing | | |
| Cash inflow from decrease in liquid resources | | |
| Change in net debt resulting from cash flows | | |
| Loans and finance leases acquired with subsidiary | | |
| New finance leases | | |
| Translation difference | | |
| Movement in net debt in year | | |
| Net debt at 1 January 19XX | | |
| Net debt at 31 December 19XX | | |

270

272

## 32  Major non-cash transactions

During the year the group entered into finance lease arrangements in respect of assets with a total capital value at the inception of the leases of £____ (19YY – £ _____ ).

A certain proportion of the consideration for the acquisition and disposal of subsidiary undertakings during the year comprised shares and loan notes.  Further details are given in note 17.

# Financial commitments

**273**  *85 4 Sch 50(5)*  Particulars are required of unprovided financial commitments which are relevant to assessing the group's state of affairs. Matters to be dealt with could include unmatched forward foreign exchange contracts and guarantees given on behalf of subsidiary undertakings. Normal sales and purchase commitments, wage agreements, etc. would not generally be considered as commitments for these purposes.

**274**  *85 4 Sch 50(3)*  Details should be provided of the amount of capital expenditure contracted for but
*SSAP 5(6)*  not provided for. The estimate of capital commitments should include any irrecoverable VAT.

**275**  *SSAP 21(54)*  Commitments existing at the balance sheet date in respect of finance leases (and hire purchase contracts which have similar characteristics) entered into but commencing after that date should be disclosed.

**276**  *SSAP 21(56)*  Commitments for the next year in respect of operating leases (and hire purchase contracts which have similar characteristics) should be analysed between those leases expiring within one year, within two to five years, and over five years, distinguishing leases of land and buildings from other leases.

# Notes to the accounts (continued)

**33 Financial commitments**

Capital commitments are as follows:

| | Group 19XX £ | Group 19YY £ | Company 19XX £ | Company 19YY £ |
|---|---|---|---|---|
| Contracted for but not provided for | | | | |
| finance leases entered into | | | | |
| other | | | | |

Annual commitments under non-cancellable operating leases are as follows:

| | 19XX Land and buildings £ | 19XX Other £ | 19YY Land and buildings £ | 19YY Other £ |
|---|---|---|---|---|
| **Group** | | | | |
| Expiry date | | | | |
| within one year | | | | |
| between two and five years | | | | |
| after five years | | | | |
| **Company** | | | | |
| Expiry date | | | | |
| within one year | | | | |
| between two and five years | | | | |
| after five years | | | | |

Leases of land and buildings are typically subject to rent reviews at specified intervals and provide for the lessee to pay all insurance, maintenance and repair costs.

## Pension arrangements

| | |
|---|---|
| **277** | *85 4 Sch 50(4)*<br>*SSAP 24(87,88)* |

Information provided in respect of pension schemes should be sufficient to give an understanding of the impact of the arrangements on the accounts. For defined contribution schemes it will usually only be necessary to indicate the nature of the scheme and highlight the amounts included in the profit and loss account and balance sheet. For defined benefit schemes, further disclosures will be required because of the greater and more uncertain obligations arising. The additional disclosures needed will include the funding arrangements, the actuarial valuation method and related assumptions, explanations of the cost charged and certain actuarial valuation information. Because of the long-term commitment involved the disclosures should not only cover amounts included in the current year's accounts but should also indicate significant changes in future costs or contributions.

*SSAP 24(89)*   Except where disclosure of information about individual schemes is necessary for a proper understanding of the accounts, information about the group's pension schemes should be provided on a combined basis.

*85 4 Sch 50(4)*   Particulars should be given of any pension commitments included under provisions (this is shown in note 24 of these model accounts) and any such commitments for which no provision has been made. Where any such commitment relates wholly or partly to pensions payable to past directors of the company, separate particulars should be given of that commitment so far as it relates to such pensions.

## Post-retirement benefits other than pensions

**278**   *UITF 6(5)*   UTIF 6 requires post-retirement benefits other than pensions to be accounted for and disclosed in accordance with the principles of SSAP 24.

# Notes to the accounts (continued)

## 34 Pension arrangements

The group provides pension arrangements to the majority of full-time employees through [*number*] defined benefit schemes and the related costs are assessed in accordance with the advice of professionally qualified actuaries.

Details of the most recent actuarial valuations of the principal schemes, which were conducted as at [*date*] using the [*describe method*], are as follows:

Main assumptions (% pa):
    rate of increase in salaries
    rate of increase in pensions in payment
    rate of dividend increase
    interest rate
    return on scheme investments

Results:
    market value of scheme's assets (£)
    level of funding (%)

The deficit on the [*describe*] scheme should be eliminated by [*date*] at the current employer's contribution rate of __% of pensionable earnings. The surplus on the [*describe*] scheme should be eliminated by [*date*] as a result of [lower contributions/a pension contribution holiday].

The pension cost charge for the year for defined benefit schemes was £_____ (19YY – £_____). The significant change in cost over the previous year is due to [*explain reasons*].

The group also operates a number of defined contribution schemes for which the pension cost charge for the year amounted to £_____ (19YY – £_____).

# Contingent liabilities

**279**    *85 4 Sch 50(2)*    Unless the possibility of any payment (or other transfer of economic benefits) is
       *FRS 12(91)*    remote, disclose for each class of contingent liability at the balance sheet date a brief
description of the nature of the contingent liability and, where practicable:

(a) an estimate of its financial effect;
(b) an indication of the uncertainties relating to the amount and timing of any payment; and
(c) the possibility of any reimbursement.

*FRS 12(94)*    Contingent assets should also be disclosed but only where an inflow of economic benefits is probable. The disclosure should include a brief description of the nature of the contingent asset and, where practicable, an estimate of its financial effect.

*FRS 12(96)*    Where any of this information is not disclosed because it is not practicable to do so, that fact should be stated.

*FRS 12(97)*    In extremely rare cases, disclosure of some or all of the information about contingent liabilities and assets can be expected to prejudice seriously the position of the reporting entity in a dispute. In such cases the disclosures need not be made unless required by law. But the general nature of the dispute and the reason why the information has not been disclosed should be stated.

**280**    *85 4 Sch 50(1)*    Details are required of any charge on the assets to secure third party liabilities, including where practicable the amount secured.

*85 4 Sch 59A*    Disclosures concerning guarantees and other financial commitments must in each case distinguish between those relating to any parent or fellow subsidiary undertaking and those relating to any own subsidiary undertaking.

# Subsequent events

**281**    *SSAP 17(23–25)*    The nature, financial effect and taxation implications of material 'non-adjusting' post balance sheet events (i.e., those events which concern conditions which did not exist at the balance sheet date) should be disclosed. Similar information is required in respect of any transactions entered into before the year end, which reverse or mature after the year end, the substance of which was primarily to alter the appearance of the balance sheet.

# Related party information

**282**    *FRS 8(6)*    Material transactions with related parties should be disclosed, irrespective of whether a price is charged. The disclosure should include:

(a) the names of and the relationship between the parties;
(b) sufficient details to understand the transactions, including the amounts involved;
(c) the balances due to or from related parties at the year end and the amounts written off these balances during the year; and
(d) the provisions for doubtful debts on amounts due from related parties at the year end.

*FRS 8(2)*    Related parties are defined in the context of control and influence and include parent, subsidiary and fellow subsidiary undertakings, directors and key management (including those of parent undertakings), holders of 20 per cent or more of the voting rights, etc.

*FRS 8(3,4)*    Exemptions from disclosure are available in certain circumstances, for example, in group accounts of transactions or balances between group undertakings that have been eliminated on consolidation.

# Notes to the accounts (continued)

## 35 Post-retirement benefits other than pensions

278

The group operates unfunded non-contributory schemes for post-retirement benefits other than pensions. Defined medical benefits are provided to retired members in executive grades and above in *[list operations and countries]*. The costs of private medical care are met for pensioners, their spouses and eligible dependants. Currently, *[number]* pensioners are entitled to receive these benefits and *[number]* employees would be entitled to receive them should they reach retirement.

An actuarial valuation of post-retirement medical benefit schemes [in accordance with the requirements of the US accounting standard SFAS 106/for accounting purposes] was performed as at *[date]* by an independent professionally qualified actuary. On the basis of a gross interest rate of ___% per annum and medical benefit cost inflation of ___% per annum for *[number]* years falling linearly after a further *[number]* years to ___% per annum thereafter, the estimated accrued actuarial liability at the valuation date was £_____. The actuarial method used was the *[describe method]*.

The cost of medical benefits in the year was £_____ (19YY – £_____).

## 36 Contingent liabilities

279

A claim has been lodged by a customer against the group in respect of a major contract. The claim calls for rectification and for compensation for alleged damage to the customer's business. It has been estimated that the maximum liability should the action be successful is of the order of £_____. The group has taken legal advice to the effect that the action is unlikely to succeed and, accordingly, no provision has been made in the accounts. In the event that the claim were to succeed, the first £_____ would be covered by insurance.

280

Certain subsidiary undertakings have provided unsecured guarantees to third parties in respect of *[describe]*. At 31 December 19XX, guarantees outstanding amounted to £_____ (19YY – £_____).

## 37 Subsequent events

281

On *[date]* the premises of *[name of undertaking]* were seriously damaged by fire. Insurance claims have been put in hand but refurbishment is currently expected to exceed these by £_____.

## 38 Related party transactions

282

Transactions with the directors of Group plc are disclosed in note 8.

211, 218

During the year the group purchased goods in the ordinary course of business from *[name of undertaking]*, an associated undertaking, at a cost of £_____ (19YY – £_____). Amounts owed by and to associated undertakings are disclosed in notes 19, 21 and 22. These amounts all relate to trading balances except for short-term loans of £_____ (19YY – £_____) included in debtors.

## 39 Controlling party

283

Mr _____, a director of Group plc, and members of his close family, control the company as a result of controlling directly or indirectly, ____% of the issued share capital of Group plc.

## Controlling party

**283**

*FRS 8(5)* When the company is controlled by another party, disclosure is required of the related party relationship and the name of that party and, if different, that of the ultimate controlling party. If the controlling party or ultimate controlling party is not known, that fact should be disclosed.

*85 5 Sch 31* Where the company is itself a subsidiary undertaking, disclose the name of the company (including any body corporate, such as an overseas company) regarded by the directors as being the company's ultimate parent company. The country of incorporation should be stated if outside Great Britain.

In many instances the ultimate controlling party will be the same as the ultimate parent company. However, where the ultimate parent company is controlled by an individual (or in some cases a group of individuals acting together) the additional disclosure of the ultimate controlling party will be required.

*85 5 Sch 30* Details are required of the name (and country of incorporation if outside Great Britain or place of business if unincorporated) of the parent undertakings of the largest and smallest groups in which the company is consolidated. The address from which copies of these consolidated accounts can be obtained, if they are available to the public, should also be disclosed.

## Five-year summary

**284**

A five-year summary is recommended but not required by the Stock Exchange.

**285**

*FRS 14(76)* In order to give a fair comparison over the period, the basic and diluted EPS figures should be restated for subsequent changes in capital not involving full consideration at fair value (e.g., bonus issues, the bonus element of rights issues, share splits and share consolidations). The cumulative effect of all such events is taken into account and the resultant EPS figures are described as restated and should be clearly distinguished from other non-adjusted data.

*FRS 14(77)* Similarly, for comparison purposes, any record of equity dividends for the same period set out in the form of pence per share should be adjusted for the factors applied when restating EPS. The equity dividends should be described as restated and clearly distinguished from other non-adjusted data in the summary.

# Five-year summary

| | 19XX<br>£ | 19YY<br>£ | 19ZZ<br>£ | 19AA<br>£ | 19BB<br>£ |
|---|---|---|---|---|---|

**Results**

Turnover
Operating profit (including associates)
Profit on ordinary activities before taxation
Profit for the financial year

**Assets employed**

Fixed assets
Net current assets
Creditors: amounts falling due after more than one year
Provisions for liabilities and charges

Net assets

**Financed by**

Shareholders' funds
Minority interests

**Key statistics**

| | 19XX | 19YY | 19ZZ | 19AA | 19BB |
|---|---|---|---|---|---|
| Earnings per share | p | p | p | p | p |
| Diluted earnings per share | p | p | p | p | p |
| Dividends per share | p | p | p | p | p |
| Dividend cover † | times | times | times | times | times |
| Return on shareholders' funds* | % | % | % | % | % |
| Return on assets** | % | % | % | % | % |
| Share price: high | £ | £ | £ | £ | £ |
| low | £ | £ | £ | £ | £ |

† Dividend cover is based on the theoretical maximum dividend from the current period's earnings, allowing for any additional taxation which would become payable, divided by the actual dividend.
\* Profit for the financial year/shareholders' funds.
\*\* Operating profit/fixed and current assets excluding investments.

Earnings and dividends per share for earlier years have been restated for subsequent changes of capital not involving full consideration at fair value, including bonus issues and rights issues.

# Appendices

# Appendix 1 Statutory formats

## Balance Sheet: Format 1

| | | £ | £ | £ |
|---|---|---|---|---|

**A** Called up share capital not paid (*1*)

**B** Fixed assets      x

**I** Intangible assets
1. Development costs    x
2. Concessions, patents, licences, trade marks and similar rights and assets (*2*)    x
3. Goodwill (*3*)    x
4. Payments on account    x

         x

**II** Tangible assets
1. Land and buildings    x
2. Plant and machinery    x
3. Fixtures, fittings, tools and equipment    x
4. Payments on account and assets in course of construction    x

         x

**III** Investments
1. Shares in group undertakings    x
2. Loans to group undertakings    x
3. Participating interests    x
4. Loans to undertakings in which the company has a participating interest    x
5. Other investments other than loans    x
6. Other loans    x
7. Own shares (*4*)    x

         x

     (Total of B)      x

**C** Current assets

**I** Stocks
1. Raw materials and consumables    x
2. Work in progress    x
3. Finished goods and goods for resale    x
4. Payments on account    x

         x

**II** Debtors (*5*)
1. Trade debtors    x
2. Amounts owed by group undertakings    x
3. Amounts owed by undertakings in which the company has a participating interest    x
4. Other debtors    x
5. Called up share capital not paid (*1*)    x
6. Prepayments and accrued income (*6*)    x

         x

**III** Investments
1. Shares in group undertakings    x
2. Own shares (*4*)    x
3. Other investments    x

         x

**IV** Cash at bank and in hand    x

     (Total of C)      x

**D** Prepayments and accrued income (*6*)      x

     (Total of C and D)      x

     *carried forward*      x    x

---

| | | £ | £ | £ |
|---|---|---|---|---|
| | *brought forward* | | x | x |

**E** Creditors: amounts falling due within one year
1. Debenture loans (*7*)    (x)
2. Bank loans and overdrafts    (x)
3. Payments received on account (*8*)    (x)
4. Trade creditors    (x)
5. Bills of exchange payable    (x)
6. Amounts owed to group undertakings    (x)
7. Amounts owed to undertakings in which the company has a participating interest    (x)
8. Other creditors including taxation and social security (*9*)    (x)
9. Accruals and deferred income (*10*)    (x)

         (x)

**F** Net current assets (liabilities) (C+D–E) (*11*)      x

**G** Total assets less current liabilities (A+B+F)      x

**H** Creditors: amounts falling due after more than one year
1. Debenture loans (*7*)    (x)
2. Bank loans and overdrafts    (x)
3. Payments received on account (*8*)    (x)
4. Trade creditors    (x)
5. Bills of exchange payable    (x)
6. Amounts owed to group undertakings    (x)
7. Amounts owed to undertakings in which the company has a participating interest    (x)
8. Other creditors including taxation and social security (*9*)    (x)
9. Accruals and deferred income (*10*)    (x)

         (x)

**I** Provisions for liabilities and charges
1. Pensions and similar obligations    (x)
2. Taxation, including deferred taxation    (x)
3. Other provisions    (x)

         (x)

**J** Accruals and deferred income (*10*)      (x)

     Minority interests      (x)

         x

**K** Capital and reserves

**I** Called up share capital (*12*)    x

**II** Share premium account    x

**III** Revaluation reserve    x

**IV** Other reserves
1. Capital redemption reserve    x
2. Reserve for own shares    x
3. Reserves provided for by the Articles of Association    x
4. Other reserves    x

         x

**V** Profit and loss account    x

         x

     Minority interests      x

         x

# Balance Sheet: Format 2

| ASSETS | | £ | £ | £ |
|---|---|---|---|---|
| **A** | **Called up share capital not paid** (*1*) | | | x |
| **B** | **Fixed assets** | | | |
| I | Intangible assets | | | |
| | 1. Development costs | x | | |
| | 2. Concessions, patents, licences, trade marks and similar rights and assets (*2*) | x | | |
| | 3. Goodwill (*3*) | x | | |
| | 4. Payments on account | x | | |
| | | | x | |
| II | Tangible assets | | | |
| | 1. Land and buildings | x | | |
| | 2. Plant and machinery | x | | |
| | 3. Fixtures, fittings, tools and equipment | x | | |
| | 4. Payments on account and assets in course of construction | x | | |
| | | | x | |
| III | Investments | | | |
| | 1. Shares in group undertakings | x | | |
| | 2. Loans to group undertakings | x | | |
| | 3. Participating interests | x | | |
| | 4. Loans to undertakings in which the company has a participating interest | x | | |
| | 5. Other investments other than loans | x | | |
| | 6. Other loans | x | | |
| | 7. Own shares (*4*) | x | | |
| | | | x | |
| | | | | x |
| **C** | **Current assets** | | | |
| I | Stocks | | | |
| | 1. Raw materials and consumables | x | | |
| | 2. Work in progress | x | | |
| | 3. Finished goods and goods for resale | x | | |
| | 4. Payments on account | x | | |
| | | | x | |
| II | Debtors (*5*) | | | |
| | 1. Trade debtors | x | | |
| | 2. Amounts owed by group undertakings | x | | |
| | 3. Amounts owed by undertakings in which the company has a participating interest | x | | |
| | 4. Other debtors | x | | |
| | 5. Called up share capital not paid (*1*) | x | | |
| | 6. Prepayments and accrued income (*6*) | x | | |
| | | | x | |
| III | Investments | | | |
| | 1. Shares in group undertakings | x | | |
| | 2. Own shares (*4*) | x | | |
| | 3. Other investments | x | | |
| | | | x | |
| IV | Cash at bank and in hand | | x | |
| **D** | **Prepayments and accrued income** (*6*) | | x | |
| | | | | x |
| | | | | x |

| LIABILITIES | | £ | £ | £ |
|---|---|---|---|---|
| **A** | **Capital and reserves** | | | |
| I | Called up share capital (*12*) | | x | |
| II | Share premium account | | x | |
| III | Revaluation reserve | | x | |
| IV | Other reserves | | | |
| | 1. Capital redemption reserve | x | | |
| | 2. Reserve for own shares | x | | |
| | 3. Reserves provided for by the Articles of Association | x | | |
| | 4. Other reserves | x | | |
| | | | x | |
| V | Profit and loss account | | x | |
| | | | | x |
| | Minority interests | | | x |
| | | | | x |
| **B** | **Provisions for liabilities and charges** | | | |
| | 1. Pensions and similar obligations | x | | |
| | 2. Taxation, including deferred taxation | x | | |
| | 3. Other provisions | x | | |
| | | | | x |
| **C** | **Creditors** (*13*) | | | |
| | 1. Debenture loans (*7*) | x | | |
| | 2. Bank loans and overdrafts | x | | |
| | 3. Payments received on account (*8*) | x | | |
| | 4. Trade creditors | x | | |
| | 5. Bills of exchange payable | x | | |
| | 6. Amounts owed to group undertakings | x | | |
| | 7. Amounts owed to undertakings in which the company has a participating interest | x | | |
| | 8. Other creditors including taxation and social security (*9*) | x | | |
| | 9. Accruals and deferred income (*10*) | x | | |
| | | | | x |
| **D** | **Accruals and deferred income** (*10*) | | | x |
| | | | | x |

# Profit and loss account: Format 1 (*see note 17*)

| | | £ | £ |
|---|---|---|---|
| 1. | Turnover | | x |
| 2. | Cost of sales (*14*) | | (x) |
| 3. | Gross profit or loss | | x |
| 4. | Distribution costs (*14*) | | (x) |
| 5. | Administrative expenses (*14*) | | (x) |
| 6. | Other operating income | | x |
| 7. | Income from shares in group undertakings | | x |
| 8. | Income from participating interests | | x |
| 9. | Income from other fixed asset investments (*15*) | | x |
| 10. | Other interest receivable and similar income (*15*) | | x |
| 11. | Amounts written off investments | | (x) |
| 12. | Interest payable and similar charges (*16*) | | (x) |
| 13. | Tax on profit or loss on ordinary activities | | (x) |
| 14. | Profit or loss on ordinary activities after taxation | | x |
| | Minority interests | | (x) |
| 15. | Extraordinary income | x | |
| 16. | Extraordinary charges | (x) | |
| 17. | Extraordinary profit or loss | x | |
| 18. | Tax on extraordinary profit or loss | (x) | |
| | Minority interests | (x) | |
| | | | x |
| 19. | Other taxes not shown under the above items | | (x) |
| 20. | Profit or loss for the financial year | | x |

# Profit and loss account: Format 2

| | | £ | £ |
|---|---|---|---|
| 1. | Turnover | | x |
| 2. | Change in stocks of finished goods and in work in progress | | (x) |
| 3. | Own work capitalised | | x |
| 4. | Other operating income | | x |
| 5. | (a) Raw materials and consumables | (x) | |
| | (b) Other external charges | (x) | |
| | | | (x) |
| 6. | Staff costs | | |
| | (a) Wages and salaries | (x) | |
| | (b) Social security costs | (x) | |
| | (c) Other pension costs | (x) | |
| | | | (x) |
| 7. | (a) Depreciation and other amounts written off tangible and intangible fixed assets | (x) | |
| | (b) Exceptional amounts written off current assets | (x) | |
| | | | (x) |
| 8. | Other operating charges | | (x) |
| 9. | Income from shares in group undertakings | | x |
| 10. | Income from participating interests | | x |
| 11. | Income from other fixed asset investments (*15*) | | x |
| 12. | Other interest receivable and similar charges (*15*) | | x |
| 13. | Amounts written off investments | | (x) |
| 14. | Interest payable and similar charges (*16*) | | (x) |
| 15. | Tax on profit or loss on ordinary activities | | (x) |
| 16. | Profit or loss on ordinary activities after taxation | | x |
| | Minority interests | | (x) |
| 17. | Extraordinary income | x | |
| 18. | Extraordinary charges | (x) | |
| | Minority interests | (x) | |
| 19. | Extraordinary profit or loss | x | |
| 20. | Tax on extraordinary profit or loss | (x) | |
| | Minority interests | (x) | |
| | | | x |
| 21. | Other taxes not shown under the above items | | (x) |
| 22. | Profit or loss for the financial year | | x |

# Notes on the balance sheet formats

## (1) Called up share capital not paid

(Formats 1 and 2, items A and C.II.5.)
This item may be shown in either of the two positions given in Formats 1 or 2.

## (2) Concessions, patents, licences, trade marks and similar rights and assets

(Formats 1 and 2, item B.I.2.)
Amounts in respect of assets shall only be included in a company's balance sheet under this item if either:

(a) the assets were acquired for valuable consideration and are not required to be shown under goodwill; or
(b) the assets in question were created by the company itself.

## (3) Goodwill

(Formats 1 and 2, item B.I.3.)
Amounts representing goodwill shall only be included to the extent that the goodwill was acquired for valuable consideration.

## (4) Own shares

(Formats 1 and 2, items B.III.7 and C.III.2.)
The nominal value of such shares shall be shown separately.

## (5) Debtors

(Formats 1 and 2, items C.II.1 to 6.)
The amount falling due after more than one year shall be shown separately for each item included under debtors.

## (6) Prepayments and accrued income

(Formats 1 and 2, items C.II.6 and D.)
This item may be shown in either of the two positions given in Formats 1 or 2.

## (7) Debenture loans

(Format 1, items E.1 and H.1 and Format 2, item C.1.)
The amount of any convertible loans shall be shown separately.

## (8) Payments received on account

(Format 1, items E.3 and H.3 and Format 2, item C.3.)
Payments received on account of orders shall be shown for each of these items insofar as they are not shown as deductions from stocks.

## (9) Other creditors including taxation and social security

(Format 1, items E.8 and H.8 and Format 2, item C.8.)
The amount for creditors in respect of taxation and social security shall be shown separately from the amount for other creditors.

## (10) Accruals and deferred income

(Format 1, items E.9, H.9 and J and Format 2, items C.9 and D.)
The two positions given for this item in Format 1 at E.9 and H.9 are an alternative to the position at J, but if the item is not shown in a position corresponding to that at J it may be shown in either or both of the other two positions (as the case may require).

The two positions given for this item in Format 2 are alternatives.

## (11) Net current assets (liabilities)

(Format 1, item F.)
In determining the amount to be shown under this item any amounts shown under 'prepayments and accrued income' shall be taken into account wherever shown.

## (12) Called up share capital

(Format 1, item K.I and Format 2, item A.I.)
The amount of allotted share capital and the amount of called up share capital which has been paid up shall be shown separately.

## (13) Creditors

(Format 2, items C.1 to 9.)
Amounts falling due within one year and after one year shall be shown separately for each of these items [and for the aggregate of all of these items].

# Notes on the profit and loss account formats

## (14) Cost of sales: distribution costs: administrative expenses

(Format 1, items 2, 4 and 5.)
These items shall be stated after taking into account any necessary provisions for depreciation or diminution in value of assets.

## (15) Income from other fixed asset investments: other interest receivable and similar income

(Format 1, items 9 and 10: Format 2, items 11 and 12)
Income and interest derived from [group undertakings] shall be shown separately from income and interest derived from other sources.

## (16) Interest payable and similar charges

(Format 1, item 12: Format 2, item 14.)
The amount payable to [group undertakings] shall be shown separately.

## (17) Format 1

The amount of any provisions for depreciation and diminution in value of tangible and intangible fixed assets falling to be shown under item 7(a) in Format 2 shall be disclosed in a note to the accounts in any case where the profit and loss account is prepared by reference to Format 1.

# Appendix 2 Summary of permitted loans to, and other permitted transactions with, directors

## A. Non-relevant company

| | Type of transaction | Permitted to | Aggregation required |
|---|---|---|---|
| | **Loan** | | |
| 85 s334 | £5,000 any purpose | Directors of company and its holding company | Yes |
| 85 s337 | Unlimited directors' expenses (where approved or ratified in general meeting) | Directors of company | No |
| 85 s338, s339 | Favourable housing loan up to £100,000 | Directors of money-lending company and its holding company | Yes |
| 85 s330, s336 | Unlimited to group companies and connected persons | Group companies and directors' connected persons | No |
| 85 s338 | Unlimited normal (arm's-length) commercial loans | Directors of money-lending company and its holding company | No |
| | **Quasi-loan including guarantee or security for quasi-loan** | | |
| 85 s330 | Unlimited for any purpose | Directors of company and their connected persons and group companies | No |
| | **Credit transaction including guarantee or security for credit transaction** | | |
| 85 s330 | Unlimited for any purpose | Directors of company and their connected persons and group companies | No |
| | **Guarantee for loan** | | |
| 85 s337 | Unlimited directors' expenses (where approved or ratified in general meeting) | Directors of company | No |

| | | | |
|---|---|---|---|
| *85 s338, s339* | In connection with favourable housing loan up to £100,000 | Directors of money-lending company | Yes |
| *85 s330, s336* | Unlimited to group companies and connected persons | Group companies and directors' connected persons | No |

**Security for loan**

| | | | |
|---|---|---|---|
| *85 s330* | Unlimited in connection with directors' expenses (where approved or ratified in general meeting) | Directors of company | No |
| *85 s330* | Unlimited in connection with group companies and connected persons | Group companies and directors' connected persons | No |

# B. Relevant company

| | *Type of transaction* | *Permitted to* | *Aggregation required* |
|---|---|---|---|

**Loan**

| | | | |
|---|---|---|---|
| *85 s334* | £5,000 any purpose | Directors of company and its holding company | Yes |
| *85 s337* | Directors' expenses up to £20,000 (where approved or ratified in general meeting) | Directors of company | Yes |
| *85 s338, s339* | Favourable housing up to £100,000 | Directors of money-lending company and its holding company | Yes |
| *85 s333, s336* | Unlimited to group companies | Group companies even if 'associated' with director | No |
| *85 s338, s339* | Normal (arm's-length) commercial loans up to £100,000 | Directors of money-lending company and its holding company | Yes |

**Quasi-loan**

| | | | |
|---|---|---|---|
| *85 s332* | £5,000 any purpose, provided repayable within two months | Directors of company and its holding company | Yes |
| *85 s337* | Directors' expenses up to £20,000 | Directors of company | Yes |
| *85 s338, s339* | Favourable housing up to £100,000 | Directors of money-lending company and its holding company | Yes |
| *85 s333, s336* | Unlimited to group companies | Group companies even if 'associated' with director | No |
| *85 s338, s339* | Normal (arm's-length) commercial loans up to £100,000 | Directors of money-lending company and its holding company | Yes |

| | Credit transactions | | |
|---|---|---|---|
| *85 s335* | Unlimited at arm's length in ordinary course of business | Directors of company and their connected persons and group companies | No |
| *85 s335* | At favourable rate, subject to limit of £10,000 | Directors of company and their connected persons and group companies | Yes |
| *85 s337* | Directors' expenses, subject to limit of £20,000 | Directors of company | Yes |
| *85 s336* | Unlimited to holding company | Holding company | No |
| | **Guarantee for loan, quasi-loan, credit transaction** | | |
| *85 s338, s339* | In connection with favourable housing loan or quasi-loan up to £100,000 | Directors of money-lending company and its holding company | Yes |
| *85 s338, s339* | In connection with normal (arm's-length) commercial loan or quasi-loan | Directors of money-lending company and its holding company | Yes |
| *85 s335* | Unlimited if in connection with credit transaction at arm's length in normal course of business | Directors of company and their connected persons and group companies | No |
| *85 s337* | In connection with directors' expenses up to £20,000 | Directors of company | Yes |
| *85 s333, s336* | In connection with unlimited loan or quasi-loan to group companies | Group companies even if 'associated' with director | No |
| | **Security for loan, quasi-loan and credit transaction** | | |
| *85 s337* | Directors' expenses up to £20,000 | Directors of company | Yes |
| *85 s335* | In connection with unlimited arm's-length credit transaction | Directors of company and their connected persons and group companies | No |
| *85 s335* | In connection with favourable credit transaction up to £10,000 | Directors of company and their connected persons and group companies | Yes |
| *85 s333, s336* | In connection with unlimited loan or quasi-loan | Holding company and group companies even if 'associated' with director | No |

# Appendix 3 Statutory disclosure requirements for directors' loans and other transactions

The disclosure exemptions listed here are those in the 1985 Act. In some instances disclosure will be required to comply with FRS 8 *Related Party Disclosures*.

| *Example* | | *Disclosure*<br>*85 6 Sch 22* | | *Disclosure exemption* |
|---|---|---|---|---|
| **Loan** | | | | |
| Director borrows cash | 1 | Name of person concerned (if 'connected' with a director, name of director as well) | a | No comparatives required (*85 4 Sch 58(3)*) |
| Director has excessive travel float and repays late or infrequently | | | b | Transactions, agreements, etc. between two companies where director is only interested by virtue of being a director of both (*85 6 Sch 18*) |
| Director has current account other than for items illustrated below | 2 | Principal terms (not defined but, e.g., security, repayment, interest, credit limit) | | |
| Company provides loan for car purchase | 3 | Fact it was agreed, made or existed during year | c | Group accounts need only show amounts of loan to directors of the holding company or its holding company and people connected with them (*85 6 Sch 15*) |
| | 4 | Liability (principal and interest) at beginning and end of year | | |
| | 5 | Maximum liability during year | d | No disclosures of items 4 to 7 if reporting company is a wholly owned subsidiary and makes loan to its parent (or fellow wholly owned subsidiary of same parent), or (not necessarily being a wholly owned subsidiary) to its own wholly owned subsidiary. Disclosure relief is subject to further condition that loan would otherwise only be disclosable because recipient company was 'associated' with a director of reporting company during the financial year (*85 6 Sch 23*) |
| | 6 | Unpaid interest (if any) | | |
| | 7 | Any bad debt provision | | |
| **Quasi-loan** | | | | |
| Company pays third party on director's behalf | 1 | Name of person concerned (see under 'loans' above) | a | No comparatives required (*85 4 Sch 58(3)*) |
| Company pays for spouse (to travel with director) and director repays later | 2 | Principal terms (see above) | b | Interlocking directorships (see under 'loans' item b) |
| | 3 | Fact it was agreed, made or existed in year | c | Group exemption as for |

| | | |
|---|---|---|
| Director uses company credit card for personal expenses<br><br>Company pays for season ticket for director and is reimbursed later | 4  Value of quasi-loan (i.e., gross maximum amount liable to be repaid to company) | 'loans' item c (but including connected persons)<br><br>d  No disclosure of item 4 opposite if conditions under 'loans' item d apply |

### Credit transaction

| | | |
|---|---|---|
| Director buys goods or services from company on credit<br><br>Company leases property to director and rent paid in arrears | 1  Name of person concerned (see under 'loans' above)<br><br>2  Principal terms (see above)<br><br>3  Fact it was agreed, made or existed in year<br><br>4  Gross arm's-length value of goods, services or land concerned | a  No comparatives required (85 4 Sch 58(3))<br><br>b  No disclosure if aggregate outstanding value of all credit transactions made (or agreed) for the director (or connected person) never exceeded £5,000 during the year (85 6 Sch 24)<br><br>c  No disclosures of group transactions as under 'loans' item c above<br><br>d  Interlocking directorships (see under 'loans' item b) |

### Mutual aid

| | | |
|---|---|---|
| Company lends to a director or another company in return for similar favour<br><br>Company places business with bank in return for loan, etc. to director<br><br>Parent company lends to a director of a subsidiary which pays management charges to parent to cover cost and interest | 1  Name of person concerned (see under 'loans' above)<br><br>2  Principal terms (see above) and value<br><br>3  Fact that it was agreed, made or existed in year<br><br>4  As for loan (see above) if in connection with a loan<br><br>5  Otherwise, as for other types of transaction | a  No comparatives required (85 4 Sch 58(3))<br><br>b  As for 'credit transaction' item b (if in respect of such) (85 6 Sch 24)<br><br>c  Interlocking directorships (see under 'loans' item b)<br><br>d  Group exemptions (see under 'loans' item c) |

### Guarantee or security

| | | |
|---|---|---|
| Company guarantees director's overdraft | 1  Name of person concerned (see under 'loans' above)<br><br>2  Principal terms (see above)<br><br>3  Fact it was agreed, made or existed in year<br><br>4  Liability of company or its subsidiary (beginning and end of year)<br><br>5  Maximum potential liability of company or its subsidiary<br><br>6  Amount paid (or liability incurred) to fulfil guarantee or discharge security | a  No comparatives required (85 4 Sch 58(3))<br><br>b  As for credit transaction item b (if in respect of such) (85 6 Sch 24)<br><br>c  Interlocking directorships (see under 'loans' item b)<br><br>d  Group exemptions (see under 'loans' item c) |

## Assignment

| | | |
|---|---|---|
| Company buys or takes an existing loan (by third party) to a director | 1 As for 'loans' above (if re a loan) | a No comparative required (*85 4 Sch 58(3)*) |
| | 2 As for guarantees (if re a guarantee) | b As for credit transaction item b (if in respect of such) (*85 6 Sch 24*) |
| | 3 Otherwise, disclose details as for other types of transactions | c Interlocking directorships (see under 'loans' item b) |
| | | d Group exemptions (see under 'loans' item c) |

## Non-director officer

**85 6 Sch 29**

| | | |
|---|---|---|
| For examples see above | In respect of all such officers (not individually), the number of individuals and the aggregate amount outstanding at the year end in respect of: | a No comparatives required (*85 4 Sch 58(3)*) |
| | • loans<br>• quasi-loans<br>• credit transactions | b No disclosure in respect of any individual whose aggregate loans, quasi-loans and credit transactions, etc. did not exceed £2,500 at the year end (*85 6 Sch 29*) |
| | Note: these categories include related guarantees, security, assignment, mutual assistance, etc. (*85 6 Sch 8*) | c Connected persons ignored |

## Direct/indirect material interest

| | | |
|---|---|---|
| Director sells property to his/her company | 1 Name of person concerned (see above) and name of director with the material interest | a No comparatives required (*85 4 Sch 58(3)*) |
| Director has significant interest in or is a partner of a supplier or customer of the company | | b No disclosures if majority of other directors decide interest is not material (*85 6 Sch 17*) |
| | 2 Principal terms (see above) | |
| Company buys a house for the sole occupation of the director's family | 3 Fact it was agreed, made or existed in year | c No disclosures of employment contract between a director and his/her company or its subsidiaries (*85 6 Sch 18*) but note disclosure requirements directors' remuneration of (*SE 12.43A(c)*) |
| | 4 Nature of interest | |
| Director provides consultancy services to his/her company | 5 Arm's-length value | |
| Company sells property to a director | | d No disclosure if aggregate value of net amounts outstanding from prior years and gross transactions in year never exceeded £1,000 during the financial year (or the lower of £5,000 and 1 per cent of net assets as at year end) (*85 6 Sch 25*) |
| Director makes loan to company | | |
| | | e Interlocking directorships (see under 'loans' item b) |
| | | f Group exemptions (see under 'loans' item c) |

g Group relief 1: no
disclosure if each party to
the transaction which is a
member of the same group
entered into the transaction
at arm's length in ordinary
course of business (*s5 6 Sch
20*)

h Group relief 2: no
disclosure if transaction by
a group company which is a
wholly owned subsidiary
and director's interest only
arises because he/she was
'associated' with the
company at some time in
year (*s5 6 Sch 21*)

i Group relief 3: no
disclosure if transaction by
a group company or its
subsidiary and director's
interest only arises because
he/she was 'associated' with
the company at some time in
the year and providing no
other group company
involved (*s5 6 Sch 21*)

# Appendix 4 The Operating and Financial Review disclosure points

## Introduction

The disclosure points which follow are based on the ASB Statement *Operating and Financial Review* published in July 1993. The Statement is designed as a formulation and development of best practice. It is intended to be persuasive rather than mandatory. Its use is, however, commended by the Financial Reporting Council, the Hundred Group of Finance Directors and the London Stock Exchange.

The detailed items listed should not be regarded as a comprehensive list of all matters that might be relevant. Nor are all items listed relevant to all businesses. The checklist should be useful in determining how a company's narrative explanation of its performance and position measures up against best practice.

Disclosures required by UITF Abstract 20 in respect of the year 2000 issue and by UITF Abstract 21 in respect of the potential impact of the euro are also often made in the OFR. In the model accounts in Part II these have, however, been illustrated in the directors' report.

For accounting periods ending on or after 23 March 1999, listed companies (and certain other entities) will be required to make narrative disclosures about derivatives and other financial instruments in accordance with FRS 13. These disclosures will usually be most appropriately made in the OFR but it is important to note that, in contrast to the other contents of an OFR, they are mandatory and must be audited. For this reason the relevant requirements of FRS 13 have been summarised in a separate section at the end of this Appendix. There is some overlap between the requirements of the ASB Statement and FRS 13 but they have been listed separately so that it is clear which requirements are mandatory.

## Overall features

| | |
|---|---|
| Written in a clear style, as succinctly as possible. | |
| Readily understandable by the general reader of annual reports. | |
| Include only matters likely to be significant to investors. | |
| Balanced and objective. | |
| Deal even-handedly with good and bad aspects. | |
| Refer to comments in previous statements where not borne out by events. | |
| Contain analytical discussion (not merely numerical analysis). | |
| Show clearly how ratios or other financial information relate to financial statements. | |
| Follow 'top-down' structure (discuss individual aspects in the context of the business as a whole). | |

| | |
|---|---|
| Give reasons for, and effect of, changes in accounting policies. | |
| Focus on matters which are of greatest significance to the business. | |
| Discuss trends and factors that have affected the results but are not expected to continue and events, trends and uncertainties that are expected to have an impact in the future. (Trends and uncertainties should be explained in terms of significance to the business but their outcome should not necessarily be forecast.) | |
| Do not provide commercially sensitive information where the potential damage to the company is greater than the benefits of disclosure. If such information is omitted, ensure that the user is not misled by a discussion that is no longer complete and balanced. | |

# Operating review

The overall aim is to identify and explain the main factors that underlie the business and, in particular, those which have varied in the past or are expected to change in the future.

| Results for the period | |
|---|---|
| Discuss significant features of the operating performance for the period. | |
| Cover all aspects of the profit and loss account to the level of profit on ordinary activities before tax. | |
| Focus on overall business and segments that are relevant to an understanding of performance as a whole. | |
| Cover changes in the industry or environment and effect on results. | |
| Cover developments within the business and effect on results. | |
| Discuss special factors that have affected the results, even if their effect cannot be quantified. | |
| In particular, consider: | |
| • changes in market conditions; | |
| • new products and services introduced or announced; | |
| • changes in market share or position; | |
| • changes in turnover and margins; | |
| • changes in exchange rates and inflation rates; | |
| • new activities and acquisitions; and | |
| • discontinued operations and disposals. | |

| Material acquisitions | |
|---|---|
| Comment on the extent to which expectations at the time of acquisition have been realised. | |
| Indicate if results of seasonal businesses are not indicative of those for a full year. | |

| Dynamics of the business | |
|---|---|
| Discuss main factors that may have a major effect on future results (whether or not significant in the current period). | |

| | |
|---|---|
| Include principal risks and uncertainties in main lines of business. | |
| Discuss in qualitative terms the potential impact on the results. | |
| Comment on the approach to managing risk. | |
| The following may be relevant depending on the nature of the business. Some of these items may be included in the contingent liabilities note (to which reference can be made) but the discussion should cover a wider range of risks and uncertainties: | |
| • scarcity of raw materials; | |
| • skill shortages; | |
| • patents, licences and franchises; | |
| • dependence on major suppliers or customers; | |
| • product liability; | |
| • health and safety; | |
| • environmental protection costs and potential environmental liabilities; | |
| • self-insurance; | |
| • exchange rate fluctuations; and | |
| • rates of inflation differing between costs and revenues, or between different markets. | |

| | |
|---|---|
| **Investment for the future** | |
| Discuss how the directors have sought to maintain future income and profits. | |
| Include activities and expenditures of the period which are intended wholly or partly to enhance future profitability and can be varied by management over a wide range without significantly affecting current trading. | |
| *Capital expenditure* | |
| Discuss current levels of capital expenditure and planned future expenditure (committed and uncommitted). | |
| Indicate the overall level of expenditure. | |
| Disclose major business segments and geographical areas accounting for material elements of the total. | |
| Give details of major projects involved. | |
| Indicate likely benefits (in period and in future) expected from both previous and present capital expenditure. | |
| *Other expenditure* | |
| Discuss other activities regarded as a form of investing in the future, particularly changes in levels of activity and management policy. | |
| Refer to benefits expected from these activities. | |
| Such activities will vary from one business to another but may include: | |
| • marketing and advertising campaigns; | |
| • training programmes; | |
| • refurbishment and maintenance programmes; | |
| • rcscarch which may lead to new product and services; and | |
| • technical support to customers. | |

| Overall return to shareholders | |
|---|---|
| Discuss overall return attributable to shareholders including: | |
| • dividends; | |
| • increases in shareholders' funds; | |
| • contributions from operating performance of business units; and | |
| • other recognised gains and losses. | |
| For investment businesses, unrealised gains and losses reported in the statement of total recognised gains and losses are an essential component of overall performance and should be discussed as such. | |

| Profits, dividends and EPS | |
|---|---|
| Indicate dividend policy. | |
| Comment on the comparison between dividends and profits both in total and per share. | |
| Explain the significance of any alternative EPS figures disclosed in the profit and loss account as permitted by FRS 3 and FRS 14. | |

| Accounting policies | |
|---|---|
| Indicate and explain any subjective judgements to which the financial statements are particularly sensitive. | |

# Financial review

The overall purpose is to explain the capital structure of the business, its treasury policy, dynamics of its financial position, sources of liquidity and their application, and financing requirements arising from capital expenditure plans. The review should concentrate on matters of significance. Narrative commentary should be supported by figures, where these assist understanding.

| Capital structure | |
|---|---|
| Discuss the capital structure in terms of: | |
| • maturity profile of debt; | |
| • types of capital instruments used; and | |
| • currency and interest rate structure. | |
| Comment on ratios such as interest cover and debt/equity. | |

| Treasury policy | |
|---|---|
| State capital funding and treasury policy/objectives including: | |
| • management of interest rate risk; | |
| • maturity profile of borrowings; and | |
| • management of exchange rate risk. | |
| Cover implementation of these policies in the period in terms of: | |
| • manner in which treasury activities are controlled; | |
| • currencies in which borrowings are made and cash held; | |
| • extent to which borrowings are at fixed interest rates; | |

| | |
|---|---|
| • use of financial instruments for hedging purposes; and | |
| • extent to which foreign currency net investments are hedged. | |
| Give purpose and effect of major financing transactions up to date of approval of financial statements. | |
| Discuss potential effect of interest rate changes on profits. | |

| **Taxation** | |
|---|---|
| Where the overall tax charge is significantly different from the normal UK tax rate applied to the profit before tax, disclose and explain the main reconciling items. | |

| **Cash flows** | |
|---|---|
| Discuss cash generated from operations and other sources of cash including any special factors which influenced them. | |
| Where segmental cash flows are significantly out of line with segmental profits, indicate and explain this. | |

| **Current liquidity** | |
|---|---|
| Discuss liquidity at end of period including: | |
| • level of borrowings; | |
| • seasonality of borrowing requirements (indicated by peak level of borrowing in the period); | |
| • maturity profile of borrowing and committed facilities; and | |
| • funding requirements for capital expenditure (committed and authorised). | |
| Refer to any restrictions (e.g., exchange control or tax consequences) on the ability to transfer funds around the group where these might be a significant restraint. | |

| **Borrowing covenants** | |
|---|---|
| Indicate if negotiations with lenders on the operation of covenants are taking place or are expected to take place. | |
| Where a breach of a covenant has occurred or is expected to occur, give details of measures taken or proposed to be taken to remedy the situation. | |

| **Going concern** | |
|---|---|
| The going concern statement required by paragraph 12.43(v) of the Listing Rules may be made as part of the OFR discussion of the financial position. Other locations such as a corporate governance page or, as illustrated in the model accounts, the statement of directors' responsibilities are acceptable. | |

| **Balance sheet value** | |
|---|---|
| Comment on strengths and resources of the business whose value is not reflected fully in the balance sheet (e.g., brands and similar intangible assets). | |
| Where considered appropriate, discuss the value of such items and increases and decreases in their value. | |

# Statement of compliance

Directors are not required to include any formal confirmation that they have complied with the ASB Statement but a comment on the extent to which the Statement has been followed may be helpful.

Where it is implied, through the use of the words 'operating and financial review' or otherwise, that the directors have endeavoured to follow the ASB Statement, they should signal any fundamental departures from it.

# Derivatives and other financial instruments: disclosures

The table below sets out a summary of the narrative disclosures which are required by FRS 13 in respect of objectives, policies and strategies for holding and issuing financial instruments, including derivatives. The disclosures are mandatory for entities within the scope of FRS 13 but they need not necessarily appear in the OFR. The audited accounts should include a specific cross-reference to the location of these disclosures.

| Derivatives and other financial instruments: narrative disclosures | |
| --- | --- |
| Explain the role that financial instruments have had during the period in creating or changing the risks the company faces in its activities. These risks will typically include:<br><br>• credit risk;<br>• liquidity risk;<br>• cash flow risk;<br>• interest rate risk;<br>• currency risk; and<br>• other types of market price risk. | |
| Include an explanation of:<br><br>• the objectives and policies for holding or issuing financial instruments and similar contracts; and<br>• the strategies for achieving those objectives that have been followed during the period. | |
| Discuss the nature of, and purposes for which, the main types of financial instruments and similar contracts are held or issued. Instruments used for the following purposes should each be covered separately:<br><br>• financing;<br>• risk management or hedging; and<br>• trading or speculation. | |
| Describe the main financial risk management and treasury policies agreed by the directors, including the policies, quantified where appropriate, on: | |
| • the fixed/floating split, maturity profile and currency profile of assets and liabilities; | |
| • the extent to which foreign currency financial assets and financial liabilities are hedged to the functional currency of the business unit concerned; | |

| | |
|---|---|
| • the extent to which foreign currency borrowings and other financial instruments are used to hedge foreign currency net investments; and | |
| • any other hedging. | |
| If these objectives, policies and strategies have significantly changed from the explanation provided in the previous period this should be disclosed and the reasons for the change explained.<br><br>Include variations resulting from changes in the company's main market price risks and from changes in the way that its exposures are managed. | |
| Explain any significant change to the role that financial instruments will have in creating or changing risks, that have been agreed by the directors before the date of approval of the accounts. | |
| Provide an explanation of how the period-end numerical disclosures shown in the accounts reflect the objectives, policies and strategies that have been described. | |
| If the period-end position is regarded as materially unrepresentative of the company's position during the period or of its agreed objectives, policies and strategies, an explanation of the extent to which it is regarded as unrepresentative should be provided. | |
| If the company uses financial instruments as hedges, it should describe: | |
| • the transactions and risks that have been hedged, including the period of time until they are expected to occur; and | |
| • the instruments used for hedging purposes, distinguishing between those that have been accounted for using hedge accounting and those that have not. | |

# Appendix 5 Preliminary announcements disclosure checklist

The disclosure checklist which follows contains the requirements for a preliminary announcement as set out by the London Stock Exchange, the Companies Act 1985 and the ASB 'best practice' Statement. The checklist focuses on content; it does not discuss issues of timing and distribution. Compliance with the ASB Statement is not mandatory but its use is recommended by the Financial Reporting Council, the Hundred Group of Finance Directors and the London and Irish Stock Exchanges. (Paragraph references are to the ASB Statement.)

| PROFIT AND LOSS ACCOUNT INFORMATION | | |
|---|---|---|
| Summarised profit and loss account containing: <br> (a) turnover; <br> (b) operating profit; <br> (c) net interest payable less receivable; <br> (d) profit before taxation and extraordinary items; <br> (e) tax on profits (UK taxation and, if material, overseas and share of associated undertakings' taxation to be shown separately, also current/ deferred tax split); <br> (f) minority interests; <br> (g) profit attributable to shareholders before extraordinary items; <br> (h) extraordinary items (net of tax); <br> (i) profit attributable to shareholders; and <br> (j) rates of dividend(s) paid and proposed and amounts absorbed thereby, giving: <br>    (i) the exact net amount payable per share; <br>    (ii) the payment date; <br>    (iii) the record date where applicable; and <br>    (iv) any foreign income dividend election, together with any income tax treated as paid at the lower rate and not repayable. | SE 12.40(a)(ii); 12.52; para 36 <br><br><br><br><br> para 39 <br><br><br><br><br><br> SE 12.40(c) | |
| Earnings per shares expressed as pence per share, including basic and diluted EPS. Additional amounts per share should be presented consistently over time, reconciled to standard EPS, not given any prominence over standard EPS and the reason for calculating the additional version explained. | SE 12.40(a)(ii); 12.52(i); para 41 | |
| Comparative figures for profit and loss account information detailed above for the preceding financial year. | SE 12.40(a)(ii); 12.52(j); para 47 | |
| Turnover and operating profit for: <br> (a) acquisitions; and <br> (b) discontinued operations; <br> as defined in FRS 3 to be shown on face of profit and loss account. | para 37 | |

| | | |
|---|---|---|
| Where crucial to understanding performance:<br>(a) segment turnover, distinguishing inter-segment sales if significant; and<br>(b) segment profit on same basis as in annual accounts. | para 38 | |
| Understanding of significant changes in the effective tax rate from the prior year. | para 39 | |
| Exceptional items, either on face of profit and loss account or in notes as FRS 3, with adequate description. | para 40 | |
| **STATEMENT OF TOTAL RECOGNISED GAINS AND LOSSES (STRGL)** | | |
| STRGL if material gains or losses, e.g., revaluations, currency movements, other than profit for the year. | para 42 | |
| Reconciliation of movements in shareholders' funds if movements other than those in STRGL need to be explained. | para 43 | |
| Comparative figures. | para 47 | |
| **BALANCE SHEET** | | |
| Summarised balance sheet, using classifications similar to annual accounts, giving for Schedule 4/4A companies at least:<br>(a) fixed assets;<br>(b) current assets;<br>  (i) stock;<br>  (ii) debtors;<br>  (iii) cash at bank and in hand; and<br>  (iv) other current assets;<br>(c) creditors: amounts falling due within one year;<br>(d) net current assets;<br>(e) total assets less current liabilities;<br>(f) creditors: amounts falling due after more than one year;<br>(g) provisions for liabilities and charges;<br>(h) capital and reserves; and<br>(i) minority interests. | para 44 | |
| Comparative figures. | para 47 | |
| **CASH FLOW STATEMENT** | | |
| Cash flow statement providing main headings from FRS 1, namely:<br>(a) net cash inflow/outflow from operating activities;<br>(b) dividends received from joint ventures and associates;<br>(c) returns on investments and servicing of finance;<br>(d) taxation;<br>(e) capital expenditure and financial investment;<br>(f) acquisitions and disposals;<br>(g) equity dividends paid;<br>(h) management of liquid resources;<br>(i) financing; and<br>(j) increase/decrease in cash. | para 45 | |
| Reconciliation of operating profit to operating cash flow. | para 46 | |

| | | |
|---|---|---|
| Reconciliation of movement in cash to movement in net debt, including the effects of movements on short-term and long-term borrowings, cash and other components of net debt. | para 46 | |
| Comparative figures. | para 47 | |

| **OTHER 'NOTE' DISCLOSURES** | | |
|---|---|---|
| Statement, subject to exceptions, that the same accounting policies as the previous period's accounts have been used. | para 17 | |
| For any changes of accounting policy:<br>(a) the cumulative effects of the policy changes on opening reserves should be disclosed in the STRGL; and<br>(b) description of the changes. | para 18 | |
| Period covered by the report. | para 49 | |
| Date on which the report is approved by the board of directors. | para 49 | |
| Statement on whether the company's auditors have reported on the statutory accounts dealing with the financial year with which the preliminary announcement (i.e., non-statutory accounts) deals. | 85 s240; para 50 | |
| If valid, clear statement that the audit report has yet to be signed. | para 15 | |
| If auditors' report is likely to be qualified, details of the nature of the qualification. | SE 12.40(a)(iii) | |

| **NARRATIVE COMMENTARY** | | |
|---|---|---|
| Any significant additional information necessary for the purpose of assessing the results being announced. | SE 12.40(a)(iv) | |
| A commentary which explains the primary statements in the context of events and trends since the previous period end and interim reports.<br>Significant events and trends should be supported by the underlying figures. | para 22<br><br>para 25 | |
| Events and changes within the year that are likely to affect significantly the succeeding year. | para 28 | |
| Consideration of whether key issues in the OFR are included. | para 29 | |
| Nature of any seasonal activity useful to understanding the performance and financial position at the year end. | para 30 | |
| Highlight and explain significant changes in the summarised balance sheet and cash flow statement, particularly movements in working capital, liquidity and net debt. | para 31 | |
| Explanation of any other matters which directors believe would help users to understand the report, such as, for example:<br>(a) acquisitions and disposals of major fixed assets or investments;<br>(b) changes in contingencies, commitments and off balance sheet financial instruments;<br>(c) material changes in capital structuring or financing; | para 32 | |

| | | |
|---|---|---|
| (d)   events after the year end;<br>(e)   effect of foreign exchange movements; and<br>(f)   impact of revised actuarial valuations on pension costs. | | |
| Salient events and features of the final interim period, together with results and comparative information where appropriate. | para 34 | |
| Specific comment on final interim period's results together with comparative information where appropriate. | para 35 | |
| Any other supplemental information as the directors deem helpful, for example, analysis of fixed assets into component parts, detail on borrowings or FRS 4 equity/non-equity split. | para 24 | |

# Index